HOW TO PASS

PRACTICE & PREPARATION

HIGHER

ENGLISH

Ann Bridges

Colin Eckford

HODDER
GIBSON

AN HACHETTE UK COMPANY

Acknowledgements

The Publishers would like to thank the following for permission to reproduce copyright material:

'A threat to young minds' by Baroness Greenfield © Crown copyright material is reproduced under Class Licence Number C02P000060 with the permission of the Controller of HMSO; 'The psychology of Twitter' by Moses Ma reproduced by permission of *Psychology Today*; 'Stranded in no-man's land' by Joyce McMillan is reproduced by permission of *The Scotsman*; 'More doesn't mean better' by Minette Marrin reproduced by permission of *The Times* 21st September 2008/nisyndication.com; 'We are more than what we buy' by Neal Lawson featured as 'Essay of the Week' in the *Sunday Herald*, 20th June 2009, reproduced by permission of Neal Lawson; Extract from the introduction to *The Language of Things* © Deyan Sudjic, 2008. Reproduced by Permission of Penguin Books Ltd.; 'The first hero of mass culture' by Jonty Oliff-Cooper © *Prospect Magazine* and reprinted with permission; 'Trio' © Edwin Morgan, *Collected Poems*, Carcanet Press Ltd, 1996; 'The Thread' by Don Paterson reproduced by permission of Faber and Faber Ltd; 'Thaw' from *Jizzen* © Kathleen Jamie, 1999, reproduced by permission of Pan Macmillan, London; extract from 'The Love Song of J. Alfred Prufrock' by T. S. Eliot reproduced by permission of Faber and Faber Ltd; 'Church Going' by Philip Larkin reproduced from *Collected Poems* by Faber and Faber Ltd; 'Witch Girl' by Douglas Dunn reproduced by permission of Faber and Faber Ltd; 'O What Is That Sound' by W. H. Auden reproduced by permission of Faber and Faber Ltd; 'Brooklyn Cop' and 'Hotel Room 12th Floor' from *The Poems of Norman MacCaig* by Norman MacCaig are reproduced by permission of Polygon, an imprint of Birlinn Ltd (www.birlinn.co.uk); 'Fern Hill' © Dylan Thomas, published by Dent and reproduced from *Collected Poems* by Everyman with the permission of David Higham Associates Limited; 'Counting the Beats' © Robert Graves, *Complete Poems in One Volume*, Carcanet Press Ltd, 2000; 'Night Marriage' from *Rapture* © Carol Ann Duffy, 2005, reproduced by permission of Pan Macmillan, London; 'Valentine' is taken from *Mean Time* by Carol Ann Duffy published by Anvil Press Poetry in 1993.

Every effort has been made to trace all copyright holders, but if any have been inadvertently overlooked the Publishers will be pleased to make the necessary arrangements at the first opportunity.

Although every effort has been made to ensure that website addresses are correct at time of going to press, Hodder Gibson cannot be held responsible for the content of any website mentioned in this book. It is sometimes possible to find a relocated web page by typing in the address of the home page for a website in the URL window of your browser.

Hachette's policy is to use papers that are natural, renewable and recyclable products and made from wood grown in sustainable forests. The logging and manufacturing processes are expected to conform to the environmental regulations of the country of origin.

Orders: please contact Bookpoint Ltd, 130 Milton Park, Abingdon, Oxon OX14 4SB. Telephone: (44) 01235 827720. Fax: (44) 01235 400454. Lines are open 9.00 – 5.00, Monday to Saturday, with a 24-hour message answering service. Visit our website at www.hoddereducation.co.uk. Hodder Gibson can be contacted direct on: Tel: 0141 848 1609; Fax: 0141 889 6315; email: hoddergibson@hodder.co.uk

© Ann Bridges and Colin Eckford 2010

First published in 2010 by

Hodder Gibson, an imprint of Hodder Education,
An Hachette UK Company
2a Christie Street
Paisley PA1 1NB

Impression number   5 4 3 2 1

Year   2014 2013 2012 2011 2010

Cover photo © PhotoAlto/Alamy

Typeset in Bembo Regular 13pt by DC Graphic Design Ltd, Swanley Village

Printed and bound in Great Britain by Martins the Printers, Berwick-upon-Tweed

A catalogue record for this title is available from the British Library

ISBN: 978 1444 10837 8

Contents

Introduction to Close Reading Papers

In this section there are four complete 50-mark Close Reading Question Papers with two passages in each. They are modelled as closely as possible on recent SQA exam papers★.

They are in approximate order of difficulty, so you are advised to work through them in order.

There is extensive and detailed advice in other books about how to approach Close Reading at this level (*Higher English: Close Reading* (Hodder Gibson 2007) or Part 1 of *How to Pass Higher English Colour Edition* (Hodder Gibson 2009), so we will not reproduce it here. The most important advice is:

- **when answering "U" (Understanding) questions, keep it short and use your "own words" as far as possible★**

- **when answering "A" (Analysis) questions, there are no marks for merely identifying a word, an image or a feature of sentence structure; you must explain the connotations and/or effect of what you identify – and make sure you link it to the focus given in the question**

- **when answering "Comparison" questions, have a definite personal line of thought and structure your answer clearly; think of this answer as a short essay**

For each paper there is a section of Answer Support, in which there are examples of acceptable answers, really good answers, some bad answers for you to comment on and, when necessary, a comment on the question.

The Answer Support is explained in more detail on page 26.

★ Note that in the papers in this book, the questions never use the expression "**in your own words**", which you will find frequently in past papers up to 2009 and in practice papers in books. This is because SQA indicated in August 2009 that the general instruction on the question paper would be adapted to clarify the importance of answering "U" questions in candidates' own words, and that from 2010 onwards there would be no references in individual questions to using "own words".

Close Reading Paper 1
Social Networking

PASSAGE 1

This passage is taken from Hansard (the formal written record of proceedings in Parliament) and is part of a speech made to the House of Lords, in February 2009, by Baroness Greenfield, an eminent neuroscientist.

A THREAT TO YOUNG MINDS

The social networking site Facebook turned five years old last week. Arguably, it marks a milestone in a progressive and highly significant change in our culture as tens to hundreds of millions of individuals worldwide, including the very young, are signing up for friendship through a screen.

5 What precisely is the appeal of social networking sites? First, there is the simple issue of the constraints of modern life, where unsupervised playing outside or going for walks is now perceived as too dangerous. A child confined to the home every evening may find at the keyboard the kind of freedom of interaction and communication that earlier generations took for granted in the three-dimensional world of the street. But
10 even given a choice, screen life can still be more appealing. Building a Facebook profile is one way that individuals can identify themselves, making them feel important and accepted. I recently had a fascinating conversation with a young devotee who proudly claimed to have 900 friends. Clearly, this is a way of satisfying that basic human need to belong, to be part of a group, as well as the ability to experience instant
15 feedback and recognition – at least from someone, somewhere – 24 hours a day.

At the same time, this constant reassurance – that you are listened to, recognised, and important – is coupled with a distancing from the stress of face-to-face, real-life conversation. Real-life conversations are, after all, far more perilous than those in the cyber world. They occur in real time, with no opportunity to think up clever or witty
20 responses, and they require a sensitivity to voice tone and body language. Moreover, according to the context and, indeed, the person with whom we are conversing, our own delivery will need to adapt. None of these skills are required when chatting on a social networking site.

Although it might seem an extreme analogy, I often wonder whether real conversation
25 in real time may eventually give way to these sanitised and easier screen dialogues, in much the same way as killing, skinning and butchering an animal to eat has been replaced by the convenience of packages of meat on the supermarket shelf. Perhaps future generations will recoil with similar horror at the messiness, unpredictability and immediate personal involvement of a three-dimensional, real-time interaction.

30 I think all of this poses something of a threat to young minds. First, I would suggest that attention span is at risk. If the young brain is exposed from the outset to a world of fast action and reaction, of instant new screen images flashing up with the press of a

key, such rapid interchange might accustom the brain to operate over such timescales. It might be helpful to investigate whether the near total submersion of our culture in
35 screen technologies over the last decade might in some way be linked to the threefold increase over this period in prescriptions for the drug prescribed for "hyperactive" youngsters with ADHD.

Related to this change might be a second area of potential difference in the young 21st century mind – a much more marked preference for the here-and-now, where the
40 immediacy of an experience trumps any regard for the consequences. After all, whenever you play a computer game, you can always just play it again; everything you do is reversible. The emphasis is on the thrill of the moment, the buzz of rescuing the princess in the game. No care is given for the princess herself or for any long-term significance because there is none. Perhaps we should be paying attention to whether
45 such activities may result in a more impulsive and solipsistic attitude.

This brings us to a third possible change – in empathy. One teacher of 30 years' standing wrote to me that she had witnessed a change over the time she had been teaching in the ability of her pupils to understand others. She pointed out that previously, reading novels had been a good way of learning about how others feel and
50 think, as distinct from oneself. Unlike the game to rescue the princess, where the goal is to feel rewarded, the aim of reading a book is, after all, to find out more about the princess herself.

Finally it seems strange that in a society recoiling from the introduction of ID cards, we are at the same time enthusiastically embracing the possible erosion of our identity
55 through social networking sites. When all your private thoughts and feelings can be posted on the internet for all to see, perhaps Facebook makes you think about yourself differently. Are we perhaps losing a sense of where we ourselves finish and the outside world begins?

With fast-paced, instant screen reactions, perhaps the next generation will define
60 themselves by the responses of others; hence the baffling current preoccupation with posting an almost moment-by-moment, flood-of-consciousness account of your thoughts and activities, however banal. I believe it is called Twitter.

PASSAGE 2

This passage, written by Moses Ma, is from the journal Psychology Today *(March 2009).*

THE PSYCHOLOGY OF TWITTER

Twitter has officially become the next big thing in terms of Internet social phenomena, so I can't resist writing about it... just like everyone else. If you've never used or even heard of Twitter, don't worry, you're not alone. As of now, less than ten percent of Internet users actually Twitter, but it's growing like crazy: visitors to Twitter increased
5 1,382 percent year-over-year, from 475,000 visitors in February 2008 to seven million in February 2009, making it the fastest growing social media site in the world.

Essentially, Twitter is an automated service for the sharing of short 140-character communications. You can send tweets from your cell phone as well as your computer. Pretty much every major celebrity has a twitter channel, from Britney Spears to John
10 Cleese, as the system has become the promotional channel of choice.

In many ways Twitter is the killer app for killing time, filling any moment with useless drivel: "boy, I love lightly scrambled eggs", "appletini or dirty martini? reply now to tell what I should order", "stop & shop is out of weight watchers brownies, but price chopper has 'em." Riveting stuff indeed.

15 More interesting, however, is how the Twitter system acts to fill a deep psychological need in our society. The unfortunate reality is that we are a culture starved for real community. For hundreds of thousands of years, human beings have resided in tribes of about 30-70 people. Our brains are wired to operate within the social context of community – programming crucial for human survival.

20 However, the tribal context of life was subverted during the Industrial Revolution, when the extended family was torn apart in order to move labourers into the cities. But a deep evolutionary need for community continues to express itself, through feelings of community generated by your workplace, your church, your sports team, and now... the twitterverse. This is why people feel so compelled to tweet, to Facebook
25 or even to check their email incessantly. We crave connection.

It's sometimes fascinating to look at Twitter in the context of Abraham Maslow's concept of a hierarchy of needs, first presented in his 1943 paper "A Theory of Human Motivation".

Maslow's hierarchy of needs is most often displayed as a pyramid, with lowest levels of
30 the pyramid made up of the most basic needs, and with more complex needs at the top of the pyramid. Needs at the bottom of the pyramid are basic physical requirements including the need for food, water, sleep and warmth. Once these lower-level needs have been met, people can move on to higher levels of needs, which become increasingly psychological and social. Soon, the need for love, friendship and intimacy
35 become important. Further up the pyramid, the need for personal esteem and feelings of accomplishment become important. Finally, Maslow emphasised the importance of self-actualisation, which is a process of growing and developing as a person to achieve individual potential.

Twitter aims primarily at social needs, like those for belonging, love, and affection.
40 Relationships such as friendships, romantic attachments and families help fulfil this need for companionship and acceptance, as does involvement in social, community or religious groups. Clearly, feeling connected to people via Twitter helps to fulfil some of this need to belong and feel cared about.

An even higher level of need, related to self-esteem and social recognition, is also
45 brought into play by Twitter. At its best, Twitter allows normal people to feel like celebrities. At its worst, it is an exercise in unconditional narcissism – the idea that

others might actually care about the minutiae of our daily lives. I believe that this phenomenon of micro-celebrity is driven by existential anxiety. I twitter, therefore I am. I matter, I'm good enough, I'm smart enough, and, goddammit, people *like* me!

[END OF TEXT]

Questions on Passage 1   *Marks Code*

1. Read lines 1–15.
   - (a) In what ways, according to lines 1–4, has Facebook brought about "significant change in our culture"?   2   U
   - (b) Explain briefly the key attractions of social networking the writer gives in lines 5–15?   3   U
   - (c) What effect does the parenthetical comment in line 15 have on the tone of the sentence in which it appears?   2   A

2. Read lines 16–23.
   - (a) In what way, according to the writer, are "Real life conversations… far more perilous than those in the cyber world"? (lines 18–19)   2   U
   - (b) Show how the writer's word choice in the whole paragraph makes clear the difference between the two types of communication.   4   A

3. How effective do you find the analogy in lines 24–29 in developing the writer's ideas? Refer in your answer to the ideas contained in the analogy and to the language used by the writer to express it.   4   E

4. Read lines 30–37.

   Show how the writer's use of language emphasises the idea of screen technologies as a "threat".   2   A

5. Read lines 38–45.
   - (a) What does the writer mean by "the immediacy of an experience trumps any regard for the consequences"? (lines 39–40)   3   U
   - (b) Show how the writer's use of language in this paragraph conveys her disapproval of computer games.   3   A

6. Read lines 46–58.
   - (a) What difference does the writer identify between a novel and a computer game?   1   U
   - (b) What, in lines 53–58, does the writer find "strange"?   2   U

7. Show how the writer's use of language in lines 59–62 conveys her disapproval of the activities she is describing.   2   A

              (30)

Marks Code

Questions on Passage 2

8. Read lines 1–25.
    (a) The style of writing in lines 1–14 is very different from that in lines 15–25. Referring to examples of both styles, discuss to what extent you find the change in style effective in engaging the reader in the writer's point of view.   4 A/E
    (b) According to lines 15–25, in what ways does Twitter "fill a deep psychological need in our society"? (lines 15–16)   2 U

9. Read lines 26–49.
    (a) Outline briefly the key points of Maslow's "Theory of Human Motivation".   3 U
    (b) Explain how the writer's sentence structure in lines 29–38 helps to clarify his description of Maslow's theory.   2 A
    (c) What, according to the writer, makes Twitter relevant to Maslow's theory?   2 U
    (d) Show how the writer's use of language in lines 44–49 highlights his main criticism of Twitter?   2 A

                                                                                   (15)

Question on both Passages

10. Which writer's views on key aspects of social networking do you find more interesting?

    Justify your choice by reference to the **ideas** of **both passages**.   5 U/E

                                                                                    (5)

                                                             Total marks   (50)

Close Reading Paper 2
Responding to Change

PASSAGE 1

In this passage, Joyce McMillan, writing in The Scotsman *newspaper on 5 January 2008, reflects on the start of the New Year, and uses reaction to a suggestion that five-year-olds should be given sex education to explore some deeper thoughts about how our society responds to change.*

STRANDED IN NO-MAN'S LAND

New Year is supposed to be a time for looking both backwards and forward. But if it's a good thing to acknowledge a quiet moment of transition between past and future, it's profoundly debilitating to find yourself permanently trapped between the two, and it often seems, at the turn of the year, as if that kind of limbo is where British society 5 has found itself for the last 30 years or so, unable to move backwards, yet somehow reluctant to move on.

It's not that nothing has changed in that time, of course. There has been turbo-charged economic growth, wave upon wave of migration, a massive shift from an industrial to a service economy, and a generation of unprecedented change in sexual politics and 10 family life. Yet still, in our hearts and minds, we seem to be resisting the changes with which we live from day to day, as if every statistic recording numbers of children born out of wedlock, or numbers of migrants arriving in Britain, or numbers of teenagers enjoying an active sex life, represented a deep threat to our world, and therefore to ourselves.

15 So it could have been almost anything, this New Year, that triggered the latest round of shock-horror headlines about a nation going to hell in a handcart, but, as it was, it was a public comment by an eminent doctor, advocating that children as young as five should be receiving sex education in schools. His reasoning is simple: children, he argues, need a good, confident knowledge of the facts about sex, long before they are 20 even tempted to start experimenting themselves.

There was no chance, though, of his remarks being greeted with calm agreement all round. For this is a culture where, well within living memory, children as old as 13 or 14 were forbidden to know anything about sex at all, sometimes with tragic consequences. Put the words "five-year-olds" and "sex education" together, therefore, 25 and the old atavistic monster rears up, roaring phrases like "going to the dogs", or "pouring petrol on a fire".

Now, of course, it's possible to debate at length whether or not, under current conditions, the extension of sex education in schools would make any decisive impact on that group of vulnerable British youngsters who, for a blizzard of social reasons,

30 just can't seem to associate what they are told about sex at school with what happens in their own lives. It seems to me, though, that it's not really the substance of the issue that's in question here. In reason, we all know that five-year-olds need to know a little bit about sex, even if it's only why their own bodies are as they are. It's just that we don't like seeing that truth written down in so many words, and we don't like the idea
35 that we can't rely on families alone to do the job.

And the mood is the same in dozens of areas where our society should be moving forward to deal with the practical challenges of 21st century life, but, at some deeper level, seems to have come to the limit of its capacity for change. We know that our binge-drinking culture is dangerous, for example, but still snarl with resentment at
40 politicians who tell us so. We know that racism is wrong, but still make endless excuses for the surly dislike of foreigners that scars our society.

And when it comes to the defining issue of our age – climate change – well, we know, in some corner of our brains, that the whole basis of our economy and society has to change over the next 20 years if we are to avoid outright catastrophe, yet we continue
45 – for example – to regard personal motorised transport as some kind of birthright, and bitterly resist any effort to shift us from our cars.

So what are we to do, stranded in this no-man's-land between an old civilisation that's no longer sustainable either practically or morally, and a new one that we still resist because it seems somehow alien? Some bluster hopelessly about the need to return to
50 the past. Others talk blithely as if there was no problem about abandoning the family as a useful transmitter of wisdom, and passing the whole job on to schools.

But for the rest of us – well, we probably do best when we face the truth that all social change involves some measure of loss, but that the clock cannot be turned back towards attitudes and prejudices that were abandoned for the best of reasons. And, above all,
55 we perhaps need to strive to move forward as a whole society, rather than as a bunch of fragmented individuals demanding increasingly impossible feats from our hard-pressed public services.

For in the end, schools can teach nothing that society as a whole does not want children to learn. If our society eats junk food, schools cannot make children eat healthily. If
60 our society is full of bullying behaviour, schools catch the backwash of emotional and physical violence. And if our society remains hopelessly ambivalent about sex – so recently an unspoken taboo, now a multimedia nightmare of cheap raunch and smut – well, then it's not primarily the failure of teachers and educationists that leaves so many teenagers all at sea in this key area of their lives. It's rather our own embarrassment
65 and silence, passed on from generation to generation, and whether lessons begin at five or 15, it will take more than a change in education policy to make any difference to that.

PASSAGE 2

In this passage, Minette Marrin, writing in The Times *newspaper in September 2008, discusses government proposals to increase the amount of sex education in schools.*

MORE DOESN'T MEAN BETTER

According to the old saying, those who can, do, and those who can't, teach. I have come to think that those who can't teach, teach sex education.

Judged by its results — not a bad way of judging — sex education has been an utter failure. The increase in sex education here in recent years has coincided with an
5 explosion of unwanted pregnancies and sexually transmitted disease (STD) far worse than anywhere else in Europe. Since the government's teenage pregnancy strategy was introduced in 1999, the number of girls having abortions has soared. A culture of promiscuity among the young has driven the rate of STDs to a record. Almost 400,000 people — half of them under 25 — were newly diagnosed, 6% more than in 2006. You
10 might well be tempted to argue that sex education causes sexual delinquency.

When something fails, the usual procedure is to drop it and try something else. With sex education, however, the worse it gets, the more people cry out for more of it and earlier — to the extent that Ministers are considering making schools offer more sex education, offer it earlier and deny parents the right to withdraw their children from it.

15 Last week the Family Planning Association published a comic-style sex education booklet ("Let's Grow with Nisha and Joe") for six-year-olds to be marketed in primary schools for use in sex and relationships lessons. There's nothing wrong with the pamphlet itself. Admittedly it's more of a dreary workbook than a "fun" comic, but there's nothing that would startle a child or should upset even the most conservative of
20 "family campaigners". The rudest thing is a drawing of two children, naked, with instructions to draw lines connecting interesting bits of their bodies with the appropriate words, yet it seems to me highly unrealistic (given that 25% of children leave primary school struggling to read and write) to assume that many six-year-olds could begin to read the labels "testicles" or "vagina".

25 What I really object to about the book is what I object to about sex education as a whole. Sex education — particularly compulsory and standardised sex education — is based on mistaken assumptions. The first is the pervasive assumption of equality — that is, that all six-year-olds or all 11-year-olds or 15-year-olds can discuss the complexities of sex in the same form in the same way. That's nonsense. Children vary in intelligence
30 and progress. Children and teenagers mature at different ages and come from different backgrounds. You cannot talk the same way to a shy 13-year-old who hasn't had her first period as to another who is well acquainted with the darker recesses of the school bike shed. Some boys are men at 11 and 12, physically; others are children until much later. You cannot talk to all these children together. And it undermines the authority
35 of those parents who do not share the values of the teacher.

Another mistaken assumption is that sex education ought, necessarily, to be entrusted to teachers, given how wildly they vary in ability and in moral attitudes. The thought that the government is considering making sex and relationship education compulsory in schools is terrifying. I can hardly imagine anything worse than subjecting a sensitive
40 child to guidance on such matters from an inexperienced and politically correct teacher, who is neither well informed nor self-critical. The relationships between sex, love, babies, and disease are too explosive to be left primarily to such a person, or to any person apart from the parents.

[END OF TEXT]

Questions on Passage 1

Marks Code

1. Read lines 1–14.
    (a) Explain the situation in which, according to lines 1–6, "British society has found itself".   2   U
    (b) Show how the writer's word choice in lines 7–10 ("It's not… family life") emphasises the extent of the changes she describes.   2   A
    (c) Why, according to the writer, do we "seem to be resisting the changes" (line 10)?   2   U

2. Read lines 15–26.
    (a) Why did the doctor's statement cause such a strong reaction?   2   U
    (b) Show how the writer's use of language in these lines emphasises the strength of the reaction.   2   A

3. Read lines 27–35.
    (a) State briefly the writer's attitude to sex-education for five-year-olds.   1   U
    (b) How effective do you find the image "a blizzard of social reasons" in conveying the writer's point about the plight of some British youngsters?   2   A/E

4. Read lines 36–46.
    (a) Show how the writer's word choice conveys "our" attitude to change in each of the areas she identifies.   3   A
    (b) Show how her sentence structure helps to clarify her argument.   2   A

5. Read lines 47–57.
    (a) Show how the imagery in lines 47–49 ("So what … alien?") conveys the writer's view of the situation we find ourselves in.   2   A
    (b) The writer gives two possible responses to this situation in lines 49–51. How does her use of language convey her dissatisfaction with both responses?   2   A
    (c) What is the writer's preferred response to the situation?   2   U

6. Read lines 58–67.
    (a) Why, according to the writer, will it "take more than a change in educational policy" to improve matters?   1   U
    (b) Show how the writer's sentence structure in this paragraph helps to clarify her argument.   2   A

                                                                          (27)

Questions on Passage 2

7. Read lines 1–10.
    (a) Show how the writer's use of language in these lines creates a rather flippant, tongue-in-cheek tone.　　　　　　　　　　　　　2　　A
    (b) Show how the writer's word choice in lines 3–10 conveys her personal attitude to the statistics she is reporting.　　　　　　　　2　　A

8. Show how the writer's use of language in lines 11–14 conveys her disapproval of introducing more sex education.　　　　　　　　　　　　2　　A

9. Read lines 15–24.
    (a) Describe the writer's attitude to the sex education booklet.　　2　　U
    (b) Show how her use of language makes her attitude clear.　　　2　　A

10. Read lines 25–43.
    (a) Summarise the writer's main objections to sex education.　　4　　U
    (b) Show how the writer's use of language conveys the strength of her objections.　　　　　　　　　　　　　　　　　　　　　　4　　A

（18）

Question on both Passages

11. Which writer in your opinion comes across as the more reasonable and thoughtful person?

    Justify your choice by reference to the **ideas and style** of **both passages**.　　5　　E

（5）

Total marks　（50）

Close Reading Paper 3
Shopping

PASSAGE 1

In the "Essay of the Week" in the Sunday Herald *newspaper, Neal Lawson lays out the reasons why we must conquer our addiction to shopping.*

WE ARE MORE THAN WHAT WE BUY

We are caught up on a treadmill of turbo-consumption powered by the unfounded belief that having more will make us happy. We are part and parcel of a consumer society whose credentials are becoming more tarnished.

Increasingly, the predominant thing that you and I do is shop and plan our lives around
5   things we have to pay for: clothes, jewellery, cars, houses, holidays, restaurants and gadgets that make us what we are. Once we were a society of producers, knowing ourselves and each other by what we did and what we made. Not any more. Today we understand ourselves and project the image we want others to see through what we buy.

10 Even for those who pretend they are above fashion, every item they own is based on finely calibrated decisions about who and what they are and what they want others to think of them. With every purchasing decision, they reject thousands of other options, on other parts of the shelf, in other shops, in order to home in on the object that is "them". It might not be "fashion" but it is their fashion. Today we are all what we
15 drive and what we wear. We don't own things – they own us.

So what keeps us running on the consumer treadmill? We buy freedom, escape, love, care, excitement and comfort. We buy to belong to a particular social group and stand apart from others. And, of course we buy status. We want to be as near the top of the herd as possible. Endless consumption fuels the instinct to be "the best", to covet the
20 newest car, to wear the latest outfit, to travel to ever-more exotic places, to possess the latest gadgets and to own a prestigious home in a "desirable" area. We live in a world where, as the commercials remind us, you can be ashamed of your mobile phone and your worth is measured according to your shampoo.

The whole show is kept going by the vast laboratory of designers, producers, marketers,
25 advertisers, branding experts, psychologists and retail consultants who devise the machinery for the image factory that defines the 21st century. The best brains in the world are engaged in continually engineering new wants into new needs: more and more things we must have in order to be "normal".

But life on the treadmill is catching up with us.

30 Most frightening of all is the fact that there are so few other ways of expressing our humanity, so we increasingly take comfort in so-called "retail therapy". Yet the object

of the sellers is not to make us satisfied but dissatisfied so that we soon go back for more. Shopping rewards us just enough to leave space for more ... and the emptier we feel the more we shop. It is the most vicious of vicious circles, and the paradox at the
35 heart of Western society which is based on the pursuit of "more".

How, then, do we escape from the treadmill of consumerism? There is no going back to some rose-tinted pre-consumption era. Shopping isn't all bad, after all – it's an important means by which we can be sociable and creative. However, we need to strike a balance, and that means regaining control over a marketing machine whose
40 sole purpose is to make ever greater profits. We require a more compelling vision of what it means to be free and live a good life. Shopping sells us a powerful myth of liberty: that the car sets us free on the open road, for instance, when the reality is that we spend hours sitting in choking traffic jams that get us nowhere and pollute the environment. We must grasp the fact that what we really need and cherish can't be
45 bought.

Perhaps the state needs to step in, and we must demand that it legislates to help us rebalance our lives as social beings and citizens, rather than simply as shoppers. A good start would be legal restrictions on advertising – particularly to children, who shouldn't be subjected to the full force of the branding psychologists. Just as Sweden has banned
50 advertising to under-12s, we need to do the same.

Other governmental measures could include increased taxation on luxury goods – thus signalling that status isn't gained by buying top-end merchandise. Finally, happiness – not wealth – must become the number one priority, which means replacing the GDP (gross domestic product) with GWB (general wellbeing) as a measure of the
55 nation's prosperity. The quality of our lives, not the quantity of our consumption, should be the measure of political success.

The current recession is a wake-up call. Right now, we are being forced to shop less, but the crucial question is: what happens when the crunch is over? Will we return to a life that is all-consuming, or use the enforced consumer slowdown as a catalyst for
60 change and move to a post-consumer society, in which shopping plays a lesser role in our lives?

PASSAGE 2

The following passage is taken from the first chapter of a book on design, The Language of Things, *by Deyan Sudjic, a commentator on architecture and design. In it, the writer discusses the importance of design in influencing purchasing decisions.*

SEDUCING THE CUSTOMER

To start with the object which is closest to hand, the laptop with which I write these words was bought in an airport shop. There is no one but me to blame for my choice. Some shops are designed to seduce their customers. Others leave them to make up their own minds. Dior and Prada hire prize-winning architects to build stores on the

5   scale of Grand Opera to reduce shoppers to an ecstatic consumerist trance. Not airports. A generic discount electronics store at Heathrow is no place for the seductions, veiled or unveiled, of the more elaborate forms of retailing.

Yet even in an airport, buying is no simple, rational decision. Like an actor performing without makeup, stripped of the proscenium arch and footlights, the laptop that
10   eventually persuaded me that I had to have it did it all by itself. It was a purchase based on a set of seductions and manipulations that was taking place entirely in my head. And to understand how the laptop succeeded in making me want it enough to pay to take it away is to understand something about myself, and maybe a little about the part that design has to play in the modern world.

15   By the time I reached the counter, even if I didn't know it, I had already consigned my old Apple computer to the electronics street market in Lagos where redundant hard drives go for organ harvesting. Yet my dead laptop was no time-expired piece of transistorised Neolithic technology. In its prime, in the early weeks of 2004, it had presented itself as the most desirable, and most knowing piece of technology that I
20   could ever have wanted. It was a computer that had been reduced to the aesthetic essentials. Just large enough to have a full-size keyboard, it had a distinctive, sparely elegant ratio of width to depth. The shell and the keys were all white.

Apple's designers were quick to understand the need to make starting a computer for the first time as simple as locating the on switch. They have become equally skilled at
25   manipulating the exterior design to create visual obsolescence. They take the view that Apple's route to survival in the PC dominated world is to use design as a lure to turn its product into aspirational alternatives to what its competitors are selling. It expects to sell fewer machines, but it charges more for them. This involves serial seduction. The company has to make most of its customers so hungry for a new
30   product that they will throw away the last one every two years.

At Heathrow, there were two Apple models to choose from. The first was all white, like my last one. The other was the matt black option. Even though its slightly higher specification made it more expensive, I knew as soon as I saw it that I would end up buying it. The black version looked sleek, technocratic and composed. The purist
35   white one had seemed equally alluring when I bought it, but the black one now seemed so quiet, so dignified and chaste by comparison. The keys are squares with tightly radiused corners, sunk into a tray delicately eroded from the rest of the machine. The effect is of a skilfully carved block of solid, strangely warm, black marble, rather than the lid on top of a box of electronic components.

40   Black has been used over the years by many other design-conscious manufacturers to suggest seriousness, but it was a new colour for Apple. Black is a non-colour, used for scientific instruments that rely on precision rather than fashion to appeal to customers. To have no colour implies that you are doing would-be customers the honour of taking them seriously enough not to try fobbing them off with tinsel. Of course this is
45   precisely the most effective kind of seduction.

And in the end black too becomes an empty signal, a sign devoid of substance, and I will no doubt fall for the next model which sets out to seduce me with its exclusive and tasteful credentials.

[END OF TEXT]

Questions on Passage 1

Marks Code

1. (a) What is the main point the writer is making in lines 1–3? 2 U
   (b) Show how the writer's word choice in lines 1–3 emphasises his low opinion of "consumer society". You should refer to **two** examples in your answer. 2 A

2. Read lines 4–9.
   (a) What is the difference the writer identifies between our place in society in the past and in the present? 2 U
   (b) Show how the writer uses sentence structure in lines 4–9 to make clear the points he is making. 2 A

3. Show how the writer's use of language in lines 10–15 creates a critical tone about those who say they are "above fashion" (line 10). In your answer you could refer to word choice, imagery, sentence structure, punctuation… 2 A

4. Read lines 16–23.
   (a) There are two main areas of our lives that the writer says we attempt to satisfy by "running on the consumer treadmill". What are these two main areas? 2 U
   (b) What effect does the writer create by his choice of the two examples he uses in the last sentence of this paragraph? 2 E

5. Show how the imagery in lines 24–28 conveys the writer's view of how "The whole show" is organised. 2 A

6. What, according to the writer in lines 30–35, is the problem with our dependence on "retail therapy"? 2 U

7. Explain how the writer illustrates his claim that shopping "sells us a powerful myth" (line 41). 2 U

8. Read lines 46–56.

   Summarise the three measures which the writer suggests should be the responsibility of the Government. 3 U

9. "The current recession is a wake-up call." (line 57)

   Show how this idea is developed in the remainder of the paragraph. (lines 57–61) 2 U

   (25)

Questions on Passage 2   *Marks   Code*

10. Read lines 1–7.
     (a) The writer makes a contrast between two kinds of shops. What is the
            main difference between them?   2   U
     (b) Show how the writer's word choice in these lines creates a distinctive
            impression of **one** of these kinds of shop.   2   A

11. Read lines 8–14.
     (a) "Yet even in an airport, buying is no simple rational decision." Explain,
            with close reference to the words of the sentence, how this sentence acts
            as a link in the writer's thoughts about the temptations to buy something
            – in this case a computer.   2   U
     (b) Show how the writer's use of language in these lines helps to explain the
            power of the computer's design.   2   A

12. Show how the writer's use of language in lines 15–22 allows his attitude
     towards his old computer to emerge. In your answer you should consider at
     least two features such as imagery, word choice, humour…   4   A

13. Read lines 23–30.

     Explain fully what the Apple company hopes to achieve by the exterior design
     of its computers.   2   U

14. Show how the writer's word choice in lines 31–39 persuades you of the merits
     of the black computer. You should consider at least two examples.   2   A

15. Read lines 40–45.

     Explain fully the process by which having "no colour" becomes the "most
     effective kind of seduction" of the customer.   2   U

16. What view of the writer's attitude to his consumerist habits do you form from
     the last paragraph (lines 46–48)?   2   E
                                                                                 (20)

Question on both Passages

17. Which passage makes you think more deeply about the modern phenomenon
     called consumerism? Justify your choice by reference to the **ideas and
     attitudes** of **both writers**.   5   U/E
                                                                                  (5)

                                                        Total marks   **(50)**

Close Reading Paper 4
Victorian Celebrity

PASSAGE 1

In this article in Prospect *magazine (January 2009), Jonty Olliff-Cooper tells the story of a now-forgotten Victorian celebrity, and discusses the social background to his fame.*

THE FIRST HERO OF MASS CULTURE

When Britney Spears totters from a night club at 5am – hair askew, often drunk, often without knickers – we tend to assume her behaviour is terribly modern. But celebrities are not new. Nor is our obsession with them, as Prince Charles recently demonstrated with his 60th birthday portrait, modelled on Victorian hero Frederick Burnaby
5 (1842–85). Burnaby is almost totally forgotten now, but in his day he was so famous that Queen Victoria reportedly fainted at news of his death. *The Times* gave him a 5000-word obituary. Grown men broke down and wept in the street.

It is easy to see why. Burnaby's exploits make Rambo look wet. Few people have survived frostbite, typhus, an exploding air balloon, and poisoning with arsenic;
10 explored Uzbekistan (where it was so cold, his beard froze solid and snapped off), led the household cavalry, stood for parliament, mastered seven languages, crossed the channel by air balloon, written a string of bestsellers, commanded the Turkish army, and founded *Vanity Fair* magazine. All this before his early death aged 42.

Burnaby could break a horseshoe apart with his bare hands. His party trick was to
15 bend a poker double round a dull dinner guest's neck. Most famously, when fellow officers coaxed a pair of ponies into his room for a jape, Burnaby simply picked them up – one under each arm – and carried them downstairs "as if they had been cats."

But, like Britney, Burnaby's actual talents only half explain his fame. Then, as now, media attention was just as important. In this respect, Burnaby was lucky. His heyday
20 coincided with a new atmosphere in Britain, receptive to his brand of reckless adventuring.

The early Victorian world of Dickens and Brunel was a grimy, serious society, born out of a strong evangelical morality and the growing pains of industrialisation. Up to about 1870, no one wanted an Empire. It cost too much. In a decade, that changed.
25 Suddenly we were in the world of side-whiskers, Sherlock Holmes, and oompa bands. Empire could not be big enough.

A media revolution was crucial to this change. Before 1860, national news did not exist. Three breakthroughs changed this. First, the telegraph allowed news to reach Fleet Street in hours, not weeks. Second, new printing techniques put cheap dailies
30 within the reach of ordinary people. Thirdly, the 1870 Education Act made it compulsory to learn the somewhat perversely-termed "3 Rs": reading, 'riting, and 'rithmetic. Suddenly millions wanted news.

New media demanded new copy. The new readers of the late Victorian era had simple tastes. They wanted then what we want now: glamour. Not exactly snaps of "Nikkola, 35 23, from Essex", but certainly a good rollicking tale of daring-do. And what better stage for excitement than that colourful, exotic, mysterious space: Empire? And what better star for that stage than Frederick Burnaby? He was in the right place, at the right time.

New publications sprang up catering for gossip and Empire, like the *Daily Mail*, which 40 filled its pages with engravings of our brave boys battling swarthy foreigners, exotic dens of oriental vice, and society ladies showing a little ankle. Gossip mags like *The Graphic* – a sort of Imperial version of *Heat* – described which balls Burnaby was attending, and who he danced with. One could buy Burnaby playing cards, Burnaby toby jugs, Burnaby crockery and Burnaby comics. There were poster-sized pullouts of 45 Burnaby in *The Illustrated London News*. He inspired songs, a polka – and even a musical. Like all celebs worth their salt, Burnaby released a celebrity autobiography. He even had his own sponsorship deal, with Cockle's Cure-all Condiments. Burnaby was the first hero of mass culture.

Of course, modern celebrity is different. Burnaby did not suffer the indignity of the 50 red carpet, but the man still had to live up to intolerably high expectations and fame nonetheless took a terrible toll. With telephoto lenses, we can catalogue Britney's demise; Victorians could not see Burnaby's, so they continued to expect the impossible. As he entered middle age, Burnaby increasingly struggled to keep up with his dashing image.

55 Eventually, the weight of expectation became too much. Resolving not to die old, Burnaby set out on one last mission. Ignoring orders, he joined the attempt to rescue General Gordon from Khartoum. On leaving, he wrote "I am very unhappy. I do not mean to come back." Sure enough, during an ambush by Sudanese warriors, he pushed through his ranks and rode out alone, determined to meet the public expectation of 60 heroic death.

So ended the life of a Victorian icon.

PASSAGE 2

The following account of Burnaby was posted, in January 2008, on the website "Great British Nutters: a celebration of the UK's pluckiest adventurers".

FRED AND THE KHAN OF KHIVA

By Jingo, they don't make chaps like Colonel Frederick Gustavus Burnaby any more. Which is a shame, or possibly a relief, I can't quite make up my mind. In the Victorian age of larger-than-life heroes, the wildly eccentric colonel towered above the lot of them. He stood 6ft 4ins tall, weighed 15 stone and boasted a 47-inch chest. Fred joined 5 the army aged 17, and quickly became recognised as the strongest man in its ranks. A first-rate boxer, swordsman, rider and runner, his party tricks included vaulting over billiard tables and twisting pokers into knots with his bare hands. You didn't want to mess with Fred Burnaby.

But he was more than just a meathead of mountainous proportions. Far more. Early in
10 his short life, Fred became something of a popular hero in Britain, famous for a bizarre 1,000-mile journey he made into Central Asia, accompanied by a dwarf. The mad trip was seen as a kind of one-man victory over the mighty Russian empire, which had tried to block his progress.

And here's how he did it.

15 On a roasting February day in Sudan, he found himself flicking through an English newspaper in a Khartoum café, absently chatting to some mates about where they all fancied going next time their leave came around. His eye fell upon a paragraph in the paper to the effect that the Russian government at St Petersburg had given an order that no foreigner was to be allowed to travel in Russian Asia, and that an Englishman
20 who had recently attempted a journey in that direction had been turned back. As a stout-hearted patriot, Fred wasn't at all keen on Russians at the best of times. Now those pesky Russians were trying to ban Englishmen from travelling in the region, too. You can imagine what Burnaby of the Guards thought of that. How dare they! What was that rotten Tsar up to? More importantly, who was going to stop him?

25 Before he'd finished his coffee, Fred's mind was made up. He would ignore the ban, travel to the heart of central Asia (somehow), and find out for himself exactly what was going on there. He saw it as his personal duty to open Britain's eyes to the menace of the Russian bear. It wasn't going to be easy of course. Apart from the possibility of being arrested, Fred's army leave inconveniently fell during winter – so it would be
30 blizzards, snowdrifts and killer temperatures every step of the way. If the Russians didn't get him, frostbite or exposure probably would.

His goal was the mysterious city of Khiva, and he wasn't exactly guaranteed a warm welcome if he made it. The Khivans were a fierce and independent lot who had been fighting Russian invaders for centuries, slaughtering the men and enslaving the
35 women in harems. Their leader, the Khan of Khiva, had a reputation for cruelty. He will "very likely order his executioner to gouge out your eyes", a friendly Russian warned Fred.

Fred's account of his wild journey – "A Ride to Khiva" – turned him into a celebrity. It sold out. Even today it's a smashing, swashbuckling read.

40 Wrapped up in a smelly sheepskin suit, his military moustache frozen stiff on his face, he sets off with a "faithful little Tartar" servant, Nazar, who stands less than five foot tall and sticks with Fred through thick and thin. At one remote settlement, the unlikely duo find all the horses have either died or are starving to death. So they hire three gigantic, shaggy camels instead, harnessing the unruly beasts to their tiny sleigh and
45 push on through the snowdrifts in bizarre fashion.

On another occasion, the motley team run into six armed Khivans who insult the guide, abusing him for working for "dogs and unbelievers" from abroad. The guide lashes out with his whip; a Khivan hits back with a camel-stick; knives are drawn; Fred pulls out his pistol.

50 In the end, of course, Fred's pluck and bravery win the day. After two months of hard travelling he rocks up outside the ancient city walls of Khiva. With characteristic optimism, Fred has already sent a messenger ahead to request an audience with the mighty Khan of Khiva, the old eye-gouger himself. To his surprise, this is granted and Fred finds himself being led into the ruler's palace.

55 A curtain is pulled back and Fred is face to face with a powerfully built guy in his late twenties, with irregular teeth and a coal-black beard and moustache: the Khan. He raises his hand to his forehead in greeting; Fred touches his cap.

And what does our dashing adventurer make of this most feared of Asian rulers? Fred writes: "I must say I was greatly surprised to find him such a cheery sort of fellow."

[END OF TEXT]

Questions on Passage 1   *Marks Code*

1. Read lines 1–17.

   (a) In what key way do Burnaby and Britney Spears differ as celebrities?   1   U

   (b) What overall impression of Burnaby is created in lines 8–13?   1   U

   (c) Show how the writer's use of language in lines 8–13 adds impact to the impression he is creating. You should refer in your answer to sentence structure and tone.   4   A

   (d) What overall impression of Burnaby is created in lines 14–17?   1   U

2. Read lines 18–32.

   (a) What similarity does the writer identify between Burnaby and Britney Spears?   1   U

   (b) In what ways was Burnaby "lucky" (line 19)?   2   U

   (c) Explain the difference the writer identifies between the "early Victorian period" and the years after 1870.   2   U

   (d) How effective do you find the imagery in the sentence "The early... industrialisation" (lines 22–23) in describing early Victorian society?   2   A/E

   (e) In what way is each of the "breakthroughs" described in lines 27–32 a "media revolution".   3   U

3. Read lines 33–48.

   (a) In what sense, according to lines 33–38, was Burnaby "in the right place, at the right time" (lines 37–38)?   2   U

   (b) Explain how the writer creates a less than serious tone in lines 33–38.   2   A

   (c) To what extent do the details in lines 39–48 justify the writer's claim that "Burnaby was the first hero of mass culture"?   2   E

   (d) How effective do you find the writer's use of colloquial language in lines 39–48. Refer in your answer to more than one example.   2   A/E

4. Read lines 49–61.

Why, according to the writer, did Burnaby die in the way he did?   2   U

(27)

	Marks	Code

Questions on Passage 2

5. Read lines 1–13.

    (a) Explain in detail how the writer creates a rather tongue-in-cheek tone in lines 1–8.   **4**   **A**

    (b) Why did Burnaby's journey into Central Asia make him "something of a popular hero" (line 10)?   **2**   **U**

6. Read lines 14–39.

    (a) Describe the impact of line 14 in terms of the structure and tone of the passage as a whole.   **2**   **A**

    (b) Why did Burnaby make the journey to Central Asia?   **2**   **U**

    (c) Choose one example of humour from lines 15–37, and explain to what extent you find it appropriate in its context.   **2**   **A/E**

7. Read lines 40–59.

    (a) In these lines the writer uses several features associated with narrative writing and story telling. Referring to specific features, show how the writer uses these to engage the reader with his description of the journey.   **4**   **A**

    (b) How effective do you find the final paragraph (lines 58–59) as a conclusion to the passage as a whole?   **2**   **E**

    (18)

Question on both Passages

8. Identify important similarities and differences in the **ideas and style** of **both passages**, making clear which passage you find more appealing and why.   **5**   **E**

    (5)

    Total marks   **(50)**

Answer Support for Close Reading Papers
Introduction

In this section there is Answer Support for each of the four practice Close Reading papers. As you will already know, the idea of working towards the "right answer" is not one which really applies to Close Reading at Higher English. There is rarely a single correct answer. In Analysis questions especially, there are often many possible areas for comment, and even when two students choose the same word or the same image or the same feature of sentence structure, it is not likely that they will both make exactly the same comment on its effect – yet both could score full marks. Despite this, we hope that what follows will be helpful.

For each question there is a suggested acceptable answer, as well as a note of any alternative or additional points which could have been made and which will gain credit. On some occasions there are examples of really sophisticated (or "insightful" as the Examiners say) responses which will certainly impress an exam marker. From time to time you will get a chance to see a really bad answer and to explain what's wrong with it. Each type of answer is identified by a simple code.

You will not see here the full "Marking Instructions" which teachers and SQA markers use. If you want to see what these look like, go to the SQA website www.sqa.org.uk (Select "Services for Learners"; then from the drop-down menu of "NQ Subjects" on the left select "English"; then from the "Subject-specific Links" on the right select "Marking Instructions"; then choose "English Higher Close Reading".) These Marking Instructions, however, are written with teachers and lecturers in mind and are not necessarily very helpful to candidates.

Also, in the Answer Support there is no general advice about how to approach specific types of Close Reading question (imagery, sentence structure, the link question, etc.), since we assume your teacher will be dealing with these regularly in class. However, for some good advice and practice, look at Section One of *Higher English: Close Reading* (Hodder Gibson 2007) or Part 1 of *How to Pass Higher English Colour Edition* (Hodder Gibson 2009). There is advice and practice material for the comparison question in Section Two of *Higher English: Close Reading* and on pages 93–96 of *How to Pass*.

Finally, it is really important to remember that there is much more to reading than a 50-mark Close Reading test, and there are many other ways of developing your ability to read and respond to "non-fiction print text which conveys complex information" (in the words of the official "Arrangements" for Higher English). Above all, you should read widely in the types of material from which the passages tend to be drawn: opinion and comment pieces from quality national newspapers; essays in periodicals and published collections; serious works of non-fiction. The more of this you read, the more you will assimilate the language and style of this type of writing, the more you will recognise the ways in which writers introduce, exemplify and develop key ideas, and the more comfortable you will be with the passages you eventually face in the exam. There is more detailed advice about this aspect of reading in *How to Pass* pages 3–14. The book *Higher English: Close Reading Preparation* (Hodder Gibson 2008) provides a range of opportunities to read and think about suitable extracts, but without the toil of answering a string of questions, and is a useful way of easing yourself into the demands made at this level.

An explanation of the codes used in this section

For each question you will find the question (along with the Mark and the U/A/E Code) repeated from the Question Paper. After that there will be two or more of the following coded boxes:

📖	*passage extract*	*This will give you the relevant lines from the Passage and will save you looking back to the Question Paper. Occasionally, if the extract is very long, it has been omitted.*
✓	straightforward acceptable answer	This will give you an example of an answer which would be enough to score the marks available. Remember, it's only an example; there are always many ways of answering these questions.
★	really good answer	This will give you an example of an outstanding and sophisticated answer which would score full marks comfortably. You should make these answers something you aspire to.
✗	weak/misguided answer	(Papers 1 to 3 only) This will present you with answers which make basic mistakes. You should figure out what's wrong, and then check with the explanations given at the back of the book on pages 179–180.
✚	other possible points	In some Analysis questions, there are many points which can be made, so this gives you points not covered in the other answers.
⬅	similar questions already tackled	You can use this to check back to questions of the same type you have already looked at. It is not exhaustive – simply a selection of questions which require a similar approach.
❗	important advice	This gives you any other points which are important about a particular question. Repetition has been avoided here, so it is important to work through the questions and the papers in order.

Close Reading Paper 1
Social Networking

Questions on Passage 1

1.　Read lines 1–15.

(a) In what ways, according to lines 1–4, has Facebook brought about "significant change in our culture"? **2　U**

📖	*The social networking site Facebook turned five years old last week. Arguably, it marks a milestone in a progressive and highly significant change in our culture as tens to hundreds of millions of individuals worldwide, including the very young, are signing up for friendship through a screen.*
✓	Because it has caused huge numbers (of all ages/all over the world) (1 mark) to embrace the idea of friendship via the internet. (1 mark)
✗	It has brought about significant change in our culture because tens to hundreds of millions of individuals worldwide are signing up for friendship through a screen. *Why is this a bad answer? See page 179*
➕	The second part of the answer could have been put the other way, i.e.: "… friendship that is impersonal or no longer face to face".

(b) Explain briefly the key attractions of social networking the writer gives in lines 5–15? **3　U**

📖	*What precisely is the appeal of social networking sites? First, there is the simple issue of the constraints of modern life, where unsupervised playing outside or going for walks is now perceived as too dangerous. A child confined to the home every evening may find at the keyboard the kind of freedom of interaction and communication that earlier generations took for granted in the three-dimensional world of the street. But even given a choice, screen life can still be more appealing. Building a Facebook profile is one way that individuals can identify themselves, making them feel important and accepted. I recently had a fascinating conversation with a young devotee who proudly claimed to have 900 friends. Clearly, this is a way of satisfying that basic human need to belong, to be part of a group, as well as the ability to experience instant feedback and recognition – at least from someone, somewhere – 24 hours a day.*
✓	• eliminates the dangers children are thought to face in the outside world • allows for the exchange of views/ideas among friends • allows for a sense of belonging to a group
➕	Other acceptable point: • it is available around the clock
!	Bullet point answers perfectly acceptable here.

(c) What effect does the parenthetical comment in line 15 have on the tone of the sentence in which it appears? **2 A**

📖	*Clearly, this is a way of satisfying that basic human need to belong, to be part of a group, as well as the ability to experience instant feedback and recognition – at least from someone, somewhere – 24 hours a day.*
✓	It changes the tone from positive to negative. "At least" has the effect of making the benefit seem less important than it was.
★	The inclusion of the comment has the effect of undercutting the writer's previous enthusiastic description of social networking. The words "someone, somewhere" have a hint of desperation about them as if anyone, anywhere will do, and they also emphasise the sense of anonymity this kind of communication involves.
✗	The parenthetical comment is in between dashes and it adds extra information. *Why is this a bad answer? See page 179*
❗	Start by comparing the tone without the extra statement with the tone as it is in the passage. Then try to see (or better still "hear") how the words in the parenthesis affect the tone.

2. Read lines 16–23.

At the same time, this constant reassurance – that you are listened to, recognised, and important – is coupled with a distancing from the stress of face-to-face, real-life conversation. Real-life conversations are, after all, far more perilous than those in the cyber world. They occur in real time, with no opportunity to think up clever or witty responses, and they require a sensitivity to voice tone and body language. Moreover, according to the context and, indeed, the person with whom we are conversing, our own delivery will need to adapt. None of these skills are required when chatting on a social networking site.

(a) In what way, according to the writer, are "Real life conversations... far more perilous than those in the cyber world"? (lines 18–19) **2 U**

✓	In real life conversations you have little or no time to come up with smart replies and could cause offence as a result. Also in the cyber world you are not heard or seen, so there are no dangers of giving out unclear signals.
✗	Real life conversations are actually happening at that moment, while in a social network you don't need to have any special abilities. *Why is this a bad answer? See page 179*
❗	Quite a lot of work has been needed here to achieve "own words", but it has to be done.

(b) Show how the writer's word choice in the whole paragraph makes clear the difference between the two types of communication. **4 E**

✓	When talking about real life conversations she refers to "stress", which suggests the pressure it can cause, and calls it "perilous", which suggests something extremely dangerous.
	When talking about the other type she uses the word "reassurance" which suggests something comforting, and talks of this type "distancing" people from real life, which makes it sound as if you're protected from it.
★	"Stress" indicates the strain and anxiety the writer feels can be caused in face to face conversation, which is described as "perilous", suggesting extreme danger and threat. The use of "chatting" when referring to the safer world of cyberspace connotes a warm, easy-going relationship, as does "re-assurance", which connotes something calming, comforting and almost encouraging.
✗	The writer says that real life conversation causes "stress", but in chat rooms there is "constant reassurance".
	Why is this a bad answer? See page 179
✚	Comment could also be made on:
	"sensitivity" – suggests possibility of upset
	"constant" – suggests something which can be relied on
!	4 marks, so four words needed – two for each "side"; a really good point on one word might get 2 marks, but it would not be sensible to assume your answer is as good as that!

3. How effective do you find the analogy in lines 24–29 in developing the writer's ideas? Refer in your answer to the ideas contained in the analogy and to the language used by the writer to express it. **4 E**

📖	*Although it might seem an extreme analogy, I often wonder whether real conversation in real time may eventually give way to these sanitised and easier screen dialogues, in much the same way as killing, skinning and butchering an animal to eat has been replaced by the convenience of packages of meat on the supermarket shelf. Perhaps future generations will recoil with similar horror at the messiness, unpredictability and immediate personal involvement of a three-dimensional, real-time interaction.*
✓	The writer is saying that people are forgetting what real conversation is like just like meat in the supermarket makes you forget that animals have actually died. She describes the "convenience" of shop food suggesting it is easy and safe just like online chat. However, face to face conversation has "messiness" – it is uncontrolled and untidy. Also "killing, skinning and butchering an animal" makes it out to be a cruel, harsh activity.
★	This analogy effectively allows the writer to compare the difference between "real" conversation and "cyber" conversation to the difference between the harsh reality of slaughtering animals and the neatly packaged meat in shops. She suggests that people feel more comfortable being protected from what is "real" and may even forget or not realise what is "real".
	The words "sanitised" and "butchering" bring out the contrast clearly: "sanitised" something unnaturally clean, with any possible offence or upset removed; "butchering" is an uncompromising description of what actually happens to animals being slaughtered suggesting a sense of cruelty and brutality, in the midst of blood and guts.

(X)	It is really effective because it really helps you to understand what she is saying. She is describing what happens in a slaughterhouse and how there is "killing, skinning and butchering". This lets you know exactly what it is like. *Why is this a bad answer? See page 179*
(+)	Comment could also be made on: "recoil" – suggests the shocked reaction when people realise what is actually happening "unpredictability" – suggests chaotic, hectic, uncertain, unsafe…
(!)	The question is coded "E" (Evaluation) – partly because you are asked "How effective do you find…", but also because it asks about **ideas and language**. "U/A/E" would look a bit silly, so it's simply coded "E". You should realise that what matters in this type of question is a clear understanding of the ideas and good analysis of the language. Notice, however, how the good answer uses words such as "effectively" and "clearly" to convey some sense of evaluation – but be careful not to overdo this approach.

4. Read lines 30–37.

Show how the writer's use of language emphasises the idea of screen technologies as a "threat". **2 A**

(book)	I think all of this poses something of a threat to young minds. First, I would suggest that attention span is at risk. If the young brain is exposed from the outset to a world of fast action and reaction, of instant new screen images flashing up with the press of a key, such rapid interchange might accustom the brain to operate over such timescales. It might be helpful to investigate whether the near total submersion of our culture in screen technologies over the last decade might in some way be linked to the threefold increase over this period in prescriptions for the drug prescribed for "hyperactive" youngsters with ADHD.
(✓)	"exposed" suggests that the young brain is unprotected and rather vulnerable; "submersion" suggests that our culture is completely surrounded by new technologies, almost as if it's drowning.
(★)	The string of words "fast… instant… flashing… rapid" emphasises speed, as if the screen is uncontrollable, almost dominating the user. The word choice of "exposed" has connotations of being defenceless, vulnerable and open to any threat or danger.
(X)	The repetition of "young" emphasises that she is concerned about boys and girls who can't look after themselves. "Investigate" has connotations of a very serious probing look at something. *Why is this a bad answer? See page 179*
(+)	An acceptable comment could be made about "action and reaction", where the repetition suggests the rapidity of the activity as a threat to those who can't control it.
(!)	"Writer's use of language…" usually allows you choose any features you think are suitable. In an exam, choose straightforward examples; don't risk anything too elaborate.

ANSWER SUPPORT FOR CLOSE READING PAPERS

5. Read lines 38–45.

> *Related to this change might be a second area of potential difference in the young 21st century mind – a much more marked preference for the here-and-now, where the immediacy of an experience trumps any regard for the consequences. After all, whenever you play a computer game, you can always just play it again; everything you do is reversible. The emphasis is on the thrill of the moment, the buzz of rescuing the princess in the game. No care is given for the princess herself or for any long-term significance, because there is none. Perhaps we should be paying attention to whether such activities may result in a more impulsive and solipsistic attitude.*

(a) What does the writer mean by "the immediacy of an experience trumps any regard for the consequences"? (lines 39–40) **3 U**

✓	She means that for many young people the pleasure they get at the moment something happens is more important that what might happen because of it.
★	Young people are totally caught up in he thrill and excitement of doing something in the present and that this surpasses any concern for what might happen in the future as a result.
!	Unusual to have 3 marks for explaining so few words, but there are three important ideas to be understood: "the immediacy of an experience", "trumps", and "regards for the consequences".

(b) Show how the writer's use of language in this paragraph conveys her disapproval of computer games. **3 A**

✓	• "buzz" suggests an artificial excitement similar to taking certain drugs • the dash before "because there is none" creates a dramatic pause which emphasises the selfishness of those who play these games • "impulsive" suggests they are thoughtless and reckless
★	The writer chooses young people's vocabulary such as "thrill" and "buzz" to suggest self-indulgent behaviour, pleasure for its own sake, and also very short-lived. She also employs a rather colloquial register in "After all", and "you can always just" to suggest sloppy thinking, and an irresponsible attitude. She concludes the paragraph in her own adult vocabulary: "solipsistic", to emphasises the totally self-centred outlook of the people she is describing.
✗	The semicolon after "again" creates a pause which allows her to show her disapproval. She uses a lot of dashes to add extra information. There are lots of big words like "immediacy", "impulsive" and "solipsistic" which show how important she thinks it is. *Why is this a bad answer? See page 179*
✚	Comment could also be made on the use of "No… none", where the use of negatives to start and finish a sentence emphasise the negative, critical attitude the writer has.
⬅	Very similar to Question 4 in this paper.

6. Read lines 46–58.

   (a) What difference does the writer identify between a novel and a computer game? **1 U**

📖	*This brings us to a third possible change – in empathy. One teacher of 30 years' standing wrote to me that she had witnessed a change over the time she had been teaching in the ability of her pupils to understand others. She pointed out that previously, reading novels had been a good way of learning about how others feel and think, as distinct from oneself. Unlike the game to rescue the princess, where the goal is to feel rewarded, the aim of reading a book is, after all, to find out more about the princess herself.*
✓	She says that reading a novel leads to a concern for others, while a computer game is all about concern with self.
✛	The idea of "reward", i.e. gaining something for yourself, could have been used in the "game" part of the answer.
!	Only one mark, but both "sides" needed. You might get away with: "Computer games make you selfish, novels don't", but it wouldn't be worth the risk!

   (b) What, in lines 53–58, does the writer find "strange"? **2 U**

📖	*Finally it seems strange that in a society recoiling from the introduction of ID cards, we are at the same time enthusiastically embracing the possible erosion of our identity through social networking sites. When all your private thoughts and feelings can be posted on the internet for all to see, perhaps Facebook makes you think about yourself differently. Are we perhaps losing a sense of where we ourselves finish and the outside world begins?*
✓	She finds it strange that on one hand we object to the introduction of ID cards, while on the other we are willing to give out information freely on social networking sites.

7. Show how the writer's use of language in lines 59–62 conveys her disapproval of the activities she is describing. **2 A**

📖	*With fast-paced, instant screen reactions, perhaps the next generation will define themselves by the responses of others; hence the baffling current preoccupation with posting an almost moment-by-moment, flood-of-consciousness account of your thoughts and activities, however banal. I believe it is called Twitter.*
✓	"instant" tends to imply it is perhaps too fast and doesn't allow for any thought; "baffling" suggests she finds it rather bemusing, almost as if it is designed to confuse.
★	Word choice: "preoccupation" suggests an unhealthy excess of attention, and "banal" conveys her belief that these "thoughts and activities" are dull and trite. Tone: The final sentence is very flat and lifeless in contrast with previous longer, more involved sentence. This creates a tone of distaste or mockery (almost self-mockery). There is a sense of a person from an older generation guardedly referring to some alien modern phenomenon.
✛	Comment could also be made on: "moment-by-moment" and/or "flood-of-consciousness", where the hyphenated forms suggest breakneck speed or unnecessary compression
↩	Very similar to questions 4 and 5(b) in this paper.

Questions on Passage 2

8. Read lines 1–25.

   (a) The style of writing in lines 1–14 is very different from that in lines 15–25. Referring to examples of both styles, discuss to what extent you find the change in style effective in engaging the reader in the writer's point of view.　　　**4 A/E**

✓	The style of 1–14 is very colloquial, e.g. "next big thing", "pretty much", "killer app". The style of 15–25 is much more formal, e.g.: "psychological need", "tribal context", "subverted". This is quite effective as the informal language draws the reader in by using an everyday style the reader is familiar with and not threatened by to describe a new technology the reader will almost certainly know. Having drawn in the reader, the writer can then move on to the more complicated part of his argument about social changes, where the vocabulary has to be more sophisticated.
★	The register in lines 1–14 is informal and imprecise ("next big thing", "don't worry", "like crazy", "pretty much", "killer app", "riveting stuff"), whereas in lines 15–25 it is much more formal, academic, at times quite jargonised, e.g.: "psychological need", "a culture starved", "resided, "the social context of community", "tribal context", "subverted", "evolutionary need". On the one hand it can be seen as effective in that the informal register in the opening paragraphs seems to mock the scale and success of Twitter and is appealing to reader's sense of the ordinary; this engages the reader's support and interest before moving into the more sophisticated, psychological argument about changes in the makeup of society and how Twitter helps to fill a void created by these. On the other hand it is ineffective in that such casual language is simply out of place in a serious piece of writing; it devalues the topic and it makes the writer sound as if he's trying to be trendy. Also, such casual, slang language misleads the reader (into thinking whole passage will be the same throughout) and the sudden shift to a much more sophisticated academic style is too much of a shock, causing the writer's argument about changes in the makeup of society and how Twitter helps to fill a void created by these to be unnecessarily hard to follow.
!	The "good" answer above is obviously much more than would be needed for 4 marks, but it is included to give you an example of how to argue both sides, which the words "to what extent" encourage you to do.

   (b) According to lines 15–25, in what ways does Twitter "fill a deep psychological need in our society"? (lines 15–16)　　　**2 U**

📖	*More interesting, however, is how the Twitter system acts to fill a deep psychological need in our society. The unfortunate reality is that we are a culture starved for real community. For hundreds of thousands of years, human beings have resided in tribes of about 30–70 people. Our brains are wired to operate within the social context of community – programming crucial for human survival.* *However, the tribal context of life was subverted during the Industrial Revolution, when the extended family was torn apart in order to move labourers into the cities. But a deep evolutionary need for community continues to express itself, through feelings of community generated by your workplace, your church, your sports team, and now... the twitterverse. This is why people feel so compelled to tweet, to Facebook or even to check their email incessantly. We crave connection.*
✓	Deep down, we have a need to be together in small societies but this is not easy in the modern world so Twitter fills the gap.

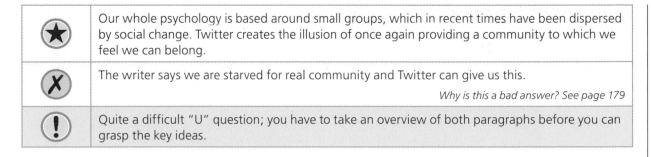

★	Our whole psychology is based around small groups, which in recent times have been dispersed by social change. Twitter creates the illusion of once again providing a community to which we feel we can belong.
✗	The writer says we are starved for real community and Twitter can give us this. *Why is this a bad answer? See page 179*
ⓘ	Quite a difficult "U" question; you have to take an overview of both paragraphs before you can grasp the key ideas.

9. Read lines 26–49.

(a) Outline briefly the key points of Maslow's "Theory of Human Motivation". **3 U**

✔	Human beings have many needs but some are more important than others. It is like a pyramid with the important ones at the bottom and the less important ones at the top. The ones at the bottom are needed for survival and have to be achieved before people can start thinking about the others, which are about feeling good and getting on with other people.
★	According to Maslow's theory, humans have a range of physical and emotional needs (which he represented as a pyramid), the most essential of which are those for physical survival. Once these are satisfied, humans desire to be fulfilled in the way they feel and the way they interact with others.
⬅	Similar to 1(b) in this paper.
ⓘ	Three marks, so three points.

(b) Explain how the writer's sentence structure in lines 29–38 helps to clarify his description of Maslow's theory. **2 A**

📖	*Maslow's hierarchy of needs is most often displayed as a pyramid, with lowest levels of the pyramid made up of the most basic needs, and with more complex needs at the top of the pyramid. Needs at the bottom of the pyramid are basic physical requirements including the need for food, water, sleep and warmth. Once these lower-level needs have been met, people can move on to higher levels of needs, which become increasingly psychological and social. Soon, the need for love, friendship and intimacy become important. Further up the pyramid, the need for personal esteem and feelings of accomplishment become important. Finally, Maslow emphasised the importance of self-actualisation, which is a process of growing and developing as a person to achieve individual potential.*
✔	If you look at the beginnings of most of the sentences, you notice that the writer is in a way giving a picture of a "pyramid", with words like "at the bottom", "lower-level needs", "further up" and "Finally" – as if they are steps up a pyramid.
★	The writer effectively structures the sentences to help convey the idea of stages in a process. This can be seen in the way most sentences begin: "Needs at the bottom", "Once these lower-level needs have been met", "Soon", "Further up", "Finally" – all giving the impression of regular steps upward, which matches perfectly the "pyramid" idea..
✗	The writer uses a lot of long sentences because he has a lot to say about the subject. *Why is this a bad answer? See page 179*
➕	It could be pointed out that, after the first sentence, all the sentences are of a relatively similar length, suggesting a structured, clear approach.

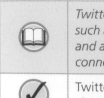

(c) What, according to the writer, makes Twitter relevant to Maslow's theory?   **2 U**

📖	*Twitter aims primarily at social needs, like those for belonging, love, and affection. Relationships such as friendships, romantic attachments and families help fulfil this need for companionship and acceptance, as does involvement in social, community or religious groups. Clearly, feeling connected to people via Twitter helps to fulfil some of this need to belong and feel cared about.*
✓	Twitter is relevant to Maslow's theory because it gives people the chance to feel that others care about them, which is one of the things Maslow says they need.
★	Twitter provides a means of meeting certain needs at the top of Maslow's pyramid, i.e. in the sphere of interpersonal relations, thus allowing people to believe they are a valued part of a community

(d) Show how the writer's use of language in lines 44–49 highlights his main criticism Twitter?   **2 A**

📖	*An even higher level of need, related to self-esteem and social recognition, is also brought into play by Twitter. At its best, Twitter allows normal people to feel like celebrities. At its worst, it is an exercise in unconditional narcissism – the idea that others might actually care about the minutiae of our daily lives. I believe that this phenomenon of micro-celebrity is driven by existential anxiety. I twitter, therefore I am. I matter, I'm good enough, I'm smart enough, and, goddammit, people* like *me!*
✓	• "minutiae" makes it clear that the writer thinks that the details people put on Twitter are trivial and insignificant • repetition of "I" and "me" reinforces the idea of self-centredness
★	"I Twitter, therefore I am" – is a distortion of Descartes' "I think, therefore I am"; comparing Twitter to a famous philosophical statement is so ridiculous that it makes Twitter sound absurd. Saying Twitter is "an exercise in unconditional narcissism" shows clearly the writer's criticism as "narcissism" is the ultimate in egotism, a word which could never have any positive connotations.
➕	Comment could also be made on: "At its best … at its worst" - suggestion of extremes "might actually care" - tone of incredulity "goddammit" - almost accusatory, self-righteous, childlike tone "good enough … smart enough" - rather petulant sounding
⬅	Very similar to questions 4, 5(b) and 7 in this paper.

Question on both Passages

NB The "Comparison" question will be dealt with slightly differently from other questions. There is an example of reasonably good answer, worth 3 out of 5, and of a really good answer which would get full marks. There is a brief commentary about both answers.

Some general points about tackling the Comparison Question:

- You should think of your answer as being a "mini-essay": write in formal continuous prose (no notes or bullet points) and have a clear "line of thought" as you would in a Critical Essay.

- Stick closely to the instruction in the question about whether or write about ideas or style or both; even if it's on style only (the least likely option) you have to show understanding of the main ideas in both passages – you can't simply write about random examples of tone, imagery etc.

- Stick closely to the "focus" in the question; it is there to help you – you are never asked just to compare the passages.

- There is no "right" answer – you can prefer either passage and still score well – it all depends on the quality of your argument.

- These answers are not marked according to length or according to the number of "points" made: they are judged on their overall quality.

- Don't be afraid to have a strong personal input, but make sure you base everything on the ideas or language features of the passages.

For more detailed advice, refer to Section Two of *Higher English: Close Reading* (which includes practice material dedicated to answering the comparison question) and pages 93–96 of *How to Pass*.

10. Which writer's views on key aspects of social networking do you find more interesting? Justify your choice by reference to the **ideas** of **both passages**.   **5   U/E**

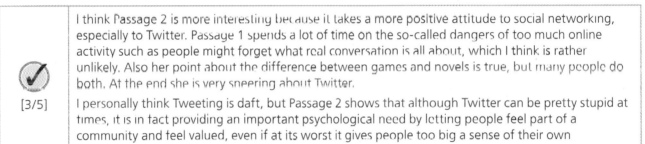

✓ [3/5]	I think Passage 2 is more interesting because it takes a more positive attitude to social networking, especially to Twitter. Passage 1 spends a lot of time on the so-called dangers of too much online activity such as people might forget what real conversation is all about, which I think is rather unlikely. Also her point about the difference between games and novels is true, but many people do both. At the end she is very sneering about Twitter. I personally think Tweeting is daft, but Passage 2 shows that although Twitter can be pretty stupid at times, it is in fact providing an important psychological need by letting people feel part of a community and feel valued, even if at its worst it gives people too big a sense of their own importance.

Commentary

This answer is fairly short, but packs in a lot of acceptable comment and reference to the Passages. The line of thought is clear (Passage 1 is negative; Passage 2 is positive), there is a clear structure and there is evidence from both Passages. There is some sensible personal comment. The answer certainly meets the typical criterion for this type of question: "understanding of both passages; some ability to compare/contrast relevant ideas is discernible" – in fact it might just score 4 out of 5.

The main weakness in this answer is the degree of vagueness: the point about "real conversation" is not explained clearly enough and the point about "games and novels" is not explained at all – although it is potentially a very valid criticism of the writer's argument. Similarly, the points about Passage 2 are just too "bald".

[5/5]

I find Baroness Greenfield's point of view much more interesting.

The piece from "Psychology Today" does little more than explain what Twitter is, demonstrating its widespread appeal and giving some, admittedly amusing, examples of its totally trivial content. After that it attempts to link aspects of Twitter to a 65-year-old academic paper about Human Motivation. It is not too hard to see that Twitter can be seen as satisfying some of the higher level needs, but why Moses Ma is bothering to tell us is less easy to understand. He calls it "fascinating", but I can't agree. Perhaps the point is that supposedly "new" technology doesn't really do anything new.

Baroness Greenfield, on the other hand, seems to me to touch on a number of genuinely interesting and provocative ideas. Firstly, she provides some sensible explanations for the explosion in social networking and I find the idea that in a way it is a response to fears (among young people and parents) of the "real world" very possibly true. Even more interesting is the idea that cyber-chat is less "perilous" than real life and the way she raises the idea that people retreat into a style of communication which is safe and uncomplicated by nuance of tone or body language. Her analogy with the slaughterhouse and the processed meat is a bit extreme but is graphic enough to make the point strongly that many people shy away from the brutal realities of life and prefer the safe and the undemanding. Her final theory – about the lack of empathy encouraged by computer games – is perhaps the scariest. The essentially self-centred nature of computer games as opposed to the engagement with the fate of others in "traditional" stories could well be in danger of causing a fundamental shift in the way young people (and hence the older generation of the future) behave. I'm not entirely convinced that it is cause and effect – it could be that manufacturers of computer games are simply responding to a change in outlook already taking place – but, unlike Moses Ma's rather pointless links to Maslow and his pyramid, it is certainly worth thinking about.

Commentary

The typical description of a full mark answer is "intelligent understanding of both passages; ability to compare/contrast relevant ideas is strong". There is no doubt this answer does that – and more. The line of thought is clear and followed consistently. There is an effective structure, in which the "less interesting" passage is dealt with (and dismissed) first, allowing the student to concentrate, at greater length, on what she finds interesting about Passage 1, finishing neatly with a swipe at the inadequacies of Passage 2.

There is clear personal engagement with the ideas all the way through and the answer is written in sophisticated and fluent English.

Close Reading Paper 2
Responding to Change

Code:

📖	*passage extract*
✓	straightforward acceptable answer
★	really good answer
✗	weak/misguided answer
✛	other possible points
←	similar questions already tackled
❗	important advice

Questions on Passage 1

1. Read lines 1–14.
   (a) Explain the situation in which, according to lines 1–6, "British society has found itself".   2 U

📖	*New Year is supposed to be a time for looking both backwards and forward. But if it's a good thing to acknowledge a quiet moment of transition between past and future, it's profoundly debilitating to find yourself permanently trapped between the two, and it often seems, at the turn of the year, as if that kind of limbo is where British society has found itself for the last 30 years or so, unable to move backwards, yet somehow reluctant to move on.*
✓	It is stuck between the past and the future. It knows it can't go back the way, but is unwilling to accept the future.
★	British society is seriously weakened by being caught between two ideas: a fondness for a past it knows can't be revisited and an unwillingness to embrace new ideas.
✗	It is unable to move backwards, yet somehow reluctant to move on.
	Why is this a bad answer? See page 179

(b) Show how the writer's word choice in lines 7–10 ("It's not… family life") emphasises the extent of the changes she describes.　　**2　A**

📖	*It's not that nothing has changed in that time, of course. There has been turbo-charged economic growth, wave upon wave of migration, a massive shift from an industrial to a service economy, and a generation of unprecedented change in sexual politics and family life.*
✔	She describes economic growth as "turbo-charged", which suggests an engine made for power and speed. She describes the shift from industry to the service economy as "massive", which suggests a huge, unstoppable force.
★	"turbo-charged" suggests something specially designed for excessive, abnormal power and speed with a hint of something reckless and dangerous. "unprecedented" suggests it is completely new – unparalleled and hard to come to terms with.
✘	She emphasises the extent of the changes she describes with very good word choice. She says "turbo-charged" and "massive" which give the reader a very clear picture of how big the changes have been. *Why is this a bad answer? See page 179*
➕	Comment could also be made on: "wave after wave" – suggests constant, repeated surging movement, relentless…
⬅	Paper 1: question 2(b)

(c) Why, according to the writer, do we "seem to be resisting the changes" (line 10)?　**2　U**

📖	*Yet still, in our hearts and minds, we seem to be resisting the changes with which we live from day to day, as if every statistic recording numbers of children born out of wedlock, or numbers of migrants arriving in Britain, or numbers of teenagers enjoying an active sex life, represented a deep threat to our world, and therefore to ourselves.*
✔	Because the changes seem to be a danger to society as a whole and to each of us individually.
✘	Because we live with them all the time and a lot of teenagers are having sex. *Why is this a bad answer? See page 179*
⬅	Paper 1: questions 1(a), 2(a), 8(b).

2. Read lines 15–26.

📖	*So it could have been almost anything, this New Year, that triggered the latest round of shock-horror headlines about a nation going to hell in a handcart, but, as it was, it was a public comment by an eminent doctor, advocating that children as young as five should be receiving sex education in schools. His reasoning is simple: children, he argues, need a good, confident knowledge of the facts about sex, long before they are even tempted to start experimenting themselves.* *There was no chance, though, of his remarks being greeted with calm agreement all round. For this is a culture where, well within living memory, children as old as 13 or 14 were forbidden to know anything about sex at all, sometimes with tragic consequences. Put the words "five-year-olds" and "sex education" together, therefore, and the old atavistic monster rears up, roaring phrases like "going to the dogs", or "pouring petrol on a fire".*

(a) Why did the doctor's statement cause such a strong reaction?   **2 U**

✓	Because sex education is a subject on which people hold strong views, and suggesting it for children as young as five was bound to shock some people.
★	Because many people have deep-seated, almost primitive fears about children knowing anything about sex, so the proposal to offer it to five-year-olds inevitably led to outrage.
✗	The doctor wanted to make sure that young children know all about sex, because in the past when teenagers weren't allowed to know anything about sex there were unfortunate results such as unwanted pregnancies.

Why is this a bad answer? See page 179

(b) Show how the writer's use of language in these lines emphasises the strength of the reaction.   **2 A**

✓	"shock-horror headlines" gives the idea that the papers were giving the stories a lot of attention and trying to scare the public. "monster" suggests something huge and evil as if the reaction were alive and threatening us.
★	The writer uses a range of clichéd, predictable responses, e.g. "going to hell in a handcart… going to the dogs… pouring petrol on a fire", as if every possible "angry" response is being trotted out. The image of the monster which "rears up, roaring" gives the impression of something fierce, angry and poised to attack; something aggressively and loudly threatening everything around it.
+	Comment could also be made on: "atavistic" – suggests something ancient, deeply felt, primal, reactionary; a primitive reversion to ancestral ways
←	Paper 1: Questions 4, 5(b), 7, 9(d)
!	Note that it's "the reaction" that's being asked about, not "the writer's reaction".

3. Read lines 27–35.

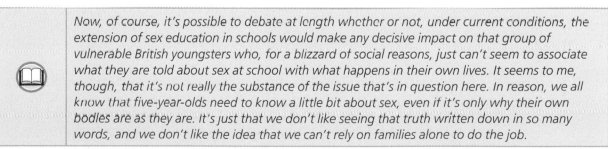

> *Now, of course, it's possible to debate at length whether or not, under current conditions, the extension of sex education in schools would make any decisive impact on that group of vulnerable British youngsters who, for a blizzard of social reasons, just can't seem to associate what they are told about sex at school with what happens in their own lives. It seems to me, though, that it's not really the substance of the issue that's in question here. In reason, we all know that five-year-olds need to know a little bit about sex, even if it's only why their own bodies are as they are. It's just that we don't like seeing that truth written down in so many words, and we don't like the idea that we can't rely on families alone to do the job.*

continued ➢

(a) State briefly the writer's attitude to sex-education for five-year-olds.　　**1　U**

✓	She thinks it is perfectly reasonable for five-year-olds to get sex education.
✛	It would also be acceptable to say: She thinks it is a suitable subject for debate.
⬅	Paper 1, Question 6 is also a "1 U" question.
❗	The use in the question of "briefly" means your answer can (and should) be very short. You usually won't lose marks for writing too much, but it's a waste of precious time – and being succinct is a valuable skill to learn in itself.

(b) How effective do you find the image "a blizzard of social reasons" in conveying the writer's point about the plight of some British youngsters?　　**2　A/E**

✓	If you're literally in a blizzard you can't see because of the amount of snow. The writer is suggesting that young people today have to face so many problems that it is as if they can't see and are helpless.
★	A "blizzard" is literally a snowstorm which overwhelms and makes vision almost impossible. The image effectively illustrates the writer's point that there are so many social reasons (causing young people not to heed the advice they get on sex) coming from many different directions such that they are blinding the young people, making it impossible to distinguish one from the other, making them seem threatened and lost.
✗	In a blizzard there is lots of snow and you can't see where you are going. It is very frightening. So it is very effective in conveying the writer's point. *Why is this a bad answer? See page 179*
❗	When answering on imagery, always start with the literal meaning and then explain how this helps the writer make a point. Remember also to show that you know what the "point" is.

4. Read lines 36–46.

📖	*And the mood is the same in dozens of areas where our society should be moving forward to deal with the practical challenges of 21st-century life, but, at some deeper level, seems to have come to the limit of its capacity for change. We know that our binge-drinking culture is dangerous, for example, but still snarl with resentment at politicians who tell us so. We know that racism is wrong, but still make endless excuses for the surly dislike of foreigners that scars our society.* *And when it comes to the defining issue of our age – climate change – well, we know, in some corner of our brains, that the whole basis of our economy and society has to change over the next 20 years if we are to avoid outright catastrophe, yet we continue – for example – to regard personal motorised transport as some kind of birthright, and bitterly resist any effort to shift us from our cars.*

(a) Show how the writer's word choice conveys "our" attitude to change in each of the areas she identifies. **3 A**

✓	She says we "snarl" when told that binge-drinking is bad for us – this suggests we are angry and a bit like a dog frightening off a threat.
	The "surly" attitude to immigrants suggests we are rude and try to ignore the way society is changing.
	Her use of "bitterly" when describing the way people fight against reducing car use, shows us to be deeply resentful of anything we don't like.
★	"snarl with resentment" suggests we react to warnings about excessive drinking like an aggressive animal, making us sound inarticulate.
	"endless excuses" about racism suggests an ability to dream up reason after reason, to argue away our dislike of immigrants.
	when we claim car travel as a "birthright" we are elevating it to something as important as inherited status, as if it is some kind of God-given entitlement.
✗	She says binge-drinking has become a "culture" which suggests it is bad for us; racism causes "scars" which shows how deeply it affects society; climate change is a "defining issue", which shows how outstandingly important it is. *Why is this a bad answer? See page 179*
✚	Comment might just be made on: "culture" – suggesting that we think it is an accepted, unquestioned part of our way of life. "foreigners" – our attitude is to lump them all together as aliens, not to see them as individuals. "shift" – suggests we are so attached to our cars it will take some effort to move us.
❗	The fact that it's for three marks should tell you that there are three "areas" to be looked at: drinking, racism, climate change. However, this is a difficult question which focuses you not so much on the **writer's** attitude as what she suggests is the **reader's** attitude.

(b) Show how her sentence structure helps to clarify her argument. **2 A**

✓	The repeated pattern of "We know... but" shows that we know what the problems are, but can always find an excuse to ignore them
★	The "We know" followed by "but/yet" emphasises the idea that while we are aware of our weaknesses, we come up with excuses not to do anything about them. The slight variation in the pattern when she comes to climate change (the insertion of "well" and the use of "yet" in place of "but") points it up as the most serious of all.
✗	She uses a lot of dashes to add extra information. This shows us she has a lot to say on the subject. Both paragraphs start with the word "And" which is unusual and ungrammatical. This makes it sound more conversational and help to clarify her argument. *Why is this a bad answer? See page 180*
←	Paper 1, question 9(b)
❗	Remember you must link the features of sentence structure to the "argument", i.e. to what the writer is actually saying.

5. Read lines 47–57.

(a) Show how the imagery in lines 41–43 ("So what… alien?") conveys the writer's view of the situation we find ourselves in.　　　　　　　　　　　**2　A**

📖	*So what are we to do, stranded in this no-man's-land between an old civilisation that's no longer sustainable either practically or morally, and a new one that we still resist because it seems somehow alien?*
✔	No-man's land is the area between two armies. The writer is suggesting that we don't seem to belong to either side, in this case the past and the future, and that we don't know which "side" to be on.
★	"no man's land": literally the space between two warring armies; suggests we are caught and trapped between two forces (the old and the new), uncertain about which way to go, committed to neither side.
➕	The answer doesn't *have* to see "no-man's land" in terms of warfare as the two answers above do. It could be seen as an area where "no man" actually goes or belongs, in which case the writer is suggesting we are metaphorically in an unknown, slightly scary dilemma unsure of where safety lies.
↩	This paper, question 3(b)

(b) The writer gives two possible responses to this situation in lines 49–51. How does her use of language convey her dissatisfaction with both responses?　　　　**2　A**

📖	*Some bluster hopelessly about the need to return to the past. Others talk blithely as if there was no problem about abandoning the family as a useful transmitter of wisdom, and passing the whole job on to schools.*
✔	"hopelessly" suggests those who want to return to the past and don't have any real argument and are a bit pathetic. "abandoning" suggests those who want to ignore the past are deserting something, leaving behind something precious.
★	One side "bluster"; the other side "talk blithely". She is condemning both since "bluster" suggests speaking with false confidence, spouting hot air, and "blithely" suggests they are happy to accept anything and ignore any problems.
➕	Comment could also be made on: "passing… on" – suggestion of giving up responsibility, passing the buck. "whole job" – informal register suggests contemptuous, couldn't-care-less attitude. the "some"/"others" balance suggesting one lot are as bad as the other.
↩	Paper 1, questions 5(b), 7, 9(d); this paper, question 4(a)

(c) What is the writer's preferred response to the situation? **2 U**

📖	*But for the rest of us – well, we probably do best when we face the truth that all social change involves some measure of loss, but that the clock cannot be turned back towards attitudes and prejudices that were abandoned for the best of reasons. And, above all, we perhaps need to strive to move forward as a whole society, rather than as a bunch of fragmented individuals demanding increasingly impossible feats from our hard-pressed public services.*
✓	Her preferred response is to accept change because it is a natural process and usually happens for good reasons. We should aim to act as a community not as individuals.
★	We should realise that change always causes some things we cherish to disappear and we should accept that old attitudes change for good reasons. Most importantly, we should accept change and approach it collectively.

6. Read lines 58–67.

📖	*For in the end, schools can teach nothing that society as a whole does not want children to learn. If our society eats junk food, schools cannot make children eat healthily. If our society is full of bullying behaviour, schools catch the backwash of emotional and physical violence. And if our society remains hopelessly ambivalent about sex – so recently an unspoken taboo, now a multimedia nightmare of cheap raunch and smut – well, then it's not primarily the failure of teachers and educationists that leaves so many teenagers all at sea in this key area of their lives. It's rather our own embarrassment and silence, passed on from generation to generation, and whether lessons begin at five or 15, it will take more than a change in education policy to make any difference to that.*

(a) Why, according to the writer, will it "take more than a change in educational policy" to improve matters? **1 U**

✓	Because it is society not schools that decides how children behave.
★	Because schools cannot bring about change in children's attitudes unless society as a whole wants it.
✛	Credit would probably be given for an answer which dealt only with attitudes to sex (i.e. the "ambivalent" attitude), but the writer is making a slightly bigger point.
⬅	Paper 1, question 6(a); this paper, question 3(a)

(b) Show how the writer's sentence structure in this paragraph helps to clarify her argument. **2 A**

✓	Three of the sentences have a very similar structure, with "If our society" at the start and "schools" or a reference to teachers in the middle. This makes clear her point that what schools do is completely tied up with society's attitudes. Also the repetition of "our" emphasises the idea that these ideas are coming from all of us, not some outside influence.

continued ➢

⭐	The parallel structure "If our society… schools" emphasises that schools' responses are dependent on the actions of society. The parenthesis "so recently… raunch and smut" elaborates on and demonstrates the idea of society being "ambivalent" about sex – contrasting "recently" with "now", and contrasting the secretiveness of "taboo" with wide broadcasting of "multimedia".
➕	Comment could also be made on the use of a topic sentence ("For in the end…") which establishes clearly the idea that schools themselves have little or no influence.
⬅	Paper 1, question 9(b); this paper, question 4(b)
❗	Remember to make it clear you understand what "her argument" actually is.

Questions on Passage 2

7. Read lines 1–10.

> According to the old saying, those who can, do, and those who can't, teach. I have come to think that those who can't teach, teach sex education.
>
> Judged by its results – not a bad way of judging – sex education has been an utter failure. The increase in sex education here in recent years has coincided with an explosion of unwanted pregnancies and sexually transmitted disease (STD) far worse than anywhere else in Europe. Since the government's teenage pregnancy strategy was introduced in 1999, the number of girls having abortions has soared. A culture of promiscuity among the young has driven the rate of STDs to a record. Almost 400,000 people – half of them under 25 – were newly diagnosed, 6% more than in 2006. You might well be tempted to argue that sex education causes sexual delinquency.

(a) Show how the writer's use of language in these lines creates a rather flippant, tongue-in-cheek tone. **2 A**

✔	The writer adds in parenthesis "not a bad way of judging" as if she is surprised that she has to make such an obvious statement and suggesting that there might actually be people who think otherwise.
⭐	The way she extends "the old saying" to "those who can't teach, teach sex education" is a throwaway suggestion that sex education is carried out by complete incompetents, and the unusual repetition in "teach, teach" sounds very odd.
	When she says "you might well be tempted to argue…" she is being deliberately euphemistic, pretending to be polite, when she really means it's blindingly obvious to her.
❌	She says that" those who can't teach, teach sex education" which is rather flippant.
	She talks about an "explosion" of unwanted pregnancies, which is not literally true.
	Why is this a bad answer? See page 180
❗	It is always difficult to explain humour. The best strategy is to think about how particular words/expressions *sound* when read aloud. (Look back to the "tone" point in the good answer to Paper 1, question 7.)

(b) Show how the writer's word choice in lines 3–10 conveys her personal attitude to the statistics she is reporting. **2 A**

✓	She refers to the increase in unwanted pregnancies as an "explosion" – this suggests she sees it as a massive increase, completely out of control. The number of abortions has "soared" – this suggests it has climbed unstoppably and with great ease.
★	She uses very emotive, unscientific language when referring to statistics: "explosion" gives the impression that the rise in unwanted pregnancies is like a bomb going off – not just with force, but damaging to all around; "soared" gives the impression that the number of abortions has not just gone up, but risen rapidly like a bird flying high into the sky until out of sight.
✗	The writer gives lots of frightening statistics, such as 400,000 cases of STDs, up 6%. *Why is this a bad answer? See page 180*
➕	Comment could also be made on: "far (worse)" – emphasising it's not just worse but significantly so. "culture" – (in this context) used in a negative way to suggest something rather self-indulgent. "driven" – suggestion of force, oppression, controlled by someone else… "record" – emphasising it's the worst ever, ironic sense of achievement.
⬅	Paper 1, questions 5(b), 7; this paper, questions 4(b), 5(b)

8. Show how the writer's use of language in lines 11–14 conveys her disapproval of introducing more sex education. **2 A**

📖	*When something fails, the usual procedure is to drop it and try something else. With sex education, however, the worse it gets, the more people cry out for more of it and earlier – to the extent that Ministers are considering making schools offer more sex education, offer it earlier and deny parents the right to withdraw their children from it.*
✓	She says that the people who want more sex education "cry out" for it – this makes them sound loud and unruly, which implies she disapproves of what they want. According to her, the Government plan will "deny… the right" which suggests the Government is being dictatorial and taking away something parents are entitled to.
★	The writer tells us what "the usual procedure" is, implying that to do otherwise must be abnormal or illogical – a point strengthened by the use of "however" in the next sentence to highlight the contrast. The dash in line 13 creates a pause before she launches her attack on the Government: the words used to introduce the attack, "to the extent that", give the idea of Ministers pushing forward something even more unacceptable; they have a tone of "would you believe it!"
➕	Comment could also be made on: the repetition of "more" – to echo the simplistic arguments of the proponents "making" – implications of compulsion.
⬅	This paper, questions 4(b), 5(b), 7(b)

9. Read lines 15–24.

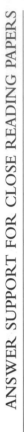

> *Last week the Family Planning Association published a comic-style sex education booklet ("Let's Grow with Nisha and Joe") for six-year-olds to be marketed in primary schools for use in sex and relationships lessons. There's nothing wrong with the pamphlet itself. Admittedly it's more of a dreary workbook than a "fun" comic, but there's nothing that would startle a child or should upset even the most conservative of "family campaigners". The rudest thing is a drawing of two children, naked, with instructions to draw lines connecting interesting bits of their bodies with the appropriate words, yet it seems to me highly unrealistic (given that 25% of children leave primary school struggling to read and write) to assume that many six-year-olds could begin to read the labels "testicles" or "vagina".*

(a) Describe the writer's attitude to the sex education booklet.   **2 U**

✓	It is rather dull but there is nothing actually wrong with it.
+	The point could also be made that she thinks it has unrealistic expectations of what children of that age can understand.
←	This paper, question 5(c)

(b) Show how her use of language makes her attitude clear.   **2 A**

✓	"dreary" suggests it's dull and uninteresting. The repetition of "nothing" emphasises the lack of anything that would offend anybody.
★	"nothing wrong with the pamphlet itself" has a tone of rather grudging approval, in which "itself" implies there is in fact something more fundamental to which the writer objects. "interesting bits" is a rather coy way to describe body parts/sexual organs – perhaps in imitation of the childish nature of the pamphlet or suggesting that the only language today's children will understand.
+	Comment could also be made on: "highly" – to extend the idea of it as "unrealistic"; shows how far removed the language of the pamphlet is from they kind of English most children can understand. "assume" – implies the writers of the pamphlet are taking things for granted, don't realise the difficulties…
←	Paper 1, question 9(d); this paper question 4(a)

10. Read lines 25–43.

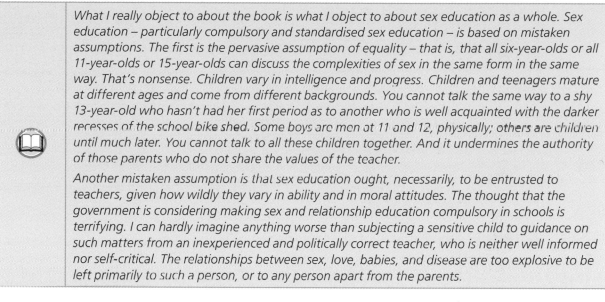

> *What I really object to about the book is what I object to about sex education as a whole. Sex education – particularly compulsory and standardised sex education – is based on mistaken assumptions. The first is the pervasive assumption of equality – that is, that all six-year-olds or all 11-year-olds or 15-year-olds can discuss the complexities of sex in the same form in the same way. That's nonsense. Children vary in intelligence and progress. Children and teenagers mature at different ages and come from different backgrounds. You cannot talk the same way to a shy 13-year-old who hasn't had her first period as to another who is well acquainted with the darker recesses of the school bike shed. Some boys are men at 11 and 12, physically; others are children until much later. You cannot talk to all these children together. And it undermines the authority of those parents who do not share the values of the teacher.*
>
> *Another mistaken assumption is that sex education ought, necessarily, to be entrusted to teachers, given how wildly they vary in ability and in moral attitudes. The thought that the government is considering making sex and relationship education compulsory in schools is terrifying. I can hardly imagine anything worse than subjecting a sensitive child to guidance on such matters from an inexperienced and politically correct teacher, who is neither well informed nor self-critical. The relationships between sex, love, babies, and disease are too explosive to be left primarily to such a person, or to any person apart from the parents.*

(a) Summarise the writer's main objections to sex education.　　　　**4　U**

✓ ★	• It is forced on children, there is no choice • It's the same for everyone, one size fits all • It is founded on beliefs which are simply wrong • It is delivered by teachers
✚	A point could also be made about the disempowerment of parents.
←	Paper 1, questions 1(b), 9(a)
!	Keep "summary" questions short; bullet points strongly recommended.

(b) Show how the writer's use of language conveys the strength of her objections.　　**4　A**

✓	• The very short sentence: "That's nonsense" creates a blunt, dismissive tone as she rejects one of the assumptions behind sex education. • The repetitive use of "children" emphasises how young, vulnerable they are in her eyes. • The use of "terrifying" suggests she is almost physically scared at the thought of it. • The use of "subjecting" gives the idea of forcing people to undergo something harmful.

continued ➤

★	The writer uses the word "assumption" more than once, underlining the idea that to her the whole argument for sex education is based on lazy thinking and a lack of intellectual rigour.
	The pattern of repetition at the start of several sentence ("Children vary… Children mature"; "You cannot… You cannot…") creates a very assertive, hectoring tone as if she is arguing forcefully, jabbing a finger at her opponents.
	The word "undermines" in "it undermines the authority of those parents" suggests a deliberately subversive tactic, eating away at and devaluing parents' status.
	The use of "politically correct" when describing teachers is a definite put-down as it implies the writer finds them excessively compliant with trendy rules.
✚	Comment could also be made on:
	"pervasive" – suggests something insidious, gets into the whole philosophy
	"(how) wildly (they vary)" – idea that differences in quality of delivery are extreme, almost dangerous
↩	Paper1, question 4; this paper, question 2(b)
!	Being hit with a "**4 A**" at this stage might seem a bit cruel, but there are plenty of features to comment on (as is always the case with a "**4 A**"), so it's really not all that difficult. If you're remembering to pace yourself sensibly, you should have enough time to earn four marks in this question.

Question on both Passages

NB The "Comparison" question is dealt with slightly differently from other questions. There is an example of reasonably good answer, worth 3 out of 5, and of a really good answer which would get full marks. There is a brief commentary about both answers.

For some general points about tackling the Comparison Question, see page 37.

11. Which writer in your opinion comes across as the more reasonable and thoughtful person?

Justify your choice by reference to the **ideas and style** of **both passages**.   **5 E**

[3/5]	I think Minette Marrin is a more reasonable and thoughtful person.
	She objects to compulsory sex education, which I think is reasonable – it should be a matter for parents, since not all have the same background and beliefs and, as Marrin argues, children vary hugely in their maturity so are not all ready for sex education at the same time. She gives us clear statistics about the problem, which I think makes her reasonable and thoughtful because she shows how frightening the situation is. She criticises the government for doing more of a policy that has failed, and I think she is right to do so. Another way she is thoughtful is that she criticises bad teachers and ones with bad moral attitudes, instead of simply believing they are all wonderful.
	Joyce McMillan is not nearly as thoughtful and reasonable. She seems to think it is ok for five-year-olds to have sex education and even makes fun of those who object, comparing them to "old monsters". She also makes fun of attitudes to drinking and climate change, which I think is unreasonable because we know something has to be done about these problems. Her last point about schools only being able to teach what society wants children to know is pretty reasonable, but I still think that Minette Marrin is more thoughtful.

Commentary

Just enough for 3 marks. There is a clear structure, a clear point of view, and a basic understanding of what each writer is saying. However, there is only one direct reference to style, and there is an awful lot of unsupported assertion ("... and I think she is right to do so.").

The student has taken a very shallow view of Joyce McMillan's argument and at times seems not to have fully understood her stance, e.g. "makes fun of attitudes to drinking and climate change".

From these passages, I think Joyce McMillan comes across as a much more reasonable and thoughtful individual. She appears sensitive and open-minded, whereas Minette Marrin comes across as rather dogmatic and narrow-minded.

There is, from the start of Passage 2, a rather sneering tone, where Marrin is dismissive of a whole profession and even suggests there is a subset of teachers who are even more incompetent than the rest. When reporting the statistics about sexual health, she limits herself to "shocking" ones which will advance her case, and even then puts her own spin on them: "soared", "culture of promiscuity". According to her, this is all the fault of teachers and politicians – as before, she condemns everyone, without any hint that the young people themselves might have to shoulder some of the blame. She is relatively even-handed when describing the FPA pamphlet ("There's nothing wrong with the pamphlet itself."), and in her general condemnation of sex education she starts out with reasonable arguments about the "mistaken assumptions" which she claims underpin the whole policy, but seems unable to resist sniping at her favourite targets: teachers ("vary wildly in ability and moral attitudes") and the Government, whose plans are "terrifying".

[5/5]

Joyce McMillan, on the other hand, strikes me as a much more reasonable and reflective person. Her article uses the furore over a suggestion to have sex education for five-year-olds to explore the ambivalent feelings of society as a whole when it comes not just to sex education but to a number of issues where we face a need to change. She acknowledges that we are apprehensive about accepting change and that often we would like to retreat to the safety of the past – hence her image of us as "stranded in no-man's land" – even though we know it is not really possible. For example, adults *know* that young people need to know about sex, it's just that they're uncomfortable about it, because it has for so long been a subject treated almost as a taboo. It is an indication of McMillan's sensitivity that she criticises not just those who retreat into the past ("bluster hopelessly") but also those who fully embrace the new ideas ("talk blithely... as if there is no problem"). This even-handedness and deep understanding of people's fears is what makes McMillan, for me, a far more reasonable and thoughtful person.

The contrast with Minette Marrin can be seen at its sharpest when you realise that when referring to teenagers, all Marrin ever does is sneer at their lifestyle ("explosion of unwanted pregnancies"), while McMillan sees them as "vulnerable" and – in a metaphor of much more subtlety – having to face a "blizzard" of social problems, making clear that they cannot be held wholly responsible and should be shown some sympathy.

Commentary

A very full and thoughtful response. It is well structured: basic statement; criticism of Marrin; praise for McMillan; a very neat conclusion which illustrates the contrast by referring to one key aspect. The final paragraph is a real bonus; the answer would almost certainly still get full marks without it. Notice how the structure allows the student to present a clear line of thought. The answer focuses more on the writers' ideas (this is nearly always the sensible approach), but there is sufficient reference to style, even without the showiness of the final paragraph.

Close Reading Paper 3
Shopping

Code:

📖	*passage extract*
✓	straightforward acceptable answer
★	really good answer
✗	weak/misguided answer
✚	other possible points
⬅	similar questions already tackled
❗	important advice

Questions on Passage 1

1.

> 📖 *We are caught up on a treadmill of turbo-consumption powered by the unfounded belief that having more will make us happy. We are part and parcel of a consumer society whose credentials are becoming more tarnished.*

(a) What is the main point the writer is making in lines 1–3? **2 U**

✓	We buy too many things in the false belief that this will make us more contented.
★	We are all fully committed to the consumer society and its promise of fulfilment, but the whole idea is now discredited and we are not satisfied with our lives.
✗	We believe that having more will make us happy and society's credentials are becoming more tarnished. *Why is this a bad answer? See page 180*
❗	The question asks for a "point" (singular) but it is for 2 marks, so you need to try and ensure your answer has two elements which are close enough to be part of the main "point".

(b) Show how the writer's word choice in lines 1–3 emphasises his low opinion of "consumer society". You should refer to two examples in your answer. **2 A**

✔	He says that because of the consumer society we are "caught up" – this suggests we are trapped by it. He also says we are on "treadmill" which makes you think of endless unpleasant work.
★	"tarnished" suggests that the gloss, the attractiveness has gone from something (in this case the appeal of consumerism) – that it was once bright and shining, but is now tainted. "part and parcel" suggests that we are nothing more than commodities in a warehouse, all the same, wrapped up ready for someone to use.
✘	His word choice emphasises his low opinion of "consumer society" by using words like "we are caught up on treadmill of turbo-consumption" – this makes out that we are all doing the same thing and have no choice. *Why is this a bad answer? See page 180*
✚	Comment could also be made on: "turbo-consumption" – idea of super-charged, almost out of control, too powerful. "unfounded" – idea of being illusory, unsupported.
⬅	Paper 1, question 2(b); Paper 2, questions 1(c), 4(a), 7(b)
ⓘ	The answer on "treadmill" is enough for this question, which is about word choice; if it had been on imagery, then a more detailed explanation of what a treadmill actually is would have been expected.

2. Read lines 4–9.

Increasingly, the predominant thing that you and I do is shop and plan our lives around things we have to pay for: clothes, jewellery, cars, houses, holidays, restaurants and gadgets that make us what we are. Once we were a society of producers, knowing ourselves and each other by what we did and what we made. Not any more. Today we understand ourselves and project the image we want others to see through what we buy.

(a) What is the difference the writer identifies between our place in society in the past and in the present? **2 U**

✔	In the past our place in society was formed by what our job was and what we produced. Now it is all about what we buy
★	Today we are defined by our possession of material goods and luxury services, whereas in the past we were seen in terms of our trade or profession – in other words what we contributed to society, not our pattern of consumption.
✘	In the past we could only produce things, we didn't have enough money to buy things like holidays and plasma TVs. *Why is this a bad answer? See page 180*

(b) Show how the writer uses sentence structure in lines 4–9 to make clear the points he is making. **2 A**

✓	The list of things we do as consumers shows just how many there are, emphasising how big the consumer society has become. The short minor sentence "Not any more" is a sudden and abrupt way to introduce the big change that has happened to our way of life.
★	The long list of typical consumer items (mostly luxury ones) emphasises the sheer extent of the spending opportunities open to us today in contrast to the simplicity of the past. The writer illustrates the sharpness of the contrast by his use of the short sentence "Not any more" which sort of jolts the reader into a sense of the complete change in society's attitude to an individual's worth.
✗	The writer uses a colon to introduce a list made up of many commas and he uses a minor sentence in among a lot of long sentences to make clear the points he is making. *Why is this a bad answer? See page 180*
✚	Reference could also be made to the use of "time markers" at the start of sentences ("Once", "Today") to emphasise the contrast.
↵	Paper 1, question 9(b); Paper 2, question 4(b)
❗	Note that a "minor sentence" is not automatically the same as a "short sentence". In this case "Not any more." is both, but not all short sentences are "minor", and a minor sentence could be quite long.

3. Show how the writer's use of language in lines 9–14 creates a critical tone about those who say they are "above fashion" (line 9). In your answer you could refer to word choice, imagery, sentence structure, punctuation… **2 A**

📖	*Even for those who pretend they are above fashion, every item they own is based on finely calibrated decisions about who and what they are and what they want others to think of them. With every purchasing decision, they reject thousands of other options, on other parts of the shelf, in other shops, in order to home in on the object that is "them". It might not be "fashion" but it is their fashion. Today we are all what we drive and what we wear. We don't own things – they own us.*
✓	The writer says they "pretend" they are above fashion, suggesting they are being false and claiming to be something they are not. The repetition of the word "other" emphasises the way these people pick and choose, they keep looking for the right item even though they say they are above fashion.
★	The writer's critical tone is clear when he describes how these hypocrites who claim to be "above fashion" actually make endless fashion-based decisions about what to buy: "finely-calibrated" implies that their decisions are almost trivial, as if there is virtually no difference between the options. The final sentence in the paragraph ("We don't own things – they own us.") not only sums up the point succinctly, it uses effective features of sentence structure to drive it home: the inverted structure built around the dash changes the idea of us being in control, e.g. "we" are no longer the subject, but the object ("us"), and the "things" have become the subject.

✚	Comment could also be made on: "calibrated" as imagery – idea of carefully crafted measuring tool, with tiny distinctions being made "reject thousands" – exaggeration to emphasise extent of picking and choosing "home in on" – idea of predatory conclusion to long search use of inverted commas around "them" – as if separated from rest of society, a breed apart use of inverted commas around "fashion" – to ridicule the fashions of the masses as compared with their more sophisticated preferences
←	Paper 1, questions 5(b), 7; Paper 2, questions 5(b), 8
❗	Remember to stay focused on the words "critical tone" in the question.

4. Read lines 16–23.

(a) There are two main areas of our lives that the writer says we attempt to satisfy by "running on the consumer treadmill". What are these two main areas? **2 U**

📖	*So what keeps us running on the consumer treadmill? We buy freedom, escape, love, care, excitement and comfort. We buy to belong to a particular social group and stand apart from others. And, of course we buy status. We want to be as near the top of the herd as possible. Endless consumption fuels the instinct to be "the best", to covet the newest car, to wear the latest outfit, to travel to ever-more exotic places, to possess the latest gadgets and to own a prestigious home in a "desirable" area. We live in a world where, as the commercials remind us, you can be ashamed of your mobile phone and your worth is measured according to your shampoo.*
✓	According to the writer, we attempt to satisfy the way we feel about ourselves and the way other people think about us.
★	Our own emotional well-being and our status in others' eyes.
←	Paper 1, question 6(b); Paper 2, question 1(a)
❗	Note how short the "good" answer is.

(b) What effect does the writer create by his choice of the two examples he uses in the last sentence of this paragraph? **2 E**

✓	The effect he creates is slightly humorous, because he uses two rather unimportant items (mobile phones and shampoo) and shows how ridiculously important they can become in our consumer society.
★	The writer satirises the shallowness and excesses of consumer-dominated living where an important concept such as shame can be attached to what is after all merely a device for communication and, even more absurdly, something as trivial as shampoo becomes a means of establishing your status.
✗	The writer uses two examples, mobile phones and shampoo. He says you can be made to feel ashamed of your phone and that you can be judged by which shampoo you use. *Why is this a bad answer? See page 180*

5. Show how the imagery in lines 24–28 conveys the writer's view of how "The whole show" is organised.

2 A

📖	*The whole show is kept going by the vast laboratory of designers, producers, marketers, advertisers, branding experts, psychologists and retail consultants who devise the machinery for the image factory that defines the 21st century. The best brains in the world are engaged in continually engineering new wants into new needs: more and more things we must have in order to be "normal".*
✓	A "laboratory" is literally a place where scientific experiments are carried out; the writer is suggesting that the people involved in production and marketing are as dedicated to finding the "solution" as a trained scientist would be.
	A "factory" is literally a place where goods are mass-produced; the writer is suggesting that the images are churned out in the organised, mechanical way you would associate with a factory.
★	The writer employs an extended metaphor, using words such as "laboratory… machinery… factory… engineering" to create an image of a vast industrial complex, suggesting that all aspects of production and retailing are part of one organised mechanism dedicated to producing the latest "image". He gives a highly critical view of the process by making it sound like a soulless enterprise, devoid of human involvement, producing goods to order in a robotic way.
➕	It would acceptable to comment on the image of "show" (i.e. an entertainment, suggesting something deliberately put together to satisfy …). However, the extended metaphor is much more important – and easier to write about.
⬅	Paper 2, questions 3(b), 5(a)
❗	The "good" answer doesn't laboriously deal with each word, but the understanding of the imagery is clear and the comments are sophisticated.

6. What, according to the writer in lines 30–35, is the problem with our dependence on "retail therapy"?

2 U

📖	*Most frightening of all is the fact that there are so few other ways of expressing our humanity, so we increasingly take comfort in so-called "retail therapy". Yet the object of the sellers is not to make us satisfied but dissatisfied so that we soon go back for more. Shopping rewards us just enough to leave space for more… and the emptier we feel the more we shop. It is the most vicious of vicious circles, and the paradox at the heart of Western society which is based on the pursuit of "more".*
✓	It doesn't make us as happy as we expect and so we have to go and buy more.
★	Retail therapy doesn't really succeed in making us content, but it works well enough for us to want to buy more – which also doesn't work, creating a never-ending cycle of unsatisfactory buying.
✗	We keep going back for more; it is a vicious circle.

Why is this a bad answer? See page 180 |
| ➕ | The answer could have been approached in this way: The fewer mental/spiritual resources we have to fall back on the more we need to buy things but it doesn't really fill the gap, so we need to buy more. |
| ⬅ | Paper 1, questions 2(a), 9(c); Paper 2 question 5(c); this Paper, question 2(a) |

7. Explain how the writer illustrates his claim that shopping "sells us a powerful myth" (line 41). **2 U**

📖	*How, then, do we escape from the treadmill of consumerism? There is no going back to some rose-tinted pre-consumption era. Shopping isn't all bad, after all – it's an important means by which we can be sociable and creative. However, we need to strike a balance, and that means regaining control over a marketing machine whose sole purpose is to make ever greater profits. We require a more compelling vision of what it means to be free and live a good life. Shopping sells us a powerful myth of liberty: that the car sets us free on the open road, for instance, when the reality is that we spend hours sitting in choking traffic jams that get us nowhere and pollute the environment. We must grasp the fact that what we really need and cherish can't be bought.*
✓	He uses the example of a car, which is sold to us with the fantasy that cars allow us to travel anywhere, when in fact a car does not give us any real freedom, only traffic jams.
★	He illustrates it by referring the mythic nature car advertising which creates the illusion of the car as a symbol of freedom, when in reality a car confers no such freedom or access to the good life at all, merely confines us in damaging traffic jams. This is an example of how you cannot achieve happiness by buying material objects.
✗	He uses a rhetorical question to ask how we can escape the treadmill of consumerism. He concedes that shopping isn't all bad. The myth is created in order to increase profits for manufacturers and retailers. *Why is this a bad answer? See page 180*

8. Read lines 46–56.

Summarise the three measures which the writer suggests should be the responsibility of the Government. **3 U**

✓ ★	• they should stop advertisements aimed at children • they should put up taxes on non-essential goods • they should measure happiness not wealth
✗	• bring in legal restrictions on advertising • increase the taxation on luxury goods • replace gross domestic product with general well-being as a measure *Why is this a bad answer? See page 180*
⬅	Paper 1, question 9(a); Paper 2, question 10(b)

9. "The current recession is a wake–up call." (line 57)

Show how this idea is developed in the remainder of the paragraph. (lines 57–61)   **2**   **U**

📖	*The current recession is a wake-up call. Right now, we are being forced to shop less, but the crucial question is: what happens when the crunch is over? Will we return to a life that is all-consuming, or use the enforced consumer slowdown as a catalyst for change and move to a post-consumer society, in which shopping plays a lesser role in our lives?*
✓	Because of the recession we don't have lots of money to spend, so when it is over we will have the choice to go back to the way we behave now or to learn our lesson and cut down on over-consumption.
★	The recession means we have less money to buy with and is a "wake-up call" in the sense that it is a warning alerting us the choice we have when economic recovery has happened: return to turbo-consumerism or become a more contented society which puts much less emphasis on retail consumption.
⬅	This paper, question 4(a)
!	Slightly unusual use of "Show how…" in a "U" question, but it is quite legitimate. You must stay alert and never go into "auto-pilot" such that you assumed this was an Analysis question.

Questions on Passage 2

10. Read lines 1–7.

(a) The writer makes a contrast between two kinds of shops. What is the main difference between them?   **2**   **U**

📖	*To start with the object which is closest to hand, the laptop with which I write these words was bought in an airport shop. There is no one but me to blame for my choice. Some shops are designed to seduce their customers. Others leave them to make up their own minds. Dior and Prada hire prize-winning architects to build stores on the scale of Grand Opera to reduce shoppers to an ecstatic consumerist trance. Not airports. A generic discount electronics store at Heathrow is no place for the seductions, veiled or unveiled, of the more elaborate forms of retailing.*
✓	Some try to influence customers into buying things; others leave customers to choose for themselves.
★	Up-market designer shops have tempting surroundings to persuade you into buying the products on display. More mundane ones such as at airports are more utilitarian, and don't go in for beguiling displays and surroundings.
➕	It would be possible to approach the question in this way: the responsibility for what you choose in some shops is entirely your own, whereas in others you can blame the methods used by the shop to influence your choice. Also possible: some shops are very sophisticated; others are plain and basic. [This answer captures the distinction between "elaborate" and "generic", but misses out on the idea of influence – however, it would probably get the marks.]
⬅	This paper, question 4(a)

(b) Show how the writer's word choice in these lines creates a distinctive impression of one of these kinds of shop. **2 A**

✓	The writer says the shops like Dior and Prada are designed to "seduce" customers, implying they are almost misleading customers by offering them something hugely appealing. Also that they put customers into a "trance" as if they have had a magical spell put on them.
★	The "elaborate" retailers "reduce shoppers to an ecstatic trance": "reduce" suggests they are diminishing their customers' individuality and "trance" gives the impression of a hypnotic spell to make them susceptible to their tricks. The comparison of their buildings to "Grand Opera" exaggerates their scale by comparing it to a lavish building which stages elaborate works of art.
✗	A building "on the scale of Grand Opera" is very different from a "generic discount store". *Why is this a bad answer? See page 180*
✚	Comment could also be made on: "Dior/ Prada" – names associated with the most up-market, expensive brands "ecstatic" – suggests the customers are put in an almost trance-like state "discount" – suggestion of cheapness, down-market
⬅	Paper 1, question 2(a); this paper, question 1(b)

11. Read lines 8–14.

(a) "Yet even in an airport, buying is no simple rational decision."
Explain, with close reference to the words of the sentence, how this sentence acts as a link in the writer's thoughts about the temptations to buy something – in this case a computer. **2 U**

📖	*Yet even in an airport, buying is no simple, rational decision. Like an actor performing without makeup, stripped of the proscenium arch and footlights, the laptop that eventually persuaded me that I had to have it did it all by itself. It was a purchase based on a set of seductions and manipulations that was taking place entirely in my head. And to understand how the laptop succeeded in making me want it enough to pay to take it away is to understand something about myself, and maybe a little about the part that design has to play in the modern world.*
✓ ★	"Yet even in an airport" refers back to the "no frills" nature of the airport shop; "buying is no simple rational decision" looks forward to this paragraph in which he describes his rather illogical decision to choose his new laptop.
✗	"Airport" refers back to what he said about shopping in an airport. The rest of the sentence leads into what he describes in the rest of this paragraph. *Why is this a bad answer? See page 180*
✚	It is possible to focus the answer on the word "Yet" as introducing a contradiction of what has gone before, but there must be specific understanding of the thrust of both paragraphs. [This approach to link questions is not recommended.]
❗	Answers to "link" questions must show understanding of the key idea in both paragraphs – in this case that airport shops don't go out of their way to influence purchases, but still the writer knows something influenced his purchase of the laptop.

ANSWER SUPPORT FOR CLOSE READING PAPERS

(b) Show how the writer's use of language in these lines helps to explain the power of the computer's design. **2 A**

✓	"manipulations" suggests the writer is aware that he is being worked on by the laptop's design, that it had the power to influence his thoughts. He also says the laptop "succeeded in making me" almost as if was a person who had compelled him to do something.
★	The image of the laptop as an "actor" suggests it has the qualities of a human trained and skilled in convincing you it is something it is not. The personification is continued throughout the paragraph: it is the laptop which "persuaded" him, as if it was an expert salesman, and "succeeded" as if it got the upper hand in a dispute.
✗	The word "rational" means sensible and well thought out, suggesting the writer thinks that the computer's design is powerful. *Why is this a bad answer? See page 180*
✚	Comment could also be made on: the extended theatre metaphor: "actor… makeup… proscenium arch and footlights" – the purity of the design, no need for embellishment, yet still convincing the way a good actor is "seductions" – suggesting the laptop has a slightly dangerous allure "entirely" – emphasising the way the laptop's design was all important in the writer's mind the structure of the sentence "Like … all by itself" – delayed main clause/periodic sentence puts emphasis on the importance, hence power, of the object

12. Show how the writer's use of language in lines 15–22 allows his attitude towards his old computer to emerge. In your answer you should consider at least two features such as imagery, word choice, humour… **4 A**

📖	*By the time I reached the counter, even if I didn't know it, I had already consigned my old Apple computer to the electronics street market in Lagos where redundant hard drives go for organ harvesting. Yet my dead laptop was no time-expired piece of transistorised Neolithic technology. In its prime, in the early weeks of 2004, it had presented itself as the most desirable, and most knowing piece of technology that I could ever have wanted. It was a computer that had been reduced to the aesthetic essentials. Just large enough to have a full-size keyboard, it had a distinctive, sparely elegant ratio of width to depth. The shell and the keys were all white.*
✓	Imagery: "organ harvesting" is literally the removal of human organs suitable for transplant after someone has died; the writer is suggesting that his old computer is now no better than a corpse from which bits and pieces can be used. Word Choice: "redundant" suggests it is not of any use now, surplus to requirements; when he bought it he thought it was "distinctive" – he was proud of its specialness. Humour: "Neolithic technology" – mentioning Neolithic at the same time as computer technology is a humorous exaggeration, since Neolithic was thousands of years ago and computer technology is very modern.

★	The writer's attitude to his old computer is a mixture of fondness as if it was an old friend and guilt at his speedy rejection of it. To begin with, it was "the most desirable… most knowing", as if a sophisticated and alluring lover; it was "distinctive" and "elegant" suggesting individuality and grace. The unembellished sentence "The shell and the keys were all white" has an almost breathless sense of awe at the simplicity of its appearance.
	That, however, was when it was in its "prime", like an athlete at the peak of his performance. Now he imagines, with a sense of regret, it being stripped of its remaining components in a distant (Lagos) "street market" – suggestive of somewhere rather basic and possibly shady – in a process he compares to "organ harvesting" as if it is a dead body being stripped for transplantation. It is as if he is struck by the speed with which something once treasured ends up on the scrap heap.
✚	Comment could also be made on: "transistorised Neolithic" – the comic mixing of modern terminology ("transistorised") with prehistory ("Neolithic") "aesthetic essentials" – suggestion of minimalist but beautiful
⬅	Paper 1, question 9(d); Paper 2, questions 4(a), 10(b); this Paper, question 3
ⓘ	Even the "basic" answer requires a fair bit of work, since this is for 4 marks. Note that the basic answer very sensibly and methodically follows the advice given in the question. The "good" answer here is very sophisticated – it is like a little essay with lots of detailed language points being made all the way through.

13. Read lines 23–30.

Explain fully what the Apple company hopes to achieve by the exterior design of its computers.

2 U

📖	*Apple's designers were quick to understand the need to make starting a computer for the first time as simple as locating the on switch. They have become equally skilled at manipulating the exterior design to create visual obsolescence. They take the view that Apple's route to survival in the PC dominated world is to use design as a lure to turn its product into aspirational alternatives to what its competitors are selling. It expects to sell fewer machines, but it charges more for them. This involves serial seduction. The company has to make most of its customers so hungry for a new product that they will throw away the last one every two years.*
✔	They hope to come up with new designs which make earlier ones look out of date and they want the design to offer something so different from other companies' products that people feel they have to have it
★	They aim for "visual obsolescence" – designs which will quickly look out of date even if the computing power and operations are not much different. They feel they must given their customers "aspirational alternatives" – their products must offer customers something to desire which is different from their competitors. They involve their customers in "serial seductions" – they make them constantly feel the need to own the latest model (even though their old one is absolutely still serviceable)
ⓘ	The approach in the "good" answer of quoting the key phrases and then explaining them is quite a useful one in "U" questions, which rely very much on putting key ideas into "own words". It is fine, as long as you remember to give the explanation and don't just rely on the quotations.

14. Show how the writer's word choice in lines 31–39 persuades you of the merits of the black computer. You should consider at least two examples. **2 A**

📖	*At Heathrow, there were two Apple models to choose from. The first was all white, like my last one. The other was the matt black option. Even though its slightly higher specification made it more expensive, I knew as soon as I saw it that I would end up buying it. The black version looked sleek, technocratic and composed. The purist white one had seemed equally alluring when I bought it, but the black one now seemed so quiet, so dignified and chaste by comparison. The keys are squares with tightly radiused corners, sunk into a tray delicately eroded from the rest of the machine. The effect is of a skilfully carved block of solid, strangely warm, black marble, rather than the lid on top of a box of electronic components.*
✓	It is "sleek", which gives the impression of something smooth and shiny, and it is "dignified" as if it is a wise, distinguished person.
★	The computer is personified by the words "composed", "dignified" and "chaste" – "composed" suggests control and elegance; "dignified" has suggestions of a revered elder statesman; and "chaste" gives the impression of something pure and unspoiled.
✗	He describes it as "alluring" which suggests it cast a spell on him. *Why is this a bad answer? See page 180*
➕	Reference could be made to: "technocratic" – suggests highest level of knowledge, commitment to the technology "quiet" – emphasis on lack of any off-putting noise "delicately" – suggests refinement, subtlety of the process "eroded" – as if a slow almost natural process, nothing as crude as "cut away" "skilfully" – emphasis on the expertise, care involved "carved" – suggestion of craftsmanship, artistic creation "warm" – sensuous appeal "marble" – association with elegant statues, temples, etc.
⬅	This paper, questions 1(b), 3, 10(b)

15. Read lines 40–45.

Explain fully the process by which having "no colour" becomes the "most effective kind of seduction" of the customer. **2 U**

📖	*Black has been used over the years by many other design-conscious manufacturers to suggest seriousness, but it was a new colour for Apple. Black is a non-colour, used for scientific instruments that rely on precision rather than fashion to appeal to customers. To have no colour implies that you are doing would-be customers the honour of taking them seriously enough not to try fobbing them off with tinsel. Of course this is precisely the most effective kind of seduction.*
✓	The customers are made to feel special because they haven't been given anything as shallow as bright colours.
★	Because it panders to the customer's sense of superiority: lesser people might be impressed by colour, but the sophisticate knows this is merely gaudy decoration.
⬅	Paper 1, question 9(c); Paper 2, questions 1(a), 1(c)

16. What view of the writer's attitude to his consumerist habits do you form from the last paragraph (lines 46–48)? **2 E**

📖	*And in the end black too becomes an empty signal, a sign devoid of substance, and I will no doubt fall for the next model which sets out to seduce me with its exclusive and tasteful credentials.*
✓	He admits that he will be taken in by whatever the manufacturers come up with next, believing it to be special and sophisticated.
★	He realises that what is the height of sophistication now will soon become common and he himself will follow the next so-called "superior" fashion. There is wry, self-deprecating humour in his admission of his own weakness in face of the power of design.
✗	Black will become outdated and so will white and the manufacturers will bring out another model to force people to spend their money just to be at the cutting edge of fashion and style.

Why is this a bad answer? See page 180

Question on both Passages

NB. The "Comparison" question is dealt with slightly differently from other questions. There is an example of reasonably good answer, worth 3 out of 5, and of a really good answer which would get full marks. There is a brief commentary about both answers.

For some general points about tackling the Comparison Question, see page 37.

17. Which passage makes you think more deeply about the modern phenomenon called consumerism? Justify your choice by reference to the **ideas and attitudes** of **both writers**. **5 U/E**

✓ [3/5]	I feel Passage 1 reflects more deeply on consumerism. Passage 2 focuses mainly on the design of products and what he feels persuades us to buy. Passage 1 looks at the bigger picture and focuses on the entire consumer market, including marketers, advertisers and retailers. This makes me think more deeply because it shows the process of how and why we end up buying a particular product and the people who contribute to this, whereas passage 2 goes into more depth about the product design aspect alone. But passage 1 looks at how excessive consumption has an effect on all areas of life, such as our general well-being and attitudes to others, and not simply shopping.
	The attitudes of both writers are very different – in Passage 1 the writer is far more opinionated, whereas in Passage 2 the writer appears to be more relaxed in his views. However the end result is the same in both. Both writers feel consumerism is largely affected by product design.

Commentary

This answer shows clear understanding of the issues and identifies the main difference between the two passages. A clear preference is expressed and there is some attempt to justify this with reference to both passages. There is an obvious structure and the assistance offered in the question has been used sensibly.

The most obvious shortcoming is that the second paragraph, about attitudes, is very thin. The basic difference is correctly identified, but there is no exemplification at all.

[5/5]

Perhaps because it is wider in scope, Passage 1 makes me think more deeply about aspects of consumerism. Passage 2, nevertheless, has an interesting take on one aspect (design), and Sudjic's attitude I find a little more appealing than Lawson's. In fact I find myself disagreeing with Lawson at a number of points.

In Lawson's argument there is no room for debate: he asserts early on that we define ourselves (and are viewed by others) in terms of what we own and buy. He points to our belief that contentment and status can be achieved by owning the best car or by travelling to the most exotic holiday destination. I think he presents a rather extreme point of view, however. Yes, there are some people for whom this type of consumer obsession is a vital activity, but there also many who, without actually living like hermits, get by without the latest mobile or must-have gadget – not least because they simply can't afford them. To my mind, his assertion that everyone has bought into the consumerist nightmare rather weakens his whole argument.

The villains, according to Lawson, are the manufacturers and advertisers, who conspire like a monstrous evil machine to make us so dissatisfied with life that we constantly want "more". Again, I think he overstates his case: manufacturers have a legitimate interest in developing and marketing new products; individuals surely have some power to resist the temptations offered.

He is at his most reasonable when he concedes that "shopping isn't all bad" and suggests we "strike a balance", but then argues that the only thing that can save us is government action. This is typical of his very pessimistic view that people themselves are powerless and can't be trusted or expected to do anything for themselves. He claims earlier in the passage that, other than shopping, "there are so few other ways of expressing our humanity", which seems to me a seriously wrong view of society.

Sudjic is similarly critical of manufacturers' ability to seduce customers into unnecessary purchases. Using the example of Apple laptops, he explains how the power of design, of superficial appearance, makes people belief they have found the perfect product, only to have that belief undermined a couple of years later when a new product is put on the market offering new and even more appealing attractions.

While both writers make me think about various aspects of consumerism, I find Sudjic's general attitude, that manufacturers are clever and we knowingly fall for their tricks, much more appealing than Lawson's, that manufacturers are evil and we are all too stupid to do anything about it.

Commentary

This is a detailed and intelligent response to the question. It is neatly structured, with the basic line of thought laid out at the start and then followed through clearly and methodically. The writer of this answer is prepared to "take on" one of the writers, and this is perfectly acceptable, indeed something to be encouraged.

Perhaps there is not enough on Passage 2, but the writer is defending the choice of Passage 1, and there is no sense that Passage 2 has been misunderstood – indeed Passage 2 does really make only one point and that is well covered in this answer.

It is certainly skimpy on Sudjic's "attitude", but the answer would still definitely score full marks.

Close Reading Paper 4
Victorian Celebrity

Code:

📖	*passage extract*
✓	straightforward acceptable answer
★	really good answer
✗	weak/misguided answer
+	other possible points
←	similar questions already tackled
!	important advice

Questions on Passage 1

1. Read lines 1–17.

    (a) In what key way do Burnaby and Britney Spears differ as celebrities?   **1   U**

📖	*When Britney Spears totters from a night club at 5am – hair askew, often drunk, often without knickers – we tend to assume her behaviour is terribly modern. But celebrities are not new. Nor is our obsession with them, as Prince Charles recently demonstrated with his 60th birthday portrait, modelled on Victorian hero Frederick Burnaby (1842–85). Burnaby is almost totally forgotten now, but in his day he was so famous that Queen Victoria reportedly fainted at news of his death. The Times gave him a 5000-word obituary. Grown men broke down and wept in the street.*
✓	She is often seen drunk, but he was respectable enough to get an obituary in *The Times*.
★	Burnaby was held in high esteem by the Establishment, whereas Britney Spears' behaviour is often disreputable.
←	Paper 1, question 6(a)

(b) What overall impression of Burnaby is created in lines 8–13? **1 U**

📖	*It is easy to see why. Burnaby's exploits make Rambo look wet. Few people have survived frostbite, typhus, an exploding air balloon, and poisoning with arsenic; explored Uzbekistan (where it was so cold, his beard froze solid and snapped off), led the household cavalry, stood for parliament, mastered seven languages, crossed the channel by air balloon, written a string of bestsellers, commanded the Turkish army, and founded* Vanity Fair *magazine. All this before his early death aged 42.*
✓	That he had a great sense of adventure.
★	A larger-than-life figure who could turn his hand to almost anything.
✚	Reference could have been made to the fact that he achieved a lot in a short life.
↩	Paper 2, question 3(a)
!	The word "overall" in the question is important: it would be a bad mistake to refer to any of the specific achievements.

(c) Show how the writer's use of language in lines 8–13 adds impact to the impression he is creating. You should refer in your answer to sentence structure and tone. **4 A**

✓	The long list of the things he did gives an impression of just how much he did in his lifetime. The use of a short minor sentence after the long list is a big contrast which allows the writer to surprise the reader with the fact that he was only 42 when he died. The tone is light-hearted, eg using the word "wet" to describe Rambo, who is a sort of superman-figure. Also, the parenthesis about his beard gives information which is probably only there for amusement value.
★	The list of Burnaby's exploits is not just very long as a way to convey the sheer extent and variety of his achievements, it is structured in such a way that it becomes an almost comic recitation: the first short list up to "arsenic" is followed by a semicolon, which creates a sort of pause for breath before launching into another string of achievements, into which is added the quite unnecessary details about his beard, which almost turns him into a carton figure of fun. The range of detail within the list (arsenic, air balloons, parliament, *Vanity Fair*, the Turkish army) is so diverse that it creates an almost surreal impression. The tone is firmly tongue-in-cheek, comically reducing the he-man Rambo to a wimp, and summing up in mock admiration, with a brief: "All this …" as if to suggest it was simply impossible for it to be achieved in a lifetime, let alone one so short.
✚	Comment could also be made on: the extensive use of verbs in the list ("explored… led… stood… mastered… crossed… written… commanded… founded") to emphasise/exaggerate the frantic activity of the man.
↩	Paper 2, question 10(b); Paper 3, question 12
!	A very difficult question, but one in which marks can be built up; in "4 A" questions, a lot of work is needed.

(d) What overall impression of Burnaby is created in lines 14–17? **1 U**

📖	*Burnaby could break a horseshoe apart with his bare hands. His party trick was to bend a poker double round a dull dinner guest's neck. Most famously, when fellow officers coaxed a pair of ponies into his room for a jape, Burnaby simply picked them up – one under each arm – and carried them downstairs "as if they had been cats."*
✓	A man of great strength.
★	You get the impression that he was something of a show off.
✚	Other possible answers: sociable not one to be bested
←	This paper, question 1(b)

2. Read lines 18–32.

(a) What similarity does the writer identify between Burnaby and Britney Spears? **1 U**

📖	*But, like Britney, Burnaby's actual talents only half explain his fame. Then, as now, media attention was just as important. In this respect, Burnaby was lucky. His heyday coincided with a new atmosphere in Britain, receptive to his brand of reckless adventuring.*
✓	It wasn't his ability and achievements alone that made him famous – like Britney, who isn't as talented as her celebrity suggests.
★	In both cases celebrity status is not simply a matter of any special gifts or aptitudes – there is an additional element: getting the attention of the newspapers, etc.
✚	The question could have been approached in other ways: Coverage in the newspapers etc are/were vital to the celebrity status of both. or Neither has/had enough natural ability to justify the extent of their fame.
←	Paper 3, question 1(a)
!	Essentially, this question is asking you to re-write "actual talents only half explain his fame" in your own words.

(b) In what ways was Burnaby "lucky" (line 19)? **2 U**

📖	*But, like Britney, Burnaby's actual talents only half explain his fame. Then, as now, media attention was just as important. In this respect, Burnaby was lucky. His heyday coincided with a new atmosphere in Britain, receptive to his brand of reckless adventuring.*
✓	When he was doing all his famous deeds, the country was in a mood to read about his sort of daring activities.

continued ➤

★	He was lucky in that his glory days occurred, by good fortune, at a time when British people were experiencing a new mood of optimism which made the public particularly open to tales of bravery such as Burnaby's.
←	Paper 1, question 2(a); Paper 3, question 13
!	Essentially, this question is asking you to re-write the last sentence in your own words.

(c) Explain the difference the writer identifies between the "early Victorian period" and the years after 1870.　　　　　　　　　　　　　　　　　　　　　**2 U**

📖	*The early Victorian world of Dickens and Brunel was a grimy, serious society, born out of a strong evangelical morality and the growing pains of industrialisation. Up to about 1870, no one wanted an Empire. It cost too much. In a decade, that changed. Suddenly we were in the world of side-whiskers, Sherlock Holmes, and oompa bands. Empire could not be big enough.*
✓	The early Victorian period was dull and strict. After 1870, things became more lively and exciting.
★	The early Victorian period was solemn and rather claustrophobic. Life after 1870 was more flamboyant.
✛	Reference could be made to: the change in attitude to Empire the frivolity of life after 1870
←	Paper 3, question 2(a)

(d) How effective do you find the imagery in the sentence "The early… industrialisation" (lines 22–23) in describing early Victorian society?　　　　　　　　**2 A/E**

📖	*The early Victorian world of Dickens and Brunel was a grimy, serious society, born out of a strong evangelical morality and the growing pains of industrialisation.*
✓	"growing pains" are literally the muscular pains suffered by a child when physical growth is fast. The writer is suggesting that industrialisation was a fast process and that in its early stages it led to some hardships and unpleasantness for people, but that it led to something worthwhile in the end.
★	A child suffers "growing pains" when its rate of growth is so rapid that the body can barely cope. Industrialisation was similar: in its early stages it occurred so quickly that society could barely cope with the effects on, for example, the environment. The image effectively describes the turmoil brought about by industrialisation – and is supported by the use of "born" to describe society as being "the child" of the strict Biblical ethos of the time.
←	Paper 2, question 3(b); Paper 3, question 5

(e) In what way is each of the "breakthroughs" described in lines 27–32 a "media revolution". **3 U**

📖	*A media revolution was crucial to this change. Before 1860, national news did not exist. Three breakthroughs changed this. First, the telegraph allowed news to reach Fleet Street in hours, not weeks. Second, new printing techniques put cheap dailies within the reach of ordinary people. Thirdly, the 1870 Education Act made it compulsory to learn the somewhat perversely-termed "3 Rs": reading, 'riting, and 'rithmetic. Suddenly millions wanted news.*
✓ ★	• The telegraph reduced hugely the time it took for news to arrive • New printing processes made newspapers available to a vast new audience. • The Education Act created enormous numbers of people able and wanting to read.
←	Paper 3, question 8
!	Notice that each point in the answer above includes something to make it sound like a "revolution", i.e. a big change: "hugely", "vast", "enormous".

3.   Read lines 33–48.

(a) In what sense, according to lines 33–38, was Burnaby "in the right place, at the right time" (lines 37–38)? **2 U**

📖	*New media demanded new copy. The new readers of the late Victorian era had simple tastes. They wanted then what we want now: glamour. Not exactly snaps of "Nikkola, 23, from Essex", but certainly a good rollicking tale of daring-do. And what better stage for excitement than that colourful, exotic, mysterious space: Empire? And what better star for that stage than Frederick Burnaby? He was in the right place, at the right time.*
✓	It was the right time because the new media of the time needed lots of stories, and the right place because a lot of his adventures happened in the Empire, which readers were fascinated by.
★	The media revolution had created a readership avid to read about thrilling exploits, especially if connected to exotic parts of the British Empire. Burnaby's adventures fulfilled both.
←	Paper 1, question 8(b); Paper 3, question 4(a); this paper question 2(b)

(b) Explain how the writer creates a less than serious tone in lines 33–38. **2 A**

✓	"Nikkola, 23, from Essex" sounds like a model posing in The Sun and sounds out of place when talking about the late Victorian era which makes you think of very stuffy people.
★	The writer plays on the idea of "glamour", making an anachronistic reference to "Nikkola, 23" in the style of a 21st century tabloid caption to a scantily clad model and contrasts this with the Victorians' idea of fun, "a good rollicking tale", which sounds quaintly old-fashioned.
⊕	Reference could be made also to: the use of "snap" to suggest modern idea of glamour is rather trivial the use of "daring-do" to suggest exaggerated old-fashioned attitude
←	Paper 1, questions 7 [for tone], 8 [for register]; Paper 2, question 7(a)

(c) To what extent do the details in lines 39–48 justify the writer's claim that "Burnaby was the first hero of mass culture"? **2 E**

📖	*New publications sprang up catering for gossip and Empire, like the* Daily Mail, *which filled its pages with engravings of our brave boys battling swarthy foreigners, exotic dens of oriental vice, and society ladies showing a little ankle. Gossip mags like* The Graphic – *a sort of Imperial version of* Heat – *described which balls Burnaby was attending, and who he danced with. One could buy Burnaby playing cards, Burnaby toby jugs, Burnaby crockery and Burnaby comics. There were poster-sized pullouts of Burnaby in* The Illustrated London News. *He inspired songs, a polka – and even a musical. Like all celebs worth their salt, Burnaby released a celebrity autobiography. He even had his own sponsorship deal, with Cockle's Cure-all Condiments. Burnaby was the first hero of mass culture.*
✔	Burnaby appeared in magazines and on games etc. He was the subject of songs and wrote his autobiography. He promoted Cockle's Cure-all Condiments. He was the first person to appear in so many different places.
★	The claim is fully justified in relation to "mass culture" because, like today's celebrities, Burnaby's exposure to the public was vast and involved a range of media: mass market magazines, merchandise, music, publication, business sponsorship. Whether or not he was the "first" is not supported by any of the details, but the implication is clear.
❗	"To what extent..." allows for some discussion, which the "good" answer does very well. The "OK" answer virtually ignores this element, but hints at it just enough.

(d) How effective do you find the writer's use of colloquial language in lines 39–48? Refer in your answer to more than one example. **2 A/E**

✔	Colloquial words such as "mags" and "celebs" are effective because the writer is aiming at a modern audience who are familiar with such words. He is trying to make Burnaby sound just like modern celebrities.
★	The colloquial register is in keeping with the writer's light-hearted tone throughout. Using chatty abbreviations like "mags" and "celebs" is almost mimicking the style of the type of publication he is describing.
➕	Reference could also be made to: "showing a little ankle" – jokey reference to Victorian prudishness "sort of" – chatty introduction to joke comparison "worth their salt" – clichéd turn of phrase (mimicking sloppy journalism?)
⬅	This paper, question 3(b)

4. Read lines 49–61.

Why, according to the writer, did Burnaby die in the way he did? **2 U**

📖	*Of course, modern celebrity is different. Burnaby did not suffer the indignity of the red carpet, but the man still had to live up to intolerably high expectations and fame nonetheless took a terrible toll. With telephoto lenses, we can catalogue Britney's demise; Victorians could not see Burnaby's, so they continued to expect the impossible. As he entered middle age, Burnaby increasingly struggled to keep up with his dashing image.* *Eventually, the weight of expectation became too much. Resolving not to die old, Burnaby set out on one last mission. Ignoring orders, he joined the attempt to rescue General Gordon from Khartoum. On leaving, he wrote "I am very unhappy. I do not mean to come back." Sure enough, during an ambush by Sudanese warriors, he pushed through his ranks and rode out alone, determined to meet the public expectation of heroic death.* *So ended the life of a Victorian icon.*
✓	He couldn't continue providing the kind of stories he was expected to, so he decided to go to his death doing something dangerous, which would live up to his image.
★	The public expected him to go on behaving in the heroic and dazzling way they had come to expect, but his past exploits had drained him and he was getting older. When he became unable to live up to expectation he decided to go out in a blaze of glory, in one final act of reckless heroism – just as his public would have wanted.
✚	Reference could be made to the fact that the public were unaware of his physical (and mental?) decline, but it is not strictly relevant.

Questions on Passage 2

5. Read lines 1–13.

    (a) Explain in detail how the writer creates a rather tongue-in-cheek tone in lines 1–8.

4 A

📖	*By Jingo, they don't make chaps like Colonel Frederick Gustavus Burnaby any more. Which is a shame, or possibly a relief, I can't quite make up my mind. In the Victorian age of larger-than-life heroes, the wildly eccentric colonel towered above the lot of them. He stood 6ft 4ins tall, weighed 15 stone and boasted a 47-inch chest. Fred joined the army aged 17, and quickly became recognised as the strongest man in its ranks. A first-rate boxer, swordsman, rider and runner, his party tricks included vaulting over billiard tables and twisting pokers into knots with his bare hands. You didn't want to mess with Fred Burnaby.*
✓	"By Jingo" is a really old-fashioned expression – the writer is trying to sound like an old Army major "chaps" is also like something out of a War film, very stuffy and British calling him "Fred" as if he was a close friend seems rather tongue-in-cheek "vaulting over billiard tables and twisting pokers into knots" are hardly "party tricks" which sounds a lot more gentle

continued ➤

★	The register of "By Jingo" and "chaps" immediately lets the reader sense the writer is being self-mocking, trying to sound like the archetypal, stiff upper lip Brit. The pretended uncertainty about whether it is a "shame" or a "relief" continues the self-mockery and is also quite humorous – how could it possibly be a "shame"? Calling his spectacular physical exploits "party tricks" is firmly tongue-in-cheek, since "party tricks" suggests something a little less energetic. The paragraph concludes with comic understatement: "You didn't want to mess…" – in light of what has just been said about his extraordinary strength, that's putting it mildly. The use of very colloquial language ("mess") adds to the comic effect – it sounds like two ordinary blokes chatting.
←	Paper 1, questions 7, 8; Paper 2, question 7(a); this paper, question 3(b)

(b) Why did Burnaby's journey into Central Asia make him "something of a popular hero" (line 10)? **2 U**

📖	*But he was more than just a meathead of mountainous proportions. Far more. Early in his short life, Fred became something of a popular hero in Britain, famous for a bizarre 1,000-mile journey he made into Central Asia, accompanied by a dwarf. The mad trip was seen as a kind of one-man victory over the mighty Russian empire, which had tried to block his progress.*
✓	Because he was seen to have stood up against a powerful foreign empire and won.
★	He single-handedly got the better of an entire country – and one which was a powerful rival to Britain. The sheer audacity of his journey appealed to the public.
+	Reference could also be made to: the length of the journey the unusual/unlikely nature of his companion
←	This paper questions 1(a), 3(a)

6. Read lines 14–39.

(a) Describe the impact of line 14 in terms of the structure and tone of the passage as a whole. **2 A**

📖	*And here's how he did it.*
✓	Structure: it is a kind of link between a general statement about the journey and the details of actual journey. Tone: sounds like someone talking to children, keeps up the rather tongue-in-cheek tone.
★	The single paragraph sentence acts structurally as turning point linking the previous paragraph in which there is description of the impact of the journey on popular imagination with the remainder of the passage which tells the story of the journey in some detail. The light-hearted tone is continued by making it sound like a patronising adult talking to children. It acts also as an introduction to the "story-telling" style of the remainder of the passage.
!	Notice how both answers are careful to deal with "structure" and "tone" – and with the passage as a whole (both before and after the sentence).

(b) Why did Burnaby make the journey to Central Asia? **2 U**

> On a roasting February day in Sudan, he found himself flicking through an English newspaper in a Khartoum café, absently chatting to some mates about where they all fancied going next time their leave came around. His eye fell upon a paragraph in the paper to the effect that the Russian government at St Petersburg had given an order that no foreigner was to be allowed to travel in Russian Asia, and that an Englishman who had recently attempted a journey in that direction had been turned back. As a stout-hearted patriot, Fred wasn't at all keen on Russians at the best of times. Now those pesky Russians were trying to ban Englishmen from travelling in the region, too. You can imagine what Burnaby of the Guards thought of that. How dare they! What was that rotten Tsar up to? More importantly, who was going to stop him?
>
> Before he'd finished his coffee, Fred's mind was made up. He would ignore the ban, travel to the heart of central Asia (somehow), and find out for himself exactly what was going on there. He saw it as his personal duty to open Britain's eyes to the menace of the Russian bear. It wasn't going to be easy of course. Apart from the possibility of being arrested, Fred's army leave inconveniently fell during winter – so it would be blizzards, snowdrifts and killer temperatures every step of the way. If the Russians didn't get him, frostbite or exposure probably would.
>
> His goal was the mysterious city of Khiva, and he wasn't exactly guaranteed a warm welcome if he made it. The Khivans were a fierce and independent lot who had been fighting Russian invaders for centuries, slaughtering the men and enslaving the women in harems. Their leader, the Khan of Khiva, had a reputation for cruelty. He will "very likely order his executioner to gouge out your eyes", a friendly Russian warned Fred.
>
> Fred's account of his wild journey – "A Ride to Khiva" – turned him into a celebrity. It sold out. Even today it's a smashing, swashbuckling read.

✓	He had read about an Englishman who had been refused entry to Russian Asia and he wanted to show that this was unacceptable.
★	He was outraged at the idea of anyone daring to forbid an Englishman the right to travel anywhere, and set off himself to prove that the Russians could not do this. He saw it as a way of drawing attention to Russian despotism and as a true Brit he could not stand by and do nothing.
+	Other acceptable points: to prove bravery, endurance, … to outface the Russians to show off to fellow officers to reach Khiva and confront the Khan
!	A lot of text to be covered, but there are only 2 marks available, so narrow it down to the two most important general points.

(c) Choose one example of humour from lines 15–37, and explain to what extent you find it appropriate in its context. **2 A/E**

✓	Using the word "friendly" to describe the Russian who tells that the Khan will "order his executioner to gouge out your eyes" is quite funny – saying this can hardly be called "friendly", but it gives the idea that Fred isn't put off even by gruesome warnings.
★	"those pesky Russians" is effective because it reduces the Russians to the level of mild irritants, humorously reproducing the voice of someone like Burnaby who would never admit that foreigners were any sort of serious threat.

continued ➤

⊕	Reference could also be made to: "that rotten Tsar" – public school-type slang; Tsar reduced to playground bully "Before he'd finished his coffee" – exaggeration; depicts his decisive, rash nature "(somehow)" – amusing aside; as if the practicalities were the last think on his mind
⬅	This paper, questions 3(b), 3(d), 5(a)

7. Read lines 40–59.

(a) In these lines the writer uses several features associated with narrative writing and story telling. Referring to specific features, show how the writer uses these to engage the reader with his description of the journey. **4   A**

✓	The writer switches to the present tense ("he sets off") making it seem more immediate and fast-moving. There are physical descriptions of characters the way there are in stories, e.g. "stands less than five foot tall" and "powerfully built guy in his late twenties" – this makes the characters a little more clear in the reader's mind. There is a lot of descriptive detail such as "smelly sheepskin suit", "gigantic shaggy camels", "tiny sleigh", "coal-black beard", which give interesting extra description to keep the reader interested. At the end there is a sort of climax with Fred finally meeting the Khan. A climax is an effective way of keeping the reader guessing what will happen next.
★	The narrative style of writing is obvious in a number of ways. Firstly the use of time and place markers: "At one remote settlement", "On another occasion", "After two months" – these give the story as sense of progression and engage the reader with the movement of the story. Secondly, there is an element of characterization all the way through: Burnaby's "military moustache", the dwarf's loyalty, the insults from the armed Khivans – these little details enliven the narrative and bring the characters to life. Thirdly, there is the sudden rush of action in: "The guide lashes out with his whip; a Khivan hits back with a camel-stick; knives are drawn; Fred pulls out his pistol." – a terse list of actions in cinematic style to make it exciting. Lastly, the writer builds up suspense as Burnaby is led to the Khan, with dramatic details such as the curtain being drawn back and the frightening details of the Khan's appearance – only to bring the tale to an amusing anti-climax as the two greet each other like gentlemen.
ⓘ	This is a not a typical question, but there are at least half a dozen fairly obvious "narrative" features which can be commented on. Remember that no one is trying to trick you; you are being asked to read sensibly and respond to a question which is, for this passage, perfectly legitimate. Note how methodical both answers are.

(b) How effective do you find the final paragraph (lines 58–59) as a conclusion to the passage as a whole? **2   E**

📖	And what does our dashing adventurer make of this most feared of Asian rulers? Fred writes: "I must say I was greatly surprised to find him such a cheery sort of fellow."
✓	I think it is effective as it seems so typical of Burnaby's character to see the Khan as "a cheery sort of fellow" despite his fearsome appearance – Fred takes everything in his stride.
★	It is suitably humorous in line with the passage as a whole – completely unexpected that Fred, after a gruelling journey, would describe the Khan in such disarming terms, using language ("cheery sort of fellow") he might use to describe someone at his club. Also, the writer's tone in "our dashing adventurer" maintains the gentle mockery he has used all along.

| | Comment could also be made on:
the question/answer form of the paragraph
the gentlemanly tone of "I must say"
the way the paragraph sums up Burnaby's *sang froid* |

Question on Both Passages

8. Identify important similarities and differences in the **ideas and style** of **both passages**, making clear which passage you find more appealing and why. **5 E**

NB. The "Comparison" question is dealt with slightly differently from other questions. There is an example of reasonably good answer, worth 3 out of 5, and of a really good answer which would get full marks. There is a brief commentary about both answers.

For some general points about tackling the Comparison Question, see page 37.

✓ [3/5]	I find Passage 1 more appealing because it gives more information about Burnaby and his times, whereas Passage 2 is mostly about one event in his life. Passage 2 is very amusing, but Passage 1 is not dull because it has a lot of humour as well. Both passages tell us that Burnaby was famous for his extraordinary adventures, but Passage 1 tells us a lot more about him, for example the list in the second paragraph of many amazing achievements. It also tells us about how he died. Passage two is only about his "mad trip" to Khiva. In Passage 1 there is an interesting comparison with a modern celebrity and the writer explains how the idea of being a celebrity in "mass culture" came about because of a "media revolution" and how Burnaby was the first ever. He was mentioned in gossip columns and had songs about him, even posters like today's celebrities. Both passages are quite funny about Burnaby, but Passage 1 varies the tone a little with serious bits about Victorian morality and the Education Act. Passage 2, however, just makes fun of Burnaby all the way through ("How dare they? What was that rotten Tsar up to?").

Commentary

A modest answer, but it is sensibly structured and has a clear and convincing line of thought. Similarities and differences are identified; both passages have been understood. There is, however, a lack of detail at almost every stage.

Both passages present Burnaby as a larger-than-life figure who had enormous appeal to the Victorian public. There are even identical references to his "party trick" of poker-bending.

Passage 1, however, takes a more serious look at Victorian society and explains how changes in media technology allowed Burnaby's fame to spread as much as it did and the extent to which his celebrity arose from fulfilling needs brought about by these changes and by the impact of industrialisation and attitudes to Empire. Passage 2 concentrates much more on one specific event (the ride to Khiva) as a way of illustrating the bizarre and swashbuckling adventures of the man. It is more of an introduction to Burnaby's life, while Passage 1 covers his rise to fame, the height of his celebrity and his death.

Neither passage is entirely serious in its presentation of Burnaby the man. Certainly, Passage 1 is completely serious and formal when explaining the social background ("a grimy, serious society, born out of a strong evangelical morality and the growing pains of industrialisation") and the impact of the new technologies ("New media demanded new copy"), but when describing the publications which emerged, the writer becomes fairly light-hearted ("our brave boys battling swarthy foreigners"). When dealing directly with Burnaby himself, however, the writer of Passage 1 is nearly always amusing ("[his] exploits make Rambo look wet"), yet there is a wistful tone at the end when covering his demise and death ("increasingly struggled to keep up with his dashing image", "rode out alone, determined to meet the public expectation of heroic death").

The writer of Passage 2, however, has his tongue firmly in his cheek throughout. From the flippancy of the opening "By Jingo" and "You didn't want to mess with", to the gentle mockery of the conclusion (quoting Burnaby's self-effacing words), it is a string of throwaway remarks and entertaining narrative: "more than just a meathead of mountainous proportions"; the improbable account of his decision to take on the Russian empire single-handed; the fantastical description of his journey to Khiva, with its bizarre conclusion. It is obvious that the writer of Passage 2 sees Burnaby as an utter fool, yet there is beneath the surface a hint of affection, as if the writer can't help liking him, despite (or perhaps because of) the sheer absurdity of his exploits.

Passage 1 certainly has useful insights into Victorian times and the concept of celebrity, but Passage 2 is much more fun.

⭐

[5/5]

Commentary

A detailed and very sophisticated response, especially the contention that the writer of passage 2 shows "affection" underneath all the mockery.

The structure is clear and addresses the question – admittedly there is no slavish explanation of which is more "appealing", but there is a clear statement in the conclusion and engagement with and understanding of both passages is very evident throughout.

Introduction to Critical Essay Papers

There are four Critical Essay papers in this part of the book.

Each of these papers is meant to be used in its entirety to give you practice in making the correct choice of your two questions.

However, before you start Paper 1, look at **Appendix 1**, (page 165) which gives advice on how to choose the best questions.

Below is a summary of the three principles demonstrated in the Appendix:

The **first principle** is that you must look at **all** the questions in the first section you have prepared for – say Drama.

The **second principle** is that you must look carefully at the **task** (the second part of the question). The first part of the question may seem perfectly suitable, but it is the second part you have to answer.

The **third principle** is that after you have provisionally chosen the best question for you in the Drama Section, you **must** go on to read the questions in the other Sections for which you have studied. It may be that there are two other questions in the paper as a **whole**, both of which you can answer better than the one you have provisionally chosen for Drama.

The following points are a summary of the instructions given at the beginning of each examination paper. They apply, of course, to all four Critical Essay papers in this book.

You must give attention to the following in your answers:

- **relevance**
- **line of thought**
- **knowledge and understanding of your text(s) and their central concerns**
- **the ability to comment on literary features and techniques, where relevant**
- **your evaluation as required by the question**
- **the quality of your written expression (including technical accuracy)**

You can find more advice about these aspects in *How to Pass Higher English Colour Edition* (Hodder Gibson 2009, pages 107–109).

Critical Essay Paper 1

SECTION A – DRAMA

Answers to questions on drama should address relevantly the central concern(s)/ theme(s) of the text and be supported by reference to appropriate dramatic techniques such as: conflict, characterisation, key scene(s), dialogue, climax, exposition, dénouement, structure, plot, setting, aspects of staging (such as lighting, music, stage set, stage directions…), soliloquy, monologue…

1. Choose a play in which a character other than the hero/heroine plays a crucial role in affecting the thoughts and actions of the hero or heroine.

    By referring closely to the part played by your chosen character show how important he or she is in affecting the thoughts and actions of the hero/heroine in the course of the play.

2. Choose a scene from a play in which a main character is persuaded or forced to act against her/his wishes or conscience.

    Describe the scene in detail and discuss to what extent the character's decision in this scene continues to reverberate throughout the play as a whole.

3. Choose a play which has as one of its main concerns loss of respect, or of honour, or of status.

    Identify which loss you have chosen and show how the playwright's exploration of this loss is important in your appreciation of the play as a whole.

4. Choose a play portraying a seemingly strong relationship which deteriorates in the course of the play.

    Discuss to what extent the deterioration is brought about by personality and to what extent by external forces and show how the portrayal of the relationship is important to your understanding of a central concern of the text.

SECTION B – PROSE

Prose Fiction

Answers to questions on prose fiction should address relevantly the central concern(s)/theme(s) of the text(s) and be supported by reference to appropriate techniques of prose fiction such as: characterisation, setting, key incident(s), narrative technique, symbolism, structure, climax, plot, atmosphere, dialogue, imagery…

5. Choose a **novel** in which a central character stands out or differs from his/her surrounding society in some important way.

    Show how his/her individual stance or position adds to your understanding of at least one of the central concerns of the novel.

6.   Choose a **novel** or **short story** in which one of the central threads of the story concerns a love affair or marriage.

   Explain how the relationship's development is affected by the couple's personalities and show to what extent the relationship is central to the main theme(s) of the text.

7.   Choose a **novel** in which the writer's use of a particular technique such as symbolism, use of recurrent imagery, use of first person narrative… plays a significant part in adding to your understanding and appreciation of one of the central concerns of the novel.

   Identify one such technique and show how the writer uses it effectively in the exploration of a central concern.

8.   Choose a **novel** in which the ending on first reading shocks you in some way.

   Describe the events of the ending and, by referring to the novel as a whole, discuss to what extent you now feel that this ending is inevitable.

9.   Choose **two short stories** set in the future, or in a culture vastly different from your own.

   Identify an important concern the writer deals with in each story, and, by looking at content and technique, assess which you find to be more effective in conveying the writer's ideas.

Prose Non-fiction

Answers to questions on prose non-fiction should address relevantly the central concern(s)/theme(s) of the text and be supported by reference to appropriate techniques of prose non-fiction such as: ideas, use of evidence, selection of detail, point of view, stance, setting, anecdote, narrative voice, style, language, structure, organisation of material…

10.   Choose a **work of non-fiction** which has, as its main subject, the experience of travel, or exploration, or an expedition.

   Discuss whether the description of the place(s) is more or less important than the description of the people involved in the travel, or exploration, or expedition.

11.   Choose a **work of non-fiction** in which the views of the writer are presented in a biased way.

   Show how the writer's use of language promotes her/his views and discuss the effect on you of her/his biased treatment of the subject.

12.   Choose a **work of biography or autobiography** which deals with the relationship between important events and the subsequent course of the subject's life.

   Show how the writer's presentation of these events emphasises their significance and go on to show how they affect the subject's life.

SECTION C – POETRY

> *Answers to questions on poetry should address relevantly the central concern(s)/theme(s) of the text(s) and be supported by reference to appropriate poetic techniques such as: imagery, verse form, structure, mood, tone, sound, rhythm, rhyme, characterisation, contrast, setting, symbolism, word choice…*

13. Choose a poem which takes a disillusioned or a despairing look at life.

Show how effectively the disillusionment or the despair is revealed by the poet's treatment of his/her subject.

14. Choose a poem one of whose main ideas springs from the observation of a place or person(s).

Show how the poet skilfully uses her/his observation of the place or person(s) as a springboard for ideas explored in the poem.

15. Choose **two** poems which deal with the same emotion, for example, love, jealousy, pity…

By examining the ideas and style of each poem, discuss which you find to be the more effective in enlarging your understanding of the emotion you have chosen.

16. Choose a poem in which the poet creates a convincing character.

Show how the poet, by skilful use of technique, brings the character alive in a convincing way.

SECTION D – FILM AND TV DRAMA

> *Answers to questions on film and TV drama should address relevantly the central concern(s)/theme(s) of the text and be supported by reference to appropriate techniques of film and TV drama such as: key sequence(s), characterisation, conflict, structure, plot, dialogue, editing/montage, sound/soundtrack, aspects of mise-en-scène (such as lighting, colour, use of camera, costume, props…), mood, setting, casting, exploitation of genre…*

17. Choose a **film or ★TV drama** which has at its centre a destructive personality.

Show how the destructive nature of the character is revealed and how this affects your view of the character in the course of the film or TV drama.

18. Choose a **film** whose setting in time and/or place is vitally important to the main theme(s) of the film.

Show how the setting is established and discuss how it helps to develop your understanding of the main theme(s) of the film.

19. Choose a **film or ★TV drama** which deals with an issue of social or political importance.

Show how the issue is presented and discuss how effectively the issue is developed in the film or TV drama.

20. Choose from a **film or ★TV drama** a key sequence which creates an atmosphere essential to the presentation of its main character(s).

Show in detail how the sequence is created and discuss its contribution to your understanding of the role of the character(s) in the text as a whole.

★ "TV drama" includes a single play, a series or a serial.

Critical Essay Paper 2

SECTION A – DRAMA

Answers to questions on drama should address relevantly the central concern(s)/ theme(s) of the text and be supported by reference to appropriate dramatic techniques such as: conflict, characterisation, key scene(s), dialogue, climax, exposition, dénouement, structure, plot, setting, aspects of staging (such as lighting, music, stage set, stage directions…), soliloquy, monologue…

1. Choose a play in which the main character is gradually revealed as a very complex human being.

    Show how the dramatist gradually reveals the complexity of the character and discuss how this adds to your appreciation of the text as whole.

2. Choose a play which uses comedy/humour to explore a serious theme.

    Explain how the dramatist effectively combines the humour with an exploration of a serious theme.

3. Choose a play which ends in a way you find moving or upsetting or poignant.

    By detailed examination of the conclusion and with reference to the rest of the play, show how the dramatist evokes this response from you.

4. Choose from a play a scene which significantly changes your impression of a major character.

    Describe how the scene achieves this and show how your feelings towards the character in the play as a whole are influenced.

SECTION B – PROSE

Prose Fiction

Answers to questions on prose fiction should address relevantly the central concern(s)/theme(s) of the text(s) and be supported by reference to appropriate techniques of prose fiction such as: characterisation, setting, key incident(s), narrative technique, symbolism, structure, climax, plot, atmosphere, dialogue, imagery…

5. Choose a **novel** in which a central character seems restless or discontented or frustrated.

    Show how the novelist makes you aware of the character's situation, and discuss to what extent the character achieves peace of mind by the end of the novel.

6. Choose a **novel** in which there is a key incident involving one of the following: a birth, a marriage, a death.

    Explain briefly what happens in the incident and go on to discuss its importance to the novel as a whole.

7.   Choose a **novel** or **short story** in which the setting is bleak or oppressive.

Show how the setting affects one of the main characters and discuss to what extent she or he manages to overcome the difficulties which the setting poses for her or him.

8.   Choose **two short stories** with a strong central character.

Compare the ways in which the character is created in each story and discuss which you think makes a more effective contribution to the story as a whole.

9.   Choose a **novel** which has as one of its main concerns the divisions caused by class, race or religion.

Show how the writer portrays the clash caused by one of these, and discuss to what extent you gained insight into the nature of such divisions.

Prose Non-fiction

> *Answers to questions on prose non-fiction should address relevantly the central concern(s)/theme(s) of the text and be supported by reference to appropriate techniques of prose non-fiction such as: ideas, use of evidence, selection of detail, point of view, stance, setting, anecdote, narrative voice, style, language, structure, organisation of material…*

10.   Choose an **essay or piece of journalism** which takes a committed stance on a social, moral or political topic which is of major importance in the twenty-first century.

Identify the topic and discuss to what extent you think the writer presents a convincing case.

11.   Choose a **non-fiction text** which celebrates the achievements of an individual or of a society.

Explain what the achievement is and show how the writer's presentation of the material can be seen as a "celebration".

12.   Choose a **work of travel writing** which conveys the sense of an exciting or dangerous journey.

Show how the writer's presentation clearly conveys the excitement or the danger and makes it an important element in your appreciation of the text as a whole.

SECTION C – POETRY

> *Answers to questions on poetry should address relevantly the central concern(s)/theme(s) of the text(s) and be supported by reference to appropriate poetic techniques such as: imagery, verse form, structure, mood, tone, sound, rhythm, rhyme, characterisation, contrast, setting, symbolism, word choice…*

13.   Choose a poem which is, for you, a serious reflection on an important issue.

Discuss how the poet's ideas and language engage you in serious reflection on the issue.

14. Choose a poem which seems to you to end in an unexpected or mysterious way.

    Explain what is unexpected or mysterious about the way the poem ends and go on to discuss how effective you think it is as a conclusion to the poem as a whole.

15. Choose a poem in which features of structure play an important part.

    Describe these important structural features and show how they enhance your appreciation of the poem as a whole.

16. Choose **two** poems with a similar setting.

    Compare the way the setting is evoked in the poems, making clear which you find more effective in conveying the central concern(s) of the poems.

SECTION D – FILM AND TV DRAMA

Answers to questions on film and TV drama should address relevantly the central concern(s)/theme(s) of the text and be supported by reference to appropriate techniques of film and TV drama such as: key sequence(s), characterisation, conflict, structure, plot, dialogue, editing/montage, sound/soundtrack, aspects of mise-en-scène (such as lighting, colour, use of camera, costume, props…), mood, setting, casting, exploitation of genre…

17. Choose a **film or ★TV drama** which presents a disturbing or upsetting or alarming picture of a society.

    Show how the film or programme makers create the impression and discuss to what extent there is any optimism in the text as a whole.

18. Choose a **film or TV drama** which explores childhood or adolescence.

    Show how the film or programme makers explore the subject and discuss to what extent they create a convincing depiction of the stage of life.

19. Choose a **film or ★TV drama** which deals with a serious subject in a comic or light-hearted way.

    Show how the comic or light-hearted elements are created but yet allow an exploration of the serious subject.

20. Choose a **film** or **★TV drama** in which a key scene or sequence is intensified by the use of sound and/or visual effects.

    Describe how the sound and/or visual effects intensify the scene or sequence and assess the importance of the scene to the text as a whole.

★"TV drama" includes a single play, a series or a serial.

Critical Essay Paper 3

SECTION A – DRAMA

Answers to questions on drama should address relevantly the central concern(s)/ theme(s) of the text and be supported by reference to appropriate dramatic techniques such as: conflict, characterisation, key scene(s), dialogue, climax, exposition, dénouement, structure, plot, setting, aspects of staging (such as lighting, music, stage set, stage directions…), soliloquy, monologue…

1. Choose a play in which the cruelty or corruption or carelessness of a character causes difficulties within the play.

    Show how the cruelty or corruption or carelessness affects other people in the play and discuss to what extent the character reforms his/her behaviour by the end of the play.

2. Choose a play which has as a central feature a conflict between generations, or couples or social classes.

    Show how the situation and/or the personalities contribute to the conflict. To what extent do you find the resolution of the conflict satisfying in terms of the play as a whole?

3. Choose a play in which a single scene illustrates a reversal of fortune for one of the characters.

    Describe in detail how the scene shows the reversal and discuss to what extent this reversal in fortune makes the character's fate inevitable.

4. Choose a play which deals with a social or political or religious issue.

    By referring to two or more of the following features – structure, setting, language, soliloquy, use of narrator – show how each contributes to your understanding of the thematic concerns of the play.

SECTION B – PROSE

Prose Fiction

Answers to questions on prose fiction should address relevantly the central concern(s)/theme(s) of the text(s) and be supported by reference to appropriate techniques of prose fiction such as: characterisation, setting, key incident(s), narrative technique, symbolism, structure, climax, plot, atmosphere, dialogue, imagery…

5. Choose a **novel** in which the mood or atmosphere created in the opening section is important to a central theme of the novel as a whole.

    Describe how the writer creates the mood or atmosphere and show how it is important in the exploration of the theme.

6. Choose a **novel** or **short story** in which one of the central concerns is injustice or cruelty, perpetrated by the state, the community, the family or the individual.

    Show how the injustice or cruelty affects one of the main characters. Discuss how the character's attempts to cope with the injustice or cruelty add to your appreciation of injustice or cruelty in the text.

7. Choose a **novel** or **short story** in which a gradual revelation of crucial information is an important factor in your appreciation of the central concerns of the novel or short story.

    Show how crucial information is gradually revealed and how this process enhances your appreciation of the central concern(s) of the text.

8. Choose a **novel** with an incident involving two or more main characters which creates a turning point in the novel.

    Describe the incident and show how its outcome is important to your appreciation of the main concern(s) of the novel.

Prose Non-fiction

Answers to questions on prose non-fiction should address relevantly the central concern(s)/theme(s) of the text and be supported by reference to appropriate techniques of prose non-fiction such as: ideas, use of evidence, selection of detail, point of view, stance, setting, anecdote, narrative voice, style, language, structure, organisation of material…

9. Choose a **biography** or **autobiography** which presents the life of a vibrant and/or influential personality.

    Show how the writer's presentation of the person effectively conveys the vibrant and/or influential nature of her or his personality.

10. Choose an **essay** or a **piece of journalism** which employs a particular tone to reinforce the central ideas of the essay.

    Show how successfully the writer uses tone to help you to see the ideas from his/her point of view.

11. Choose a **work of non-fiction** which explores the wonder of travel, or the extremes of human endeavour.

    Show how the writer creates the sense of wonder, or an appreciation of the extreme lengths to which the participants are driven.

SECTION C – POETRY

Answers to questions on poetry should address relevantly the central concern(s)/theme(s) of the text(s) and be supported by reference to appropriate poetic techniques such as: imagery, verse form, structure, mood, tone, sound, rhythm, rhyme, characterisation, contrast, setting, symbolism, word choice…

12. Choose a poem which portrays the natural world as spiritual or uplifting.

   Identify what aspect of the natural world the poet is describing and discuss to what extent she or he is successful in bringing into focus its spiritual or uplifting effects.

13. Choose a poem in which you can recognise a point where the poem moves from description into reflection.

   Identify that point in the poem and show how effectively the poet uses the description (of place, person, or experience) to provide a springboard for his or her reflection on the central ideas of the poem.

14. Choose **two** poems on the same theme.

   Compare the approaches taken to the theme and discuss which you feel to be more effective in increasing your understanding and appreciation of the central concern(s) of the poems.

15. Choose a poem in which the writer creates an interesting character or persona.

   Show by what means the writer creates the character or persona and discuss how effectively the concerns of the poem are developed through the presentation of the character or persona.

SECTION D – FILM AND TV DRAMA

Answers to questions on film and TV drama should address relevantly the central concern(s)/theme(s) of the text and be supported by reference to appropriate techniques of film and TV drama such as: key sequence(s), characterisation, conflict, structure, plot, dialogue, editing/montage, sound/soundtrack, aspects of mise-en-scène (such as lighting, colour, use of camera, costume, props…), mood, setting, casting, exploitation of genre…

16. Choose a **film** or **★TV drama** which is set in the future.

   Show to what extent setting it in the future facilitates the discussion of an important theme.

17. Choose a **film** or **★TV drama** in which an act of betrayal (e.g. of friends, of family, of country) is central to the theme of the film or TV drama.

   Describe what impact the betrayal has on the betrayed and show how it is important in developing the theme of the text.

18. Choose a **film** or **★TV drama** in which one important sequence focuses on a moment of decision for the hero/heroine.

   By examining the sequence in detail, show how the moment of decision is portrayed, and go on to show the impact of that decision on the rest of the text.

19. Choose a **film** or **★TV drama** in which one of the main characters is a flawed hero.

   Show how the film or programme makers present the character as flawed and discuss to what extent your reactions to her or his role in the text as a whole are manipulated by the film or programme maker.

★ "TV drama" includes a single play, a series or a serial.

Critical Essay Paper 4

SECTION A – DRAMA

1. Choose a play in which a distortion of the truth (such as downright lies, mistaken identity, fabrication, disguise) plays an important part in the plot of the play.

   Explain what the distortion of truth is and then discuss to what extent it helps to reveal important aspects of character and/or theme.

2. Choose a scene from a play in which a main character is introduced.

   Describe what important aspects of the character's personality are revealed in this scene and show how far these aspects of personality are important in determining the fate of the character in the play as a whole.

3. Choose a play in which two characters shed light on each other's strengths and weaknesses.

   Show how the portrayal of these two characters makes clearer your understanding of one (or more) of the central concerns of the play.

4. Choose a play which deals with the concept of power – political, emotional, social or religious.

   Identify the power dealt with and show to what extent its exploration in the course of the play leads you to a deeper understanding of the power discussed.

SECTION B – PROSE

Prose Fiction

5. Choose a **novel** or **short story** which has as one of its central concerns the desire for power, or for love, or for wealth, or for status.

   By referring to the effects of this desire on the characters, show how the writer explores this idea in the text as a whole.

6. Choose a **novel** in which a main character is isolated from his or her society.

   Explain the reasons for his or her isolation, and discuss to what extent the character's personality and actions are themselves responsible for his or her isolation.

7. Choose a **novel** in which there is a key incident of high tension between two of the characters.

   Describe the incident, and show to what extent the outcome of the incident affects the course of the novel and illuminates a key concern of the novel.

8. Choose a **novel** or **short story** which has a happy ending.

   Discuss the extent to which you feel that the happy ending (expected or unexpected) is a satisfactory outcome to the novel or short story.

Prose Non-fiction

Answers to questions on prose non-fiction should address relevantly the central concern(s)/theme(s) of the text and be supported by reference to appropriate techniques of prose non-fiction such as: ideas, use of evidence, selection of detail, point of view, stance, setting, anecdote, narrative voice, style, language, structure, organisation of material…

9. Choose a **biography** or **autobiography** of a person who is, or has been, eminent in the field of science, or sport, or politics, or the arts.

   To what extent has the writer's presentation of the facts of the subject's life increased your understanding of the contribution of the person to his/her specialist field.

10. Choose an **essay** or a **piece of journalism** which is concerned with one of today's big issues – economic, social or political.

    Show to what extent the writer, by his or her presentation of ideas and evidence, increases your knowledge and understanding of the issue.

11. Choose a **work of non-fiction** which, while seeking to inform, relies for its attraction on the use of humour.

    Identify the writer's main ideas and show how to what extent his use of humour is effective in increasing your appreciation of these ideas.

SECTION C – POETRY

Answers to questions on poetry should address relevantly the central concern(s)/ theme(s) of the text(s) and be supported by reference to appropriate poetic techniques such as: imagery, verse form, structure, mood, tone, sound, rhythm, rhyme, characterisation, contrast, setting, symbolism, word choice…

12. Choose a poem in which the poet experiences a moment of understanding or revelation.

    Describe what the understanding or revelation was about and show to what extent the poet's depiction of the experience gives you an insight into the ideas dealt with in the poem.

13. Choose a poem which has as a central feature the gradual revelation of a situation.

    Briefly give an account of the situation and then show how the gradual revelation increases your appreciation of the poem as a whole.

14. Choose a poem which deals with childhood.

Discuss to what extent you feel the poet is successful in recreating the experience of being a child.

15. Choose **two** poems which deal with change or the passage of time.

Compare the ideas of each poem and by examining the techniques of each poet make clear which poem you feel to be more effective in conveying the central idea.

SECTION D – FILM AND TV DRAMA

Answers to questions on film and TV drama should address relevantly the central concern(s)/theme(s) of the text and be supported by reference to appropriate techniques of film and TV drama such as: key sequence(s), characterisation, conflict, structure, plot, dialogue, editing/montage, sound/soundtrack, aspects of mise-en-scène (such as lighting, colour, use of camera, costume, props…), mood, setting, casting, exploitation of genre…

16. Choose a **film** or ★**TV drama** in which a central character finds herself or himself in a frightening situation.

Explain how the character copes with the situation and discuss to what extent this enhances your understanding of the character's role in the film as a whole.

17. Choose a **film** or ★**TV drama** with an opening section which seems to you of particular importance in establishing theme **or** mood **or** character.

By referring closely to the opening section of the film, show how the theme or mood or character is established and go on to show it is developed in the film as a whole.

18. Choose a **film** which you feel to be an typical example of its genre.

By referring to specific aspects of your chosen film show why you feel it deserves this description.

19. Choose a **film** or ★**TV drama** which is concerned with portraying aspects of power.

Identify the aspect(s) of power dealt with and show to what extent your appreciation of the subject is enhanced by the use of specific features such as characterisation, use of camera, editing…

★ "TV drama" includes a single play, a series or a serial.

Answer Support for Critical Essay Papers
Introduction

For Papers 1, 2 and 3, you will find advice on the answering of each question under two headings:

Suggested Approaches:

★ You may find an opening paragraph to help you with a possible starting place, followed by a series of points which probably should form the material for the rest of the essay.

★ You may find some points, or a framework, with one or two paragraphs "written" for you, to demonstrate how the "line of thought" is maintained.

★ You may find some suggestions followed by a possible concluding paragraph.

★ There may simply be an outline or sketch for an answer.

Points to Note and Remember:

These points will be relevant to the particular questions they follow, but they generally apply to all similar questions. The most important ones are summarised below:

1. The opening paragraph should signal what the main thrust of your line of thought is going to be.

    ★ It should not simply repeat the question.

    ★ It should not make statements such as "I am going to discuss…"

    ★ It should not (unless specifically asked for in the question) list techniques or features. (This practice is detrimental to your essay because it dictates a mechanical structure which does not allow you the flexibility to create a line of thought, and which can cause you to lose sight of the central concerns. The discussion of techniques should take place naturally in the course of developing a line of thought in the answer.)

2. The concluding paragraph should reach the logical end point of your argument – e.g. "Hamlet has finally succeeded in avenging his father's death, although at a heavy price."

    ★ It should not simply restate the question.

    ★ It should not make statements such as "I have shown how…" (If your line of thought is sound, you will have shown this. And if your line of thought is not sound, a statement such as this will not make it so.)

3. Most questions demand a selection and reordering of your material.

    ★ Some questions demand a quite narrow focus which means that some of the material you have at your disposal will be irrelevant.

    ★ Some questions demand that you start from the middle of the text, or even from the end.

4. All questions require you to show your understanding of the central concerns of the text, even where this is not spelled out in the question.

5. Use of Quotation:

★ In shorter texts, such as poems, you are expected to be able to quote and comment readily from all parts of the poem which are relevant to your answer.

★ In longer texts reference can be made to the text by means of quotation or by describing specific events or incidents. Close analysis of particular words and phrases is rarely necessary. There may be times in a more "technical" question on a novel, or in poetry or film where detailed (and meaningful) analytical comment is appropriate, but, in general, when dealing with longer texts such as novels and plays, "micro-analysis" is not helpful.

It is important that you start with Paper 1 for three reasons:

★ There is general advice about each genre at the beginning of the appropriate section in Paper 1 which is not repeated in the other papers.

★ **Points to note and remember** are spelled out most fully in Paper 1 and they can be applied to questions in the other papers.

★ **Appendix 1** (Choice) uses the questions in Paper 1 to illustrate its points.

Papers 1 and 3 deal only with film in Section D.

Paper 2 deals only with TV drama in Section D.

Paper 4 has no advice offered to help you. You should use it to put into practice all that you have learned in the course of trying the first three papers.

A Note of Warning (or Advice)

While the practising of writing Critical Essay answers can be useful, it must go hand-in-hand with further reading of your texts. There is no point in trying to answer essay questions based on one reading of a text, no matter how thoroughly done in class. Each question requires you to select from your total knowledge of a text in order to construct your answer. Ideally, given an essay question, sitting at peace in your own study space, not in the pressure cooker of an exam hall, you would reread your text, highlighting the aspects you would need for *this* essay, as opposed to the essay you did last week on another question. If you want to do well, you have to have a really sound knowledge of your text(s) and you have to be aware that you will only be able to use some of that knowledge in the answer to any one question (see *How to Pass Higher English Colour Edition*, pages 126–129, and elsewhere).

In this Support section there may not be an answer corresponding to a text you have studied. But the answer given will still be useful, because it will demonstrate the basic principles involved in an answer of the type required. In the case of poems used as examples you can easily read the relevant poems (pages 172–178) and the suggestions will then make much more sense. And you will enjoy reading the poems. It could be helpful to look at synopses of longer texts which you don't know in order to profit more fully from the advice given.

Critical Essay Paper 1

Section A – Drama

For each of the four questions in this and other sections you will find:

★ a list of common texts which might be suitable for the question concerned

★ suggestions about approaches to the question using one play as an example.

The principles outlined for each play exemplified here will be applicable to the text(s) which you have studied. You should therefore read the **Suggested Approaches** carefully and attempt to apply them to your own text.

Question 1

Choose a play in which a character other than the hero/heroine plays a crucial role in affecting the thoughts and actions of the hero or heroine.

By referring closely to the part played by your chosen character show how important he or she is in affecting the thoughts and actions of the hero/heroine in the course of the play.

Technically, this question applies to all plays, because part of the dramatic function of all of the characters is to affect the central character, but there are some quite obvious choices among commonly studied plays:

> **Macbeth** (with either Macbeth or Lady Macbeth as the main character)
>
> **The Glass Menagerie** (the effect of Amanda, or Laura on Tom)
>
> **King Lear** (almost any character's effect on Lear)
>
> **A View from the Bridge** (probably Catherine's effect on Eddie)
>
> **Hamlet** (the effect on Hamlet of the Ghost of his father)
>
> **Almost any play by Pinter** (in which a menacing character has profound effects)

Such plays could provide the material for an answer to this question, depending, of course, on the depth and flexibility of your own knowledge of the play.

Suggested Approaches:

Here is how you might start an answer to this question using Iago from Othello.

> *In the play **Othello** by William Shakespeare, Iago is the most important character affecting Othello's thoughts and actions. He begins his campaign of manipulation directly after the dismissal of Cassio. But he has already begun to lay the groundwork for his plan from the moment he conceived it, just before he left for Cyprus:*

continued ➢

> *After some time to abuse Othello's ear*
> *That he (Cassio) is too familiar with his wife*

Having engineered the disgrace of Cassio in the brawl with Roderigo and Montano, he hypocritically advises Cassio to plead his case through Desdemona, intending to turn the situation to his own advantage:

> *I'll pour this pestilence into his ear.*
> *That she repeals him for her body's lust.*

From there it is an easy step to bring Othello to see the meeting between Desdemona and Cassio, and sow the first seeds of doubt in Othello's mind about his wife's faithfulness.

Here Shakespeare has Iago play his "honesty card"; and throughout the play, by having him seem to be reluctant to believe anything against Cassio, or Desdemona, or to disturb Othello's peace, Shakespeare makes more credible the deception of Othello. Iago immediately follows his, apparently surprised, "Ha! I like not that." on seeing Cassio leave Desdemona, with a disclaimer,

> *Cassio, my lord! No, sure, I cannot think it…*

This simultaneously bolsters his reputation for fairness and honesty, and also rouses suspicion in Othello, with a reference to Cassio's "steal(ing) away so guilty-like."

The answer might now develop along the following lines:

★ details of the rest of this long and eventful scene where Iago manipulates Othello's thoughts by playing on his vulnerability

★ the whole episode of the handkerchief culminating in Act 3, Scene 4, crucial to Iago's effect on Othello's thoughts and ultimately his actions

★ Iago's more direct approach in Act 4 – "Lie with her, on her; what you will" leading to Othello's first fit

★ the seeming "proof" of the Bianca scene

★ finally pushing Othello to action "Do it not with poison…"; and to his suicide.

NB This outline is not necessarily the only possibility. There are other incidents and scenes equally fruitful in providing material for an answer.

Points to Note and Remember:

1. The first paragraph **does not slavishly repeat the question**. Instead it states exactly what the essay is going to be about, referring to the main thrust of the question.

2. There is **no mention of any technique or feature**. You will, in the course of your essay, inevitably deal with characterisation, structure, dialogue. There may be other features which your argument points up, but reference to these should emerge naturally in the course of your discussion. They do not need to be mentioned in paragraph 1; indeed mention of such things in the opening paragraph is often detrimental to your essay because it dictates a mechanical structure which does not allow you the flexibility to answer the question as required.

3. The answer **does not start at the beginning of the play and go straight through it.** There is almost nothing from Act I, because Iago hasn't even devised his plan until the end of it.

Question 2

Choose a scene from a play in which a main character is persuaded or forced to act against her/his wishes or conscience.

Describe the scene in detail and discuss to what extent the character's decision in this scene continues to reverberate throughout the play as a whole.

The requirement for a scene to involve an action which is against the protagonist's wishes or conscience places limitations on the choice of play, but there are several quite obvious choices among commonly studied plays:

> ★ the court scene in Miller's **The Crucible**
>
> ★ Act 3 Scene 3 in **Romeo and Juliet** – Tybalt's death
>
> ★ Act 1 Scene 7 in **Macbeth** – Macbeth's decision to go ahead with the murder of Duncan
>
> ★ Act 1 Scene 5 in **Twelfth Night** – Viola's wooing of Olivia on Orsino's behalf, in opposition to her own love for Orsino
>
> ★ **Hamlet**, Act 1 Scene 5, where Hamlet is given the task of revenge, and accepts it unwillingly, or Act 3 Scene 1 where Ophelia returns Hamlet's gifts in accordance with her father's command
>
> ★ the scene in Act 2 of **A Man for All Seasons** by Robert Bolt where Sir Thomas More insults Norfolk in order to spare Norfolk from the King's displeasure

Suggested Approaches:

Consider Scene 4 from **The Glass Menagerie** by Tennessee Williams.

You would start by describing the scene in some detail, because you would have to show how Tom was, in this case, "persuaded" (rather than "forced" although you could make a case for either) to bring home a gentleman caller for Laura.

In this scene Tom is on the back foot as a result of two events:

(a) in the previous scene he insulted Amanda in one of the most memorable speeches in the play "…ugly, babbling old witch…"

(b) he has been drinking the night before and possibly feels guilty about it.

Amanda's persuasion consists of moral blackmail using Laura's lack of prospects as a weapon. You would finish this section by showing how reluctantly Tom agreed to Amanda's wishes, merely to stop her nagging and because he was rushing to get to work on time.

Now you have to look at the extent to which this scene "reverberates throughout the play as a whole" – in other words, the major consequences of Tom's decision to ask Jim into the household.

There are two major effects:

1. The initial encouragement and subsequent disappointment of Laura.

2. Tom's decision to leave home.

The sequence begins with Laura's realisation that "Jim" was, in fact the "Jim" she had talked to her mother about earlier as a boy who had once interested her. The effect is so strong as to make her faint. (Summer storm/thunder)

The next few paragraphs of your essay might look like this:

> *When finally Amanda manages to engineer Jim and Laura into a situation where they will be alone, Laura gradually overcomes her shyness with Jim. Jim has them both sit on cushions on the floor, offers her chewing gum, breaking the ice. Laura finally gains enough courage to ask him about his singing (which for her is an extremely bold action). It leads to the important question – "I don't suppose you remember me at all". (William prepares us for the importance of this question by using it as one of his "LEGENDS" on the screen.) Jim surprises her by, in fact, remembering her. It was the name "Blue Roses" which made her memorable to him, not her calliper, which is what Laura thought was all that people ever remembered her for. She gradually gains confidence throughout the conversation, and brings out her yearbook and the programme from* Pirates of Penzance *which Jim eventually signs for her.*
>
> *Not only has Laura, in this scene, been gaining confidence but she has unwittingly been feeding Jim's ego. She remembers him as the High School hero, which was probably the time in his life when he felt most successful. He obviously has not forged the meteoric career which was forecast for him in the year book (or he would not be working as a clerk in a shoe warehouse). The fact that his disappointment is alleviated by Laura's reminiscences contributes to the warmth which he feels for her, leading to his helping her with advice about overcoming her inferiority complex.*
>
> *When he describes his own hopes for his future career, Laura is inspired by his enthusiasm…*

You would then continue with:

★ Reference to the glass animals, including the smashing of the unicorn

★ The culmination of this scene – Jim's realisation of what he has done – "Stumble-john"

★ The revelation of Jim's engagement to Betty

★ Laura's devastation

★ Amanda's realisation that all her plans have come to nothing (Thunder again)

★ Quarrel with Tom, and Tom's final speech including the importance of "pieces of coloured glass…"

Points to Note and Remember:

1. In the course of dealing with characterisation throughout your essay, you have also touched on elements of structure, Williams' use of LEGENDS, the symbolism of the glass animals, and the pathetic fallacy of the summer storm. These techniques take their place naturally in the course of developing a line of thought in the answer. (see point 1, page 91)

2. The starting point for this essay is Scene 4, with some reference to what has happened directly before. The only other reference to the earlier part of the play is the conversation about Jim and Blue Roses, which is relevant to the later scene.

3. The balance between the space in the essay given over to the scene, and that given to "the play as a whole" would depend on the line of thought in the answer, but neither should be too brief.

Question 3

Choose a play which has as one of its main concerns loss of respect, or of honour, or of status.

Identify which loss you have chosen and show how the playwright's exploration of this loss is important in your appreciation of the play as a whole.

Possible texts for this question might be:

A Streetcar Named Desire; The Crucible; King Lear; The Birthday Party; Macbeth; Othello; A View from the Bridge; Death of a Salesman; A Doll's House

There are many more plays commonly studied which would be appropriate for this question.

Suggested Approaches:

All My Sons by Arthur Miller would provide material for an answer to this question.

The first part of the question on this occasion is very quickly answered, as all you are being asked to do is to specify which of the three "losses" you are going to deal with. In fact, the three concepts are quite closely related, especially "respect" and "status", but for this play "respect" is easiest to deal with.

The main part of your answer should explore the "loss" and show how it affects your reading (or viewing) of the whole play.

Chris's relationship with Joe is initially one of affection and respect: "Isn't he a great guy?" – a view which is shared to some extent by Ann.

Joe's neighbours appear to have a benign view of Joe, but it is later revealed that Jim has suspected (or known) what Joe had done.

Kate's position is a bit more ambiguous. She is in possession of the facts about Joe, but she has to remain in a state of denial because of her refusal to accept Larry's death. (The apple tree is an important symbol here.)

George, who brings the case back into the open, originally accepted the court's view of the apportioning of blame between his father and Joe, refusing to see or communicate with his father, thinking that Joe was the "good guy"

Your essay would then deal with when, how and why Joe loses their respect. The revelations, especially as they affect Chris, allow the audience to understand something of the conflict between duty to family and duty to society as a whole.

If you have covered all these aspects, your concluding paragraph might look like this:

> *By the final scene Joe realises that he has lost Chris's respect, but he still has a hope that he may be forgiven. When Chris returns it is obvious that he is torn between his duty and his remaining feelings for Joe. But when Larry's letter is finally read and understood Joe realises that there is no further hope that the family, on which all his hopes and actions were centred, can remain as a functioning unit and that he has forfeited not only their respect but ultimately his own self-respect. His final action in shooting himself represents perhaps a cowardly way out of his predicament, but can also be seen by the audience as an indication of his desire to be able to face his own actions and punish himself for them.*

Points to Note and Remember:

1. The list of "losses" given in the question is a **closed** list. You are not at liberty to add another "loss" which would suit you better.

2. In this conclusion there is no mere repetition of the original question. It does **not** state something to the effect that "in my conclusion, I have shown how Joe's loss is important to my appreciation of the play as a whole…".

3. Be careful to remember that the "central concern" is not just "loss" – it is "loss of respect". In any question about the theme or central/thematic concerns the definition is important – "loss of respect" not "loss"; "love betrayed" or "the power of love", not just "love".

Question 4

Choose a play portraying a seemingly strong relationship which deteriorates in the course of the play.

Discuss to what extent the deterioration is brought about by personality and to what extent by external forces and show how the portrayal of the relationship is important to your understanding of a central concern of the text.

Plays which could be used in this question are:

A View from the Bridge; All My Sons; Educating Rita; Othello; Macbeth; Serjeant Musgrave's Dance; The Glass Menagerie; Who's Afraid of Virginia Woolf?

There are many more plays commonly studied which would be appropriate for this question.

Suggested Approaches:

A Doll's House by Henrik Ibsen would be an appropriate text for this question.

The relationship between Nora and Torwald seems to be a loving one, but there are obvious weaknesses in it. The relationship deteriorates so much that Nora leaves Torwald in the end. The relationship is threatened both by external forces – Krogstad and the bond – and by personality traits in both of the characters in the relationship. You have to evaluate which of these factors (internal or external) is more important, and go on to show how the breakdown in the relationship is closely concerned with one of the main concerns – women's independence.

Selection of evidence:

Personality:

★ Torwald's controlling nature – the pet names which essentially keep Nora in a subservient role

★ Nora's playing up to his wishes (while secretly subverting them) which contrasts with the obvious efficiency with which she has gone about repaying the loan

★ The importance of "morality" and the way in which Torwald sees it as "respectability" and "position in society"

★ The importance of "practical morality" on Nora's part in arranging for her husband's stay in the south, and her wish to spare her father any anxiety. This results in the forgery of the signature

★ Nora's growing doubts about her relationship, prompted by her fears about the loan, – her conversation with Anne about the children – her symbolic performance of the tarantella: all of these point towards a major change in her view of herself

External forces:

★ Krogstad's loss of his position in the Bank leads to his attempt to manipulate Nora, and finally, to his attempt to blackmail Torwald

★ This leads to the climax where Torwald prohibits Nora from seeing her children for fear of moral contamination, and Nora's realises her husband's intransigence and selfishness

★ Mrs Linde's intervention with Kronstad takes the threat away completely, but reveals even more clearly to Nora, her husband's essentially superficial standards

★ The bold decision taken by Doctor Rand to cut off all communication and wait for death possibly encourages Nora's decisiveness

The result of both factors:

★ Nora's final decision to try to find her own personality, divorced from the "doll" role which she has played, first for her father, and then for Torwald

★ And finally, the slamming of the door, symbolising the freedom and independence which Nora now hopes for

Points to Note and Remember:

1. In this case you probably do start at the beginning of the play and end at the end, taking events in chronological order; but you should ensure that each bit of the narrative which you deal with is **related to the elements of the question** – is it to do with the deterioration in the relationship? Or the influence of personality? Or the factors brought about by external forces? It must be linked to the "independence" theme. Remember, too, that there is an evaluative task to do. Within the above framework, you will have discussed characterisation, structure, and symbolism without any explicit statement about "techniques", but you will have shown your understanding of their contribution to the text as a whole.

2. Although the **relationship** dealt with in **A Doll's House** is a marriage, the question is open to relationships of a non-romantic kind. The relationship between father and son, or between partners in a business, or comrades in arms (as in **Serjeant Musgrave's Dance**) could equally well be explored.

Section B – Prose Fiction (Novel)

Question 5

Choose a **novel** in which a central character stands out or differs from her/his surrounding society in some important way.

Show how her/his individual stance or position adds to your understanding of at least one of the central concerns of the novel.

Central character	(One of) the central concerns
Winston Smith **Nineteen Eighty-Four**	absolute power of the state
John the Savage **Brave New World**	soullessness of the "perfect" society
Ivan Denisovich **One Day in the Life of Ivan Denisovich**	the indomitable human spirit
Heathcliff **Wuthering Heights**	the destructive power of thwarted love
Jean Brodie **The Prime of Miss Jean Brodie**	the misuse of power
Casey **The Grapes of Wrath**	sacrifice for the common good
Simon **Lord of the Flies** (or Roger or Jack)	the predilection of mankind towards evil
Offred **The Handmaid's Tale**	refusal to conform/give in to society
The Priest **The Power and the Glory**	faith under pressure
Holden Caulfield **The Catcher in the Rye**	teenage angst
Mrs Scott **Consider the Lilies**	injustice/betrayal by the Church
Dennis Barlow **The Loved One**	the American way of death

There are many more novels and characters which would be appropriate, and, even in the above list, there could be other characters and other concerns in the novel which would provide equally valid answers.

Suggested Approaches:

The Trick is to Keep Breathing – Janice Galloway.

A possible opening paragraph:

> *In* **The Trick is to Keep Breathing** *by Janice Galloway we have a character who "differs" from her surrounding society in at least one important way – she is suffering from a severe mental breakdown, and can barely function in the world around her. In following her progress through the novel we can begin to gain an insight into what the world of the mentally ill involves.*

The essay would then go on to show how the back story of Michael's death is approached only very obliquely, because she keeps balking at the memory, and so does not let the reader approach it either. The minutely detailed description of the symptoms of her condition aid the reader in realising the helplessness of her condition:

"I look at the ceiling where upstairs is, then look at my hands. I have to concentrate: one finger at a time, releasing pressure…redistributing pieces of myself."

Other points to follow up:

★ Her reliance on work to keep a tenuous hold on reality "This is my workplace. This is what I am."

★ Her feeling of emptiness, symbolised by her anorexia, and by blank pages in the text. She asks her friend Marianne (who is In the USA) "What will I do while I'm lasting, Marianne, what will I do?"

★ The detailed description of other symptoms such as: lack of sleep, alcoholism, fixations with time, and cleanliness – affect the reader leading him or her further into the world of the severely depressed

★ Her use of lists to try to order the chaos of time and her faith in horoscopes and women's magazine remedies are affecting in their ordinariness

★ Her spell in hospital and its uselessness – they never even discover she is anorexic – leaves us feeling how unsolvable deep depression is.

It is important to notice that although the focus of the novel is on breakdown, Galloway lets you see that there is a dark humour which gives you an impression of something of the "original" Joy, before the "Stone" part of her name took over. Her solution is simply to "keep breathing", to "last" out the time, because that is all she can do. Eventually her increasing ability to form complete sentences and take part in ordinary activities (such as buying a Christmas tree) gives some hope that there might be an alleviation at least, if not an end, to her downward spiral.

The typographical tricks played in the book – margin notes, trailing sentences, could be mentioned in the essay where there is a relevant point to be made – as in the blank page example above; but you should avoid "tacking on" a paragraph dealing with these as a separate topic.

Points to Note and Remember:

1. In the course of dealing with this question you have dealt with characterisation throughout; you have also touched on some of the elements of structure – the story of Michael's death; typographical tricks such as blank pages; the use of dramatic form; the importance of Joy Stone's name, and the significance of the title. All of these have been shown to be relevant to the reader's deepening understanding of depression and mental illness which is a central concern of the text.

Question 6

Choose a **novel** or **short story** in which one of the central threads of the story concerns a love affair or marriage.

Explain how the relationship's development is affected by the couple's personalities and show to what extent the relationship is central to the main theme(s) of the text.

Many novels would seem to be appropriate for this question – as many novels have a "romantic interest", but, looking at the actual question you have to answer, the lovers' relationship has be set against the bigger picture of the novel's social and historical context.

> Some novels such as **The Prime of Miss Jean Brodie** do have love affairs as part of the plot, but the central concerns are more socio-political – the misuse of power…
>
> **Where Angels Fear to Tread** has at least three romantic pairings but the novel as a whole is much more concerned with culture and class issues
>
> **The Quiet American** has larger issues than the love triangle, although it is important in paralleling the political struggles
>
> More suitable would be novels where the relationship is more central:
>
> **Sunset Song; Nineteen Eighty-Four; A Room with a View; A Farewell to Arms; Jane Eyre; North and South; The Collector; Atonement; The Great Gatsby**

Suggested Approaches:

Sunset Song – Lewis Grassic Gibbon.

An outline for this essay would probably contain:

★ the beginnings of Chris and Ewan's relationship – possibly the kiss in the dark, her father's funeral, and their meeting in Stonehaven.

★ their expedition to Dunottar – important in two ways:

　　it foreshadows the difficulties that their tempers can cause;

　　the story of Sarah shows something of Ewan's compassion and experience, and looks forward, perhaps, to Chris's relationship with Long Rob

★ the night adventure with the horses, and the emergence of their passionate relationship.

★ Ewan's pride is made clear in the discussions they have about money and although he puts it behind him, there is a possible source of tension.

★ tension emerges between the Highlander and the Lowlander. Although united in their love of the land, they are separated by their different cultures.

★ the divide between them in the matter of education illustrated by the visit to Edzell Castle – "Chris laughed and looked at him, queer and sorry, and glimpsed at the remoteness that her books had made."

★ the quarrel they have when Chris realises she is pregnant – the tendency of both to say truly hurtful things, and to be stubborn about taking them back.

> *Through all these incidents, Grassic Gibbon shows their strong feelings of love and passion, for each other and for the land, but also the possibility that this very strength might become a weakness. This is revealed more clearly when society around them begins to change, and they try to hold everything as it is. They are bound up in their land, and their new baby so they shut out the war from their lives. Only when Chae comes home on leave does Ewan first raise the question of his enlisting, only to suppress it. "Ewan looked at her shamed-like and blushed and said 'Och, I was asking only'." They don't speak about it again – and the question remains suspended in the air, a threat to their happiness.*

Their relationship is a central illustration of the effects that the war has on the whole community, represented by:

★ society's goading of those men who do not go to fight

★ Long Rob's conscientious objection and his treatment by the community

★ the destruction of the land, and its old ways

The episode in which Ewan comes back on leave further highlights the parallels between their relationship and the effects of the war.

> *Although it is the war that has brought about the situation, their parting has a number of reminders that deep feelings can go either way, that Chris's coldness and contempt comes from somewhere far away (the English Chris) to "the body of a drunken lout from the plough stilts" and the stubbornness of both at parting has happened before, but the reconciliation, this time, does not come   and never will in this life:*

> *"Oh God, she had never let him go like that! And in her desolation of weeping she began to pray…and prayed for him to come back, to kiss her and hold her in kindness just once before he went down that road."*

★ you could continue to the point at which Chris realised (after speaking to Chae) what Ewan had felt at the end, and how it restored her love for Ewan

The evaluation required in the question will arise naturally from the structure of the essay you have written. Your conclusion would probably be that their relationship mirrors the destruction of the community as it was, but that the reconciliation at the end, might point to a different but not wholly negative future.

Points to Note and Remember:

1. If you use an appropriate quotation such as the one above, "Oh God, she had never… he went down that road." there is no necessity to comment on it further – no need, for example, to pick out the word "desolation" for further analysis of the kind that says the blindingly obvious – that "desolation" is an extremely strong word which lets you know that she is isolated and alone. This is what examiners call "micro-analysis" and, in answers on the novel, it is generally regarded as unnecessary. Close analysis of particular words and phrases in essays on a novel is rarely necessary. There may be times in a more "technical" question on a novel, or in poetry or film where detailed (and meaningful) analytical comment is

appropriate, but, in general, when dealing with longer texts such as novels and plays, such micro-analysis is not helpful.

2. In this case, you do not start at the beginning of the novel. Most of the material up to the death of John Guthrie is not really relevant to this question.

Question 7

Choose a **novel** in which the writer's use of a particular technique such as symbolism, use of recurrent imagery, first person narrative... plays a significant part in adding to your understanding and appreciation of one of the central concerns of the novel.

Identify one such technique and show how the writer uses it effectively in the exploration of a central concern.

There are so many possibilities and variations possible in this question that there is no point in trying to identify particularly suitable texts. You will either be prepared for this kind of question or you won't.

Suggested Approaches:

The important words in the first part of the question are 'significant... adding... understanding and appreciation... one... central concerns'. You must realise that a vague and woolly essay on "techniques" is not what is required.

The important thing to remember is to tie your technique firmly to a central concern.

One example would be when dealing with **changes in narrative perspective** in **The Inheritors** by William Golding. Any discussion of the viewpoint adopted in the first ten chapters of the novel would be aimed at showing the essential goodness displayed by the people –as the title suggests, they are "the meek who shall inherit the earth" and the observations of the New People as cruel and sacrificers of children – hardly human. The reversal of narrative perspective in the middle of chapter 11 reveals that "the people" (in their last representative, Lok) are primitive, animalistic: "the red creature" is called "it" not "he". It also reveals that the New People are "us", homo sapiens, (the next inheritors?) and through the eyes of Tuami, we gain some slight sympathy with them, in their superstition and fear of "the devils". However, we still possess the knowledge that we gained through the previous narrative perspective of the essential "darkness" which inhabits their existence.

Points to Note and Remember:

1. The technique chosen for this answer is **not** in the list suggested in the question. The list of suggested techniques is an **open** list – you are free to ignore these suggestions and consider instead other technique(s) which you feel to be appropriate.

2. It is important to tie your technique firmly to a central concern.

Question 8

Choose a **novel** in which the ending on first reading shocks you in some way.

Describe the events of the ending and, by referring to the novel as a whole, discuss to what extent you now feel that this ending is inevitable.

Suitable texts would include:

The Great Gatsby; The Cone-Gatherers; The Changeling; Nineteen Eighty-Four; Tess of the D'Urbervilles; Where Angels Fear to Tread; A Farewell to Arms; Sunset Song; Brighton Rock; Lamb

Suggested Approaches:

Where Angels Fear to Tread by E.M. Forster.

The death of the baby in the closing chapters of the book is profoundly shocking to the reader.

To what degree it is inevitable is problematic, but the "to what extent" part of the question allows you to say that the end seems to you now either inevitable, or not inevitable, or partly inevitable.

The essay should start with a description of the shocking incident:

★ the kidnapping, the weather, the claustrophobic setting

★ Philip's premonitions "filled him with sorrow and with the expectation of more sorrow to come"

★ the baby's crying (in the way Gino had described – "If he cries silently then you may be frightened")

★ Forster leads the reader to feel that at this moment the fate of the baby is terrible and somehow inevitable, as it proves to be.

Part of the shock is caused by the contrast between this incident and the only other incident in which Forster describes the baby – in glowing, warm terms, where Gino and Miss Abbott bathe him.

In the context of the novel as a whole Forster presents us with a series of apparently irreconcilable opposite which make a happy ending unlikely:

★ Sawston with Monteriano

★ Mrs Herriton and Harriet with Gino, Perfetta and the cast of characters from the village

★ Philip in England (and initially in Italy) with Philip in Italy in the latter half of the book

Philip's succumbing to Italy's spell is used by Forster to act as a bridge between the shabby portrait of Italy which we see in Lilia's marriage and the exuberance of Italian life as exemplified at the Opera.

In the conclusion you would discuss the extent to which of the clash of cultures caused the baby's death.

Points to Note and Remember:

1. "The ending" does not have to be positively the last incident in the novel – it can include, as here, the "beginning of the end".

2. Any question which asks "to what extent" allows you to say "wholly" or "partly" or "not at all".

Prose Fiction – Short Story

Question 6

Choose a **novel** or **short story** in which one of the central threads of the story concerns a love affair or marriage.

Explain how the relationship's development is affected by the couple's personalities and show to what extent the relationship is central to the main theme(s) of the text.

Suitable texts would include:

The Lady's Maid; The Boarding House; Eveline; Smeddum; Andrina; Odour of Chrysanthemums; Flight; The Yellow Wallpaper; What Becomes; A Ringin Frost

Suggested Approaches:

The Lady's Maid by Katherine Mansfield.

This would be an interesting choice. Although the marriage never happens, and the relationship is described only in retrospect, it is important as it highlights the essential selfishness of "my Lady", and the exploitation of the servant which are central concerns of the text:

★ the situation of the couple is told in retrospect by the Lady's Maid of the title: she and her suitor were to be married after a long courtship and she was going to help with his florist's shop

★ the circumstance which influences their relationship is the determination of "my Lady" not to let her servant go, which illustrates the exploitation of the servant and the implied criticism of the class system – central to the story

★ the writer's skilful use of the lady's maid as the naïve narrator, unconscious of the way in which she is being manipulated, makes her fate even more poignant to the reader.

Question 9

Choose **two short stories** set in the future, or in a culture vastly different from your own.

Identify an important concern the writer deals with in each story, and, by looking at content and technique, assess which you find to be more effective in conveying the writer's ideas.

> *"the future"*
>
> **The Murderer; A Sound of Thunder; The Pedestrian; The Star;**
> **The Nine Billion Names of God; Billennium; Nightfall**
>
> *"culture vastly different from your own"* the past, for example Edgar Allan Poe, or
> de Maupassant; writing with a colonial background – Rudyard Kipling, for example, or
> contemporary writers such as Anita Desai and Alice Walker.

This question is fairly open, because it does not demand two stories on the same theme, or two stories by the same writer, or two stories using the same techniques. Beware, however, of choosing two stories which have absolutely nothing in common. The question demands that there must be some similarity in the setting, and the closer that similarity, the easier you will find the evaluative task which you have to consider.

Suggested Approaches:

Ray Bradbury's **The Murderer** and J.G. Ballard's **Billennium**

Both of these stories deal with a time in the future where changes in circumstances put pressure on the human race.

In **The Murderer** the pressure is caused by the incessant, unremitting communication – wrist radios, intercoms, surround-sound musak, talking machinery, the complete absence of silence.

In **Billennium** the pressure is one of living space. The effects of a massive population explosion have been mitigated by the use of most of the planet for food production, leaving living space in cities severely limited.

In each case there is a protagonist through whose eyes you see the problem.

Basically, one warns us about what happens when there is no silence, and the other warns us about what happens when there is no space.

The evaluative task is to come to a conclusion as to which writer is more effective in his warning.

Points to Note and Remember:

1. Generally, although simply writing a short essay on the first short story followed by a short essay on the second, with a brief comparative comment tacked on at the end will answer the question, a better comparison is usually made by dealing with both stories together.

Prose Non-fiction

The list of features for non-fiction is markedly different from those features connected with fiction. There are some aspects in common (for example, setting) but setting in non-fiction has a slightly different function from setting in fiction. In the first place, in non-fiction the setting is real and non-negotiable, whereas in fiction the setting can be "imagined" to fulfil certain needs of the novelist. Take **Lord of the Flies** by William Golding. The island has a series of settings which take on symbolic significance – but the need for these settings in the novel brings them into being. But, if you are Bill Bryson in Hammerfest, you can't "make up" the town. A writer of non-fiction can **select**, and often the selection is very skilful in giving the desired impression, but it can't be untrue. The writer of non-fiction is often concerned to present the setting as a subject of interest in itself.

Similarly, "characterisation" in fiction is distinct from descriptions of a person in non-fiction. Again, the writer of non-fiction can select and emphasise, but he can't make it up. A character in a novel is an imagined person, whose thoughts (depending on the method of narration) can be open to the reader. A writer of non-fiction can only give you this sort of information through the use of dialogue or interview.

It is important to recognise the difference between the two genres.

Question 10

Choose a **work of non-fiction** which has, as its main subject, the experience of travel, or exploration, or an expedition.

Discuss whether the description of the place(s) is more or less important than the description of the people involved in the travel, or exploration, or expedition.

An important word here is "main". It tends to rule out a lot of Orwell (although essays such as **Marrakesh** are in essence "travel" writing). Essayists in general usually have an issue of some sort as their main subject. The background (place and culture) may be an important context, but is rarely the main subject. The following texts are just some examples of suitable texts:

Travel:

Bruce Chatwin, Colin Thubron, Paul Theroux, Rory Stewart, Michael Palin, Bill Bryson and others

Exploration/expedition:

Summit Fever Andrew Greig

Touching the Void Joe Simpson

Sisters of Sinai Janet Soskice

Older texts:

Scott's Last Expedition

Endurance: **Shackleton's Incredible Voyage** by Alfred Lansing

Question 11

Choose a **work of non-fiction** in which the views of the writer are presented in a biased way.

Show how the writer's use of language promotes his/her views and discuss the effect on you of his/her biased treatment of the subject.

Many newspaper columnists could provide material for this question:

> Keith Waterhouse, Ian Hislop, Malcolm Muggeridge, Will Self, and, depending on the subject, Polly Toynbee, Ian Bell, Melanie Phillips, Howard Jacobsen, Yasmin Alibhai Brown

Writers such as these often use language in a highly rhetorical or emotive way.

Suggested Approaches:

The first part of this question is quite narrow, requiring the kind of understanding of the uses of language as they are often explored in Close Reading Passages. The second part of the question asks you to evaluate the effect of this language on you – is it persuasive? Is it over the top? Is it off-putting in its repetitiveness, for example – or is it completely convincing?

Question 12

Choose a **work of biography or autobiography** which deals with the relationship between important events and the subsequent course of the subject's life.

Show how the writer's presentation of these events emphasises their significance and go on to show how they affect the subject's life.

> Historical biographies could fall into this category, for example, **Samuel Pepys, the Unequalled Self** by Claire Tomalin; or actors' memoirs such as Lawrence Olivier's **Confessions of an Actor**; or playwright Arthur Miller's **Timebends**; or Peter Ackroyd's **The Life of Thomas More** or **Dickens**; C.S Lewis on religious conversion; Tony Benn on his political life…

Suggested Approaches:

The first part of the question requires a detailed knowledge of the important incidents, and how the writer makes you aware that these are significant events. The second part should deal with the effect of the events on the person, and their effects in changing, intensifying, modifying, reversing, the course of the subject's life.

Section C – Poetry

The approach required for most of the poetry questions is usually slightly different from the questions on plays and novels. Unlike the Sunset Song answer in the novel section (pages 102–3) where advice is given against the "micro-analysis" approach, in the poetry section the question often demands a close analysis of some references to the poem. This is because the question often asks for comment on the poet's style, or treatment, or use of poetic techniques, or poetic skill in portraying her or his subject. However, the question will also demand an understanding of the main concern(s) of the poem, and will suggest a line of thought to be followed in your answer. A mere listing of techniques with analysed quotations will not provide a satisfactory essay.

The following discussions of particular poems will be infinitely more useful to you as examples of what to do and what not to do if you read the five poems used in this section in Appendix 3, pages 172–178. They are all quite short – and besides, you may enjoy them.

Question 13

Choose a poem which takes a disillusioned or a despairing look at life.

Show how effectively the disillusionment or the despair is revealed by the poet's treatment of her/his subject.

Suggested Approaches:

Dover Beach by Matthew Arnold (Appendix 3, page 172)

The following could be the opening:

Arnold, in **Dover Beach**, *despairs of life itself, in which sadness and human misery permeate even the most calm and beautiful moments. The poem starts on what seems to be a positive note:*

> *The sea is calm tonight.*
> *The tide is full. The moon lies fair*
> *Upon the straits*

And the poet calls his wife to the scene.

> *Come to the window, sweet is the night air!*

But the contrast of the "calm" and "fair", with the harsher words which follow — "the grating roar/of pebbles which the waves suck back and fling…" begins to suggest that all is not well. The rhythm also adds to the destabilising effect suggesting the ebb and the flow of the waves:

> *Begin, and cease, and then again begin*
> *With tremulous cadence slow, and bring…*

At this point the enjambement creates a moment's hiatus, like the top of the wave before it falls, which highlights the important climax of the verse –

The eternal note of sadness in.

Arnold remembers "Sophocles long ago", who listening to the waves beside the Aegean, encapsulated in his tragedies "the turbid ebb and flow of human misery", and parallels this with himself and his wife finding the same sounds and the same thoughts centuries later and many miles away "by this distant northern sea". By using this illustration, Arnold is emphasising the presence of human misery in all times and all places...

A similar treatment of the rest of the poem, always focusing on the despair Arnold feels will provide a good answer to a fairly straightforward question.

Points to Note and Remember:

1. Note that, as in the advice in point 1 page 91, **the first paragraph makes no mention of "techniques"**. An essay which follows a "technique led" structure will tend to become a list, and will prevent you from forming a sensible line of thought. Take care that the **analysis of any aspect of the poem's language is directed at the main thrust of the question** – the idea of disillusion or despair.

2. In the first paragraphs of this essay on Dover Beach, you will see that word choice, contrast, rhythm, enjambement and allusion have all been dealt with naturally as part of the 'argument', or line of thought, of the answer.

Question 14

Choose a poem one of whose main ideas springs from the observation of a place or person(s).

Show how the poet skilfully uses his/her observation of the place or person(s) as a springboard for ideas explored in the poem.

Suggested Approaches:

In the following outline the crucial point at which the poem moves from the particular to the general, from the experience to the reflection is expanded for you.

Trio by Edwin Morgan (Appendix 3, pages 176–7).

The first part of your essay would look at the situation and the people as Morgan describes them – you would be emphasising the happiness contained in almost every detail of the description, showing how that feeling is evoked.

Now you identify the point in the poem where the argument moves from the particular to the general:

The rhythm of the poem breaks at the line:

> *Orphean sprig! Melting baby! Warm Chihuahua!*

and this signals the beginning of the poet's reflection on the experience. The "brisk sprig of mistletoe" is the immediate trigger for these thoughts. Unlike tinsel and plastic guitar covers, mistletoe has an ancient history dating from classical times at least, as a mythical, powerful plant. It brings to the poet's mind the larger significances of Christmas, even in the modern world. Morgan again uses an ancient reference, this time a religious one, "The vale of tears" which he says is "powerless" in the face of the Trio's happiness. Regardless of whether Christ existed or not, the occasion, with its warmth and euphoria, has put out of their minds the "Monsters of the year" – the troubles and problems looming in their everyday lives. These and all the connotations of the "vale of tears" – the valley of the shadow of death - are defeated by these three people on this day. The monsters "are scattered back / can't bear this march of three". "Scattered back" and "march" both suggest the image of an irresistible military force which renders the monsters "powerless".

You would go on to look in detail at the conclusion of the poem, which further develops the impregnability of their happiness and its effect on the poet, and their lasting and unintentional effect on the poet, and on you, the reader.

Points to Note and Remember:

1. This is quite a short poem. You would be expected to quote and comment readily from all the parts of the poem which are relevant to your answer.

Question 15

Choose **two** poems which deal with the same emotion, for example, love, jealousy, pity…

By examining the ideas and style of each poem, discuss which you find to be the more effective in enlarging your understanding of the emotion you have chosen.

Suggested Approaches:

The Thread by Don Paterson and **The Thaw** by Kathleen Jamie (Appendix 3, pages 177 and 175).

These two poems have in common the emotion of "love". But that is not enough of a similarity to allow you to write a meaningful comparison. The fact that in each case the love is for a child gives much more scope for an answer. And, further, there is anxiety mixed with that love. These similarities make the task meaningful and worthwhile.

The Thread is about Jamie, a baby who is born with his life hanging on a thread. For a week it is not certain whether he is going to live or die. He survives and the poet makes a joyful contrast between the fragile nature of his hold on the world when he was born, and the healthy two year old that he now is.

The Thaw is about the homecoming of a new-born baby, with the mother delighting in his existence alongside all the familiar domestic surroundings, following the anxiety of childbirth itself "in a difficult giving".

Some of the following points could be expanded to form the basis of a comparison.

★ The description of the birth in each suggests difficulty and anxious love.

In **The Thread**,

> Jamie made his landing in the world
> so hard he ploughed straight back into the earth.

In **The Thaw**,

> ablaze with concern
> for that difficult giving,
> before we were two, from my one.

★ You might make a comment about the point of view of the poet in each case – one watching the birth, the other giving birth.

★ One of the main points of comparison is in the language of the poems highlighting the kind of delight the poets have in the safe existence of their children. In **The Thread**, there is a vigorous, active quality in the description of Jamie's later boundless energy: "roaring down the back of Kirrie Hill"/"somehow out-revving/every engine in the universe."

The language of **The Thaw** is quieter, more contemplative:

> a journey
> through darkening snow,
> arms laden with you in a blanket

★ Each title is important in that it encapsulates a metaphor which is important to the main idea of the poem. The explanation of these metaphors is important in showing your understanding of the central concerns of the poems.

★ The order of events in each poem: the birth coming first in **The Thread** but last in **The Thaw** might lead to a discussion of which order is more effective.

★ The argument of each poem highlights the love for the child, the happiness it creates, and the completion of the family and the home.

Points to Note and Remember:

1. In this case, the list of suggested techniques is an **open** list – you are free to ignore these suggestions and consider instead other emotions...anger, contempt, joy...

2. There has to be enough common ground between the themes of the two poems to make a meaningful comparison.

3. In the above outline, you are dealing with the two poems in parallel. In an evaluation such as this it is much better to treat the two texts in an integrated way. Dealing with one on its own, and then the second on its own followed by a short evaluative conclusion is not so satisfactory.

Question 16

Choose a poem in which the poet creates a convincing character.

Show how the poet, by skilful use of technique, brings the character alive in a convincing way.

Suggested Approaches:

Consider **The Love Song of J. Alfred Prufrock** by T.S. Eliot – the first section of which is printed on page 174

In this poem Eliot creates a credible character by suggesting several important characteristics: timidity; self-deprecation; lack of confidence with women; inarticulacy in the face of the big questions of existence; unease about his cultural milieu; fear about his personal appearance; and pained and resigned recognition, finally, of his limitations. Some of the techniques the poet uses are:

★ the use of first person voice

★ the "inclusion" of us as listeners

★ the use of apparently "normal" speech patterns, hesitations, repetitions…

★ the use of striking imagery

★ repetition of significant couplets and structures

★ shifting patterns of rhyme and variations in rhythm and length of line

All of these establish a tone and help to "realise" the personality of Prufrock.

The approach to this essay should be to deal with the characteristics revealed as the poem moves on, and to show how any of the techniques mentioned illustrate Prufrock's character at that point in the poem. An example of the kind of comment you might make is:

For example:

> *My morning coat, my collar mounting firmly to the chin,*
> *My necktie rich and modest, but asserted by a simple pin –*
> *(They will say: "but how his arms and legs are thin!')*

In these lines the poet presents us with someone who externally appears rich, confident, but tastefully so. The necktie is "modest", the pin, "simple". But this impression is immediately undermined by Prufrock's uncertainty – his suspicion that only his bad points are seen, The rhyming of "chin" and "pin" with "thin" suggests that to him, the last is what everyone really notices.

Points to Note and Remember:

1. The thrust of this question is on "character" rather than ideas. The techniques of characterisation provide the main source of material for your answer.

Section D – Film and TV Drama

Writing about Film or TV drama is a perfectly legitimate alternative to writing about a novel or a play or a poem. If you have actually studied a suitable text (and not just seen it once the night before the exam!), then you are at liberty to write about it in exactly the same way, and be judged by exactly the same criteria, as you would for an essay in Sections A, B or C.

Remember too that you are not expected to be any more "technical" when writing about Film or TV Drama than you would in any of the other sections. Of course you need to know *some* of the "language of film" – in the same way as you need to know *some* of the "language of poetry" for example – but it needn't be as specialised as it might be in Media Studies. In an English Critical Essay, you are still concerned about character, conflict, setting, dialogue, and, above all, theme. There will be filmic techniques which help you to explain the effectiveness of an aspect of the text where they are relevant to the question you have been asked. As in the other sections, these techniques take their place naturally in the course of developing a line of thought in the answer (see page 91).

Suggestions about TV drama appear in Paper 2.

Question 17

Choose a **film or TV drama** which has at its centre a destructive personality.

Show how the destructive nature of the character is revealed and how this affects your view of the character in the course of the film or TV drama.

Suitable texts (among many others) would be:

Psycho; **Dr Strangelove**; **The Servant**; **Knife in the Water**; **The Godfather**:

Suggested Approaches:

The Unforgiven, directed by (and starring) Clint Eastwood.

Although other characters in the film could be described as destructive, there is no point for not going for the obvious – the central character, William Munney, played by Clint Eastwood himself.

It is clear that this question lends itself to this film. In very broad terms, initially, the main character is seen to be "reformed" from his previous career as a killer, and only gradually, in the course of the film, does the destructive nature appear, coming to a head in the last sequence where he kills five men.

A possible beginning could look like this:

> In the film **The Unforgiven**, directed by Clint Eastwood, our first view of William Munney is ambiguous: we are not sure whether he is a force for good or for evil. The establishment of Munney's situation at the beginning of the film is done in two ways: the first is a narrative text which scrolls over the initial shot of the Eastwood homestead – and the second is the homestead itself seen in black silhouette with a single tree, and a newly dug grave and headstone – suggestive of a poor bare existence.

The narrative text gives the necessary information about Munney – his past as a killer, his marriage to a good woman, her influence in reforming him, and the fact of her death – reinforced by the tombstone. This quickly and neatly parcels up Munney's earlier history, without the need for flashbacks. As a result, when the film gets started the series of events does not have to be interrupted, and the story can move at speed.

The mise-en-scène sketches his present poverty, and when we cut back to the homestead after the scene in Grilley's, we see his two children, the difficulties with the hogs, reinforced by his falling several times into the pig-muck, the hopelessness of it all. This renders credible the idea that he might fall in with the Kid's invitation to join him in a "contract" killing, thus, perhaps, leading to the re-emergence of the more destructive side of his personality.

Other aspects of the story which would contribute to the argument of this answer would probably include the following:

★ the attitude to "the rule of the gun" is illustrated by the attitude of each of the three killers, and their different reactions to the opportunities for killing and the actual moments of killing

★ the Western background of the period (1880s) shows the dangers and difficulties and cruelties present in a culture where the law and the law keepers are living on the fringes of the overall lawlessness of society, having only a very tenuous control, and often themselves subject to no higher authority, dispensing a very rough, and sometimes corrupt justice

★ our reactions to those who kill, those who torture, and those who are killed are manipulated by the film. None of the characters is admirable, no-one is a hero, all are destructive in their own way, but Munney, because he is more experienced, more angry, "wins" the battle

These notes suggest a possible line of thought – but there are many other ways of answering the question.

Points to Note and Remember:

1. Note that these opening paragraphs do more than simply restate the question. They give the necessary information – film, director, character – and link the opening sequence of the film with the notion of "destructive" in the question.

2. There is reference to specific filmic techniques, but aspects such as characterisation, setting and theme figure largely in this answer.

Question 18

Choose a **film** whose setting in time and/or place is vitally important to the main theme(s) of the film.

Show how the setting is established and discuss how it helps to develop your understanding of the main theme(s) of the film.

Suitable texts (among many others) would be:

Rear Window: the ever-present setting of the back court onto which James Stewart looks, from his own apartment where he is "trapped" by his broken leg.

If…: The setting in a boys' school is crucial to the disintegration "portrayed" in the film.

Knife in the Water: the remote, bleak setting, and the isolation created by the yacht focus on the unstable and dangerous relationships within the film.

2001: A Space Odyssey or **Silent Running**: the completely cut off nature of the setting intensifies the playing out of the main concerns of the film.

Twelve Angry Men: the claustrophobic atmosphere in the jury room.

Suggested Approaches:

Dr Strangelove, directed by Stanley Kubrick.

The setting in time – the middle of the Cold War, when nuclear war was a realistic possibility (especially following the Cuba crisis of 1962) – and place – the War Room at the White House (among others) – are essential to the playing out of the main themes of American paranoia about Communism, and the massive distrust existing between the two great nuclear powers.

The question itself, in this case, simply asks you to link the setting to the themes.

Setting in time:

Silent opening with only the wind as eerie sound. Voice over giving information about an as yet unknown threat being developed by the Soviet Union in a remote island/mountain location. Footage of B52 bombers being refuelled in flight with details of their lethal potential, ironically backed by a melodic, innocent popular love song.

Very quickly, therefore, the audience realises the major opposition will be the USA versus the Soviet Union, and their respective nuclear capabilities, and we also know that the film will take a satiric stance with respect to the material.

Setting in place:

The most important setting used is the War Room at the White House, where there is a progressive revelation of all the systems in place for retaliation in case of attack, on both sides. These systems seem likely to lead to the greatest catastrophe of all, without either side making a deliberate decision to attack. The War Room's "other-worldliness" is created by its design – seen in long shot it is almost like an isolated space station – and the ever-present world map showing the relentless progress of the bombers towards their Soviet targets creates visible suspense.

This information about the settings has to be linked with "main theme(s)" – such as the paranoia of the great powers, the fallibility of leaders and systems, the morality of owning/manufacturing nuclear weapons…

Question 19

Choose a **film or TV drama** which deals with an issue of social or political importance.

Show how the issue is presented and discuss how effectively the issue is developed in the film or TV drama.

Among many suitable films:

political issues:

Schindler's List;   **Dr Strangelove**;   **Apocalypse Now**;   **The Godfather**

social issues:

Rear Window;   **Trainspotting**;   **The Servant**;   **Thelma and Louise**

Suggested Approaches:

The issue of voyeurism, or of personal privacy, is one of the issues (loneliness and isolation are others) explored in **Rear Window**, directed by Hitchcock and starring James Stewart as Jeff, a photo journalist. The presentation is gradual, from interested nosiness to obsessive surveillance – marked by use of binoculars, long-lens cameras, housebreaking…

Part of the effectiveness is due to the audience's sharing the point of view of the reporter for almost the whole length of the film and being complicit with him in his pursuit of the "murderer". The surveillance of the secondary characters, like Miss Lonelyhearts or The Composer eventually creates a shame factor in the audience. The topic is also discussed explicitly between Jeff and his girlfriend, Lisa, played by Grace Kelly, thus opening up the subject for speculation…

When Doyle announces that there has been no murder, Jeff asks him how he explains Thorwald's behaviour. Doyle replies that most people's private lives have many things in them which couldn't be explained, or are being kept hidden for private reasons – here the camera rests on Lisa's overnight bag – and the exchanged glances accept that there are some things we do keep private, but not necessarily because we are criminals.

When Doyle leaves, Jeff is still using his long-lens camera to look idly around the block. We see, in close-up, Miss Lonelyhearts getting ready to go out to meet real people – as opposed to the imaginary people we have seen her entertaining. Later we see her come back with a man, who immediately attempts perhaps rape, but at least makes an attempt to push the relationship onto a sexual level, against her will. She slaps him and makes him leave. We then see her throw herself onto the settee in despair.

At this point, Jeff and Lisa look at each other uncomfortably. Jeff says "That was pretty private stuff" and puts down the camera. They both feel guilty and come back to reality with the thought that they are both devastated and disappointed that a man has not killed his wife – which is pretty weird. Lisa pulls the blinds down – incidentally for the first time in the film the audience cannot see out – and says "The show's over for tonight" which underlines the real issue – are they legitimately trying to catch a criminal? Or is the whole experience mere entertainment at other people's expense – a sort of early "Big Brother" show?

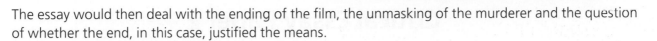

The essay would then deal with the ending of the film, the unmasking of the murderer and the question of whether the end, in this case, justified the means.

Points to Note and Remember:

1. There is reference to specific filmic techniques, such as point of view, the symbolism of the binoculars and the long-lens camera, but characterisation and setting are all-important. It is the combined effect of all of these in illuminating the central concern which forms the answer to the question.

Question 20

Choose from a **film or TV drama** a key sequence which creates an atmosphere essential to the presentation of its main character(s).

Show in detail how the sequence is created and discuss its contribution to your understanding of the role of the character(s) in the text as a whole.

Suggested Approaches:

The opening sequence of Polanski's **Knife in the Water** sets up a bleak, unforgiving atmosphere: a deserted landscape, an empty road, flat land, flat water and at a distance the figure of a young man standing in the middle of the road in the path of an oncoming car. The stand-off between the young man and the driver of the car foreshadows the rivalry and gamesmanship which will be at the core of the film.

Critical Essay Paper 2
Section A – Drama

Question 1

Choose a play in which the main character is gradually revealed as a very complex human being.

Show how the dramatist gradually reveals the complexity of the character and discuss how this adds to your appreciation of the text as whole.

Suggested Approaches:

Hamlet is a vast and complex play, and to cover it in 45 minutes in the depth you might like is simply an impossible task, but your essay will be judged on the quality of what you have chosen to include (not what you have had to leave out), provided it is relevant to the task.

Question 1 is almost perfect for **Hamlet**, whose hero has been described as the most complex character in literature. Nevertheless, this does not give you *carte blanche* simply to write whatever you want (or have prepared in advance) about Hamlet's character. There are two important "hurdles" in the question: the idea that the complexity is revealed "gradually" and the instruction to discuss "your appreciation of the text as a whole".

Note how the following opening paragraph deals with both of these.

> *In* **Hamlet** *the main character is first presented to us as a young man, slightly disillusioned with the world and out of sympathy with the world of his elders – a relatively unexceptional situation. As the play develops, we see his character grow in complexity as Shakespeare makes us aware of his wit, his intelligence, his extensive learning, his capacity for love, his morbid obsession with death, his tortured attitude to the task of revenge and finally a nobility of spirit which heightens the sense of tragedy in the final scene.*

> *When Hamlet, in Act 1 Scene 2, utters his first words ("A little more than kin and less than kind"), the wordplay on "kind" demonstrates Hamlet's wit, and we can detect a bitterness towards his uncle, who is trying to draw Hamlet in to the celebration of the marriage. To his mother as well he is scornful: "Nay, Madam, I know not seems", and in this Shakespeare is already suggesting to us a key feature of Hamlet's personality: his distaste for the superficial and his need to explore things in depth.*

> *This sense of Hamlet's distrust of his elders emerges further in his dealings with Polonius, whom he mocks mercilessly, but whom he recognises as a symbol of the deceit and corruption within the court – the corruption which eventually leads to the death of the tragic hero.*

The essay could go on to deal with the ideas outlined in the opening paragraph through exploration of Hamlet's relationship with his mother, his relationship with Ophelia, his discussions with the Players. It would be important to leave sufficient time to deal with the final scene and the "nobility of spirit" which is the essence of tragedy.

Points to Note and Remember:

1. Do not fall into the trap of writing an essay which is merely about Hamlet's complex character. You may well have written an essay like this before, but it is not a complete answer to *this* question, the one you are now being asked.

Question 2

Choose a play which uses comedy/humour to explore a serious theme.

Explain how the dramatist effectively combines the humour with an exploration of a serious theme.

> Any of Shakespeare's comedies would be suitable here: **A Midsummer Night's Dream** and **Much Ado About Nothing** explore attitudes to love. A number of plays by George Bernard Shaw might also be appropriate – **Pygmalion** as a study of class, **The Devil's Disciple** as a study of political commitment. Many contemporary Scottish dramatists make extensive use of humour: Iain Heggie, Liz Lochhead and Gregory Burke, for example.

Suggested Approaches:

A well-known Scottish example is John Byrne's **The Slab Boys**.

This play is full of comic situations, outrageously exaggerated characters, and funny one-liners, yet still succeeds in exploring some serious aspects of life in the time and place in which the play is set.

In order to tackle this question successfully, you would need to have a ready knowledge of a number of the humorous features and an ability to explain what actually makes them funny, and a clear view of what the "serious" theme is.

A possible opening:

> John Byrne's play **The Slab Boys** (first performed in 1978) is often hilariously funny but also manages to explore serious topics such as the sense of alienation felt by Phil and the social hierarchy of the period in which it is set (the late 1950s). It also touches on the treatment of the vulnerable in society (e.g. Hector and Phil's mother).
>
> The play follows a single day in the "Slab Room" at Stobo's carpet factory in Paisley. The "Slab Boys" (Phil and Spanky) work here, grinding the powder colours to be used by the designers. In a way, the work is symbolic of dull, repetitive work (a literal "grind"). Phil is in fact a talented artist and has aspirations to go to Glasgow Art School, but feels he is discriminated against because of his lower class origins. He and Spanky are natural rebels (a poster of James Dean is on display prominently) and constantly at loggerheads with their superiors Jack Hogg and Willie Curry. By the end of the day Phil is rejected by the Art School and is sacked from his job.

The comedy comes in a number of forms: clever one-liners, running gags, exaggerated characters, farcical situations and confusions. The accurately represented West of Scotland speech of working-class youth of the time can be funny in itself.

The second paragraph is not essential, but is a useful overview of the play and contains some relevant references to thematic concerns such as the dullness of the work and Phil's desire to escape it.

The third paragraph clearly sets up a structure for the next part of the essay, promising at least five paragraphs:

★ clever one-liners

★ running gags: e.g. Phil and Spanky's goading of Alan, by calling him every possible name but Alan: Archie, Andy, Amos, Alma, Albert…

★ exaggerated characters: e.g. Lucille (brash, sexy), Hector (the simple-minded butt of Phil and Spanky's humour)

★ farce: e.g. the confusions over who is taking Lucille to the Staffie, the "dressing up" of Hector"

★ language; down to earth, guttural, abrasive; contrast in speech between Alan and others to emphasise class difference

While working through these, you would almost certainly have been mentioning aspects of the key themes identified in paragraph one, but it will be best to write a least a couple of substantial paragraphs to cover these as a good way of bringing your essay to a conclusion and remaining solidly relevant to the task. This will be your opportunity to discuss what *you* think the play "as a whole is about", e.g. the sadness of Phil's situation (mention his mother, his job, his aspirations), the "class" aspect (e.g. Alan's privileged position – university education, son of a chief designer), the possible irony of the ending when Hector (who seems to have little talent) is promoted and Phil is sacked). Given time, you might consider the bleakness of the ending for Phil (there is particular nastiness that the news of his rejection by the Art school is delivered by Alan) – and possibly the ambivalent role of Spanky at the conclusion.

Points to Note and Remember:

1. Although you are cataloguing the ways in which humour operates in the play, the fact that these are always tied in with the key themes, prevents your essay becoming merely a list of humorous techniques, and the line of thought is not lost sight of.

Question 3

Choose a play which ends in a way you find moving or upsetting or poignant.

By detailed examination of the conclusion and with reference to the rest of the play, show how the dramatist evokes this response from you.

> Many plays will be suitable here – any Shakespeare tragedy for example, although other Shakespeare texts (e.g. **The Merchant of Venice**, **The Tempest**) could yield strong answers. All the commonly-studied works of Miller and Williams would also be good to work with.

Suggested Approaches:

Death of a Salesman by Arthur Miller.

The "ending" can be defined in a number of ways: (see page 105, Paper 1) perhaps from the scene in the restaurant onwards, or from the confrontation between Linda and Biff, or from the row between Willy and Biff. A really good approach, however, would be to focus on the "Requiem", which undoubtedly evokes all three of the emotions offered in the question. If you know this in detail (and you should) you should be able to use it to refer to many key ideas of the whole play.

You could begin like this:

> *The "Requiem" which concludes Arthur Miller's* **Death of a Salesman** *is an intensely moving experience for the audience. Set at the funeral for Willy (in which the audience rather disturbingly seems to become the grave into which the characters look), it has the immediately moving quality of any funeral and this is added to by its summing up of the life of the tragic character we have been watching throughout the play.*

> *The small number attending the funeral is in itself moving. Only Linda, Biff, Happy, Charley and Bernard (who doesn't speak) are present. This is a stark contrast to the dreams Willy had of emulating the death of Dave Singleman ("hundreds of salesmen and buyers were at his funeral") and underlines the sad fact that Willy is not the well-liked salesman of his dreams but an ordinary man, whose only support comes from his family, in Linda's words "a small boat looking for a harbour".*

Other topics could be:

★ the moving tribute from Charley, with its curiously elevated diction

★ Biff's tribute to his father

★ the contrasting views of Biff and Happy

★ Linda's grief

★ the visual impact – Linda alone at the end, supported finally by Biff; the "darkening stage... the hard towers of the apartment buildings"

★ the music

The point about Biff's tribute could be dealt with like this:

> *As well as Charley's touching tribute, Biff speaks simply and movingly about his father. He recalls times when Willy would come home from a trip and they would work on the house "making the stoop; finishing the cellar; putting up the new porch". The simplicity of this paints a picture of Willy as the family man, providing for and protecting his family. The skills are those associated with pioneering Americans of the old days and highlight for us just how out of place Willy really was in the harsh modern world of business, in which he was unable to make enough to live and where he is threatened and browbeaten by people such as Howard. In the scene at the start of Act 2 Miller shows most clearly the uncaring side of capitalism: Willy is patronised by Howard ("Look, kid, I'm busy this morning.") and eventually sacked. Howard appears more interested in the tape machine than in Willy and Willy's nightmare increases when he finds himself alone with the machine which seems to threaten him. It seems that his unquestioning commitment to the business world brings him no reward; Biff's emphasis during the Requiem on other skills is indeed a moving reminder of how Willy had, in Biff's words, "the wrong dreams".*

Notice how this paragraph:

★ opens with a "link sentence" and uses the word "movingly" to refer subtly to the question

★ gives detailed reference to what Biff says at the funeral

★ uses this to make a general point about the play as a whole

★ supports this with some detailed reference to a relevant scene elsewhere in the play

★ returns to the Requiem

★ sets up a possible following paragraph about the contrast between Biff and Happy ("the wrong dreams"/"a good dream")

Points to Note and Remember:

1. "detailed examination" of the conclusion and "reference to the rest of the play" would have to be in a fair balance in this answer, so it is essential that you know the scene in detail if you are going to choose this question.

Question 4

Choose from a play a scene which significantly changes your impression of a major character.

Describe how the scene achieves this and show how your feelings towards the character in the play as a whole are influenced.

In almost any play, there is probably a scene which causes you to think slightly differently about a character, so this question looks possible for whatever you have studied. As long as you know the scene in some detail, have a grasp of the character in the whole play and stick as best you can to the idea that the scene changes your impression, you should be able to write an essay which will at least pass.

However, you need to notice the important word "significantly" in the question. To write a convincing essay you have to identify a situation where you can honestly say that the scene had a big effect on your perception of the character so far. The best Critical Essays come from genuinely relevant responses, not from ones where you have to manipulate or twist things to get a "fit".

> Here are two examples of rather weak choices for this question, where the 'significance' would be quite difficult to argue convincingly:
>
> The murder of Duncan in **Macbeth**: you could argue that this changes Macbeth from the brave and loyal warrior described in Act 1 Scene 2 into a cold-blooded murderer, but the darker side of Macbeth has already emerged (in his soliloquies for example); and remember that the "murder of Duncan" does not actually happen on stage).
>
> The rape of Blanche in **A Streetcar Named Desire**: you could argue that Stanley's violence here makes you think badly of him, but throughout the play Stanley has been characterised as a rather brutal, primitive man whose antagonism towards Blanche builds slowly so that the rape scene is really an inevitable climax rather than one which causes a "significant change"; and remember that this scene is so close to the end of the play that it would make the overall discussion quite hard.

Suggested Approach:

The Merchant of Venice by William Shakespeare.

A really good scene which should work well would be the one in which Shylock pleads for equality of treatment: "Hath not a Jew eyes…" (Act 3 Scene 1).

A basic plan could include:

1. Impressions of Shylock before this scene:

   - ★ toying with Bassanio/hatred for Christians in general and Antonio in particular

   - ★ pretence that the bond is a "merry jest" (Act 1 scene 3)

   - ★ the possessive father/"dream of moneybags"/dislike of music (Act 2 scene 5)

2. The scene itself:

   - ★ context

   - ★ content

   - ★ language

   - ★ impact for rest of play

3. The trial scene and how audience feelings are affected:

   - ★ despite unrelenting attitude during first part of trial, underlying understanding of his motives

   - ★ sympathy at harsh treatment by Portia

This isn't the only way to structure your response: you could start with the scene and then go back to compare your impressions of the character before, during and after it. It is a matter of personal taste. There is not just one "correct" way of approaching a question: there definitely has to be a clear structure, but you should employ the one that suits you best – and this depends not just on the text and the question, but on you.

The main thrust of your argument here will be that to begin with we get a fairly negative impression of Shylock as a rather vindictive, hate-filled, selfish individual. The main speech in the key scene reverses this abruptly: his plea for equality (pointing out the physical similarities of Jew and Christian) is delivered with calm dignity, underscored by simplicity of the language and the sophisticated repetition of words and phrases to give it an almost hymn-like quality. As a result the audience is inclined to feel sympathy for a character they previously despised.

Points to Note and Remember:

1. Remember that small details can be important and impressive when constructing a case such as this, for example Shylock's dislike of music ("When you hear the drum/And the vile squealing of the wry-necked fife… stop my house's ears… let not the sound of shallow foppery enter my sober house") is designed to characterise him as a puritanical figure – all the more so because of the abundance of music in Belmont.

Section B – Prose Fiction

Question 5

Choose a **novel** in which a central character seems restless or discontented or frustrated.

Show how the novelist makes you aware of the character's situation, and discuss to what extent the character achieves peace of mind by the end of the novel.

For this question it will be important to choose a novel with a character who genuinely and convincingly is "restless or discontented or frustrated".

Suitable texts:

Sunset Song – Chris is often "restless" and "discontented" with her life; her attempts to find contentment (with Ewan, with the land) are key concerns of the novel

Dr Jekyll and Mr Hyde – Jekyll's frustration at his safe, respectable lifestyle is key to the ideas of the novella.

A Burnt-out Case (Graham Greene) – Querry's journey to Africa is all because of his discontentment with his life in Europe

Leila (Robin Jenkins) – the central character, Andrew Sandilands, is discontented with the outlook of the ex-patriot community and is drawn into the revolutionary politics of the beautiful Leila

A Handful of Dust (Evelyn Waugh) – Lady Brenda's restlessness at Hetton Abbey triggers her affair with Beaver, with serious consequences for her and for Tony, and allows Waugh to lay bare the shallowness of her society

Espedair Street (Iain Banks) Daniel Weir's restlessness with "star" lifestyle

Possible, but less convincing, choices:

The Cone-Gatherers – none of the words seems quite strong enough to describe Duror's anguished state of mind

Lord of the Flies – Ralph is certainly "frustrated" at times, but it is not a useful description of his character or situation as a whole, and would probably lead you away from key ideas in the novel

The Prime of Miss Jean Brodie – Jean Brodie is certainly "frustrated" (e.g. with the rigid morals of the time, with the unimaginative methods of education), but the novel centres around her relationships with her "set" and her betrayal by Sandy – it would be difficult to write convincingly on this topic.

Suggested Approaches:

The Catcher in the Rye by J.D. Salinger.

How does Salinger make the reader aware of Holden's discontentment/restlessness/ frustration:

★ his view that all adults are "phoneys"

★ his attitude to school and his school mates

★ his sense of isolation/alienation in New York

★ his dismissive, repetitive language

★ his reaction to the graffiti

★ the desire to "protect" children from the adult world

To what extent does he "find peace of mind"?

★ not at all – the novel is being narrated from a mental institution

★ he is going to start a new school – with the strong implication that the whole process will repeat itself, that he will never fit in

★ he indicates that he is cautiously optimistic about the future, but all that has gone before makes the reader suspect that this optimism is not well founded, adding to the overall pessimism of the text as a whole

Points to Note and Remember:

1. Beware treating the second part of the question as an excuse simply to "tell the story"; you will obviously have to outline what happens in the lead up to the conclusion, but the task is to discuss "to what extent the character achieves peace of mind".

2. Although the question does not explicitly ask you to deal with the "central concerns of the text", you should always make it clear that you are aware of what these are and integrate them into your response to the question.

Question 6

Choose a **novel** in which there is a key incident involving one of the following: a birth, a marriage, a death.

Explain briefly what happens in the incident and go on to discuss its importance to the novel as a whole.

There are many novels which end tragically with the death of an important character, or which have a death acting as a turning point, or a catalyst:

Lamb; **The Changeling**; **The Power and the Glory**; **Dr Jekyll and Mr Hyde**; **The Cone-Gatherers**; **Lord of the Flies**; **The Inheritors**; **The Grapes of Wrath**; **For Whom the Bell Tolls**; **Brave New World**; **The Blue Afternoon**; **A Handful of Dust**; **Cal**…

There are many where a marriage is an important element, either as the joyful end of a complex plot as in **Jane Eyre**, **Emma**, **Nicholas Nickleby**, or as an important element in representing a more sombre theme as in **Far from the Madding Crowd**, **North and South**, **Brighton Rock**, **The Woman Who Walked into Doors**…

There are novels such as Dickens' **Oliver Twist** or **Dombey and Son** where a birth provides the mainspring for the plot, and others where a birth dominates a main character as in **Grace Notes** or **The Millstone**.

And there are novels which have birth, marriage, *and* death as important elements: **Sunset Song**, **Wuthering Heights**, **Howards End**.

Suggested Approaches:

Brave New World by Aldous Huxley.

1. A brief description of the incident would contain:

   ★ The death of John the Savage which occurs at the very end of the novel

   ★ John is very much preoccupied by death, the death of Linda particularly

   ★ The precipitating incident is the appearance of Lenina among all the sightseers who are goading John into violence, either against himself or others

   ★ In shame and remorse for his loss of control in the subsequent orgy, he hangs himself

   ★ When the next group of sightseers appear they find his body swinging gently, perhaps to suggest that he has found peace at last

2. The discussion of its importance would probably begin with a statement such as:

   This incident illustrates the impossibility for a truly human character, one like us, fallible, and subject to extremes of emotion, to exist in a society where almost every really human quality has been eradicated. Huxley is warning us against a state which reveres industrialisation, encourages

128

conspicuous consumption, discourages individuality and philosophical thinking, and revels in mass entertainment of a mind-numbingly trivial kind, assisted by the systematic use of recreational drugs and sex.

3. Briefly describe how Huxley presents, in the first seven chapters of the novel, the seemingly admirable efficiency and smooth running of society

4. In the Reservation part of the book Chapters 7–9 we see such normal things as natural birth, disease and family through Lenina's eyes – and she finds them disgusting

5. Introduction of John, the pivotal character, whose reading of Shakespeare has given him a window to understanding his emotions

6. The central part of the essay would illustrate the unbridgeable gulf between John's values (and by extension, our own) and those represented by the Brave New World. Huxley lets us experience this as we revisit the Brave New World and see it this time through John's eyes

7. The ending would show how John's fate becomes inevitable as his alienation from the New World becomes complete, thus demonstrating the aridity and soullessness of the society against which Huxley is warning us

Question 7

Choose a **novel** or **short story** in which the setting is bleak or oppressive

Show how the setting affects one of the main characters and discuss to what extent he or she manages to overcome the difficulties which the setting poses for him or her.

Novels which are concerned with the following are likely to be suitable. But be careful to read the second part of the question before jumping to a choice.

War:

The Quiet American; Cold Mountain; A Farewell to Arms

Dystopia.

Never Let Me Go; The Handmaid's Tale; Nineteen Eighty-Four; A Clockwork Orange; The Road

Bleak landscape:

Consider the Lilies; Sunset Song; The Grapes of Wrath; Wuthering Heights; Hard Times; The Silver Darlings

Oppressive institutions:

Lamb; One Flew Over the Cuckoo's Nest; One Day in the Life of Ivan Denisovich; Oranges Are Not the Only Fruit

Suggested Approaches:

North and South by Elizabeth Gaskell.

1. *Physical setting:*

Margaret Hale finds Milton – the "North" of the title very gloomy and harsh.

Examples: the weather, the "hopeless" streets, different plants and flowers, poverty, the mill buildings "great doors in the dead wall" and the oppressiveness of the heavy ornamentation in the gloomy interiors.

2. *Social setting:*

She initially dislikes the people who do not seem to treat her with the deference she was used to receive in the South; especially she dislikes Mrs Thornton, and initially Mr Thornton, whom she thinks uncultured and too preoccupied with exploiting his workers in the mill.

Her conflict with Mr Thornton continues over the matter of the strike. She dislikes the open warfare between the classes which is endemic in Milton, being used to the more submissive, squirearchical interactions in the South.

The expansion of the above points would probably take up about half of your essay.

3. To what extent does she overcome these difficulties?

Gradually, but by the end, almost completely.

Evidence:

★ Later, when she befriends Nicholas and Bessy Higgins, she feels better about the place, and gradually comes to appreciate something of the more open, frank and nature of Northern society.

★ The fact that Mr Thornton takes on Higgins having found "a soft place" in his heart, makes some impact on Margaret.

★ Later she comes to understand at least something about the capitalist system when Mr Thornton's business has run into severe difficulties, threatening the livelihood of his workers as well as himself.

★ After her mother and father have died and Mr Bell has suggested she move back to Helston (The South) she finds that it is not right for her any more. When Mr Bell dies she uses his legacy to help Mr Thornton and agrees to marry him, having finally come to appreciate his real virtues.

Points to Note and Remember:

1. There is little mention of the rest of the Hale family here, or of the Frederick incident, or of Margaret's life before she came to Milton. None of these is relevant to the idea of the setting and its effect on Margaret.

Question 8

Choose **two short stories** with a strong central character.

Compare the ways in which the character is created in each story and discuss which you think makes a more effective contribution to the story as a whole.

The requirement for "strong central character" is actually quite restrictive. If you have studied a selection of short stories, rather than just one or two, you may be able to tackle this question. Otherwise, your only other short story choice is "a bleak or oppressive setting". There are likely to be some strong central characters in short stories you have studied but, remembering the advice on pages 112–113 in Paper 1 the comparison and evaluation is more worthwhile if there are other points in common. **Smeddum** (Grassic Gibbon) and **The Vendetta** (de Maupassant) both have strong women characters who set their minds at an objective and succeed in their goals. **Odour of Chrysanthemums** (Lawrence) and **The Story of an Hour** (Kate Chopin) deal with women who begin to have a hope of independence at the deaths of their husbands. **The Battler** (Hemingway) and **Through the Tunnel** (Lessing) both deal with growing courage/rites of passage themes. **The Law of Life** (Jack London) and **In Another Country** (Hemingway) both deal with the acceptance of fate.

Question 9

Choose a **novel** which has as one of its main concerns the divisions caused by class, race or religion.

Show how the writer portrays the clash caused by one of these, and discuss to what extent you gained insight into the nature of such divisions.

Suitable texts would be:

Class:

The Cone-Gatherers; **The Changeling**; **Bleak House**; **Great Expectations**, **Sunset Song**; **The Great Gatsby**; **Wuthering Heights**; **A Room with a View**; **North and South**; **Atonement**; **The Go-Between**; **The Remains of the Day**; **Howards End**…

Race:

Cry, The Beloved Country; **To Kill a Mockingbird**, **Small Island**; **Brick Lane**; **I Know Why the Caged Bird Sings**…

Religion:

The Power and the Glory; **Brideshead Revisited**; **Cal**…

Suggested Approaches:

The Cone-Gatherers by Robin Jenkins.

1. Clash portrayed by Lady Runcie-Campbell's behaviour to Neil and Callum:

   ★ her insistence that they go on the deer drive – "we cannot have them dictating to us in every way."

   ★ her decision to sack them after the deer drive –"Is it not enough that I wish them to go?"

   ★ her reaction to Roderick's greeting the brothers in Lendrick and her horror that they should be given a lift.

   ★ the incident at the beach hut "After this war the lower classes are going to be frightfully presumptuous"

   ★ her refusal, in conversation with Roderick to admit that she had done anything wrong.

2. Neil's feelings of injustice:

★ "another hindrance had been the constant sight of the mansion house chimneys, reminding him of their hut, which to him remained a symbol of humiliation"

★ "aren't the kennels at the big house bigger than our hut?"

★ his treatment after the deer drive brings out his thirst for justice for the ordinary man, on whose behalf the war was supposed to be being fought.

★ when Roderick greets him in Lendrick he is so shocked that he reverts to acting as the subservient inferior, much to his own embarrassment.

★ he is humiliated at the beach hut and asks Tulloch to take them away from the estate

★ his final refusal to help Lady Runcie-Campbell until she comes personally to ask him.

3. The discussion of the class divide would include some of the above points, but they would have to be put into the context of giving "insight" into the problems. Important for this would be:

★ Lady Runcie-Campbell's relations with other classes: Tulloch, Duror, Peggy, the Doctor…

★ Lady Runcie-Campbell's Christianity, and the dilemmas it leads her into

★ Roderick's position as mediator

★ Tulloch's position as a creator of doubt in her. "and I find no fault in them"

For example:

> *The reader's insight into these issues is further developed in the conversation Lady Runcie-Campbell has with Roderick on the morning after the storm. She tries to get Roderick to absolve her from the guilt which her Christian side is feeling because of her action in throwing the brothers out of the beach hut into the storm. Roderick refuses to do this, merely saying "We were wrong". His judgement of her sparks off a declaration of her social, as opposed to her religious creed: that these people are inferior, and that to treat them in any other way would be patronising and lead to their further humiliation. Ironically Roderick's greeting of Neil in Lendrick and his reaction seem in some way to back up that opinion. Neil is struggling against an age-old and inbred feeling of deference, but on occasions when he has time to think, he stands up for himself and his own dignity.*

Points to Note and Remember:

1. There is no necessity to become involved in this essay with the struggle between good and evil, as usually represented by Callum and Duror. The people who most obviously embody this theme are Lady Runcie-Campbell, Neil, Roderick and Tulloch.

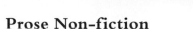

Prose Non-fiction

Question 10

Choose an **essay or piece of journalism** which takes a committed stance on a social, moral or political topic which is of major importance in the twenty first century.

Identify the topic and discuss to what extent you think the writer presents a convincing case.

> A suitable text might be concerned with climate change, or consumerism, or terrorism, or discrimination…

Question 11

Choose a **non-fiction text** which celebrates the achievements of an individual or of a society.

Explain what the achievement is and show how the writer's presentation of the material can be seen as a "celebration".

> *Texts which celebrate a society:*
>
> **London: The Biography** (Peter Ackroyd); **The Right Stuff** (Tom Wolfe); **The Audacity of Hope** (Barack Obama); **The Age of Wonder** (Richard Holmes).
>
> *Texts which celebrate a person:*
>
> A wide range of possibilities – works by Hunter Davies, Michael Holroyd, Claire Tomalin, Dava Sobel, Simon Callow and many autobiographical works.

Question 12

Choose a **work of travel writing** which conveys the sense of an exciting or dangerous journey.

Show how the writer's presentation clearly conveys the excitement or the danger and makes it an important element in your appreciation of the text as a whole.

Suitable texts would be:

Bruce Chatwin, Colin Thubron, Paul Theroux, Rory Stewart, Michael Palin, Bill Bryson and others.

Possible texts dealing with travel writing include the texts mentioned on page 108 dealing with exploration and others such as Rory Stewart's **The Places in Between**, John Simpson's **A Mad World My Masters**, James Cameron's **Witness in Vietnam** and other work by war correspondents, can mingle the excitement and the danger of their journeys.

Section C – Poetry

The following discussions of particular poems will be infinitely more useful to you as examples of what to do and what not to do if you read the five poems used in this section (Appendix 3, pages 172–178).

Question 13

Choose a poem which is, for you, a serious reflection on an important issue.

Discuss how the poet's ideas and language engage you in serious reflection on the issue.

You could argue that any poem which *doesn't* offer "serious reflection on an important issue" is not much of a poem, and in that sense any poem could be used for this question. However, that would be unwise. Not only would it that lead you into the trap of believing that you can "twist" any poem to fit any question (you can try, but the results are often hilarious), it could well make you write something that sounds very artificial and unconvincing.

Even if you find a good "fit", it is not an open invitation to write everything you know about the poem in any way you want. You still need to address the key words in the question "serious reflection", "important issue", "ideas and language", and, perhaps most important of all, "for you".

Suggested Approaches:

Church Going by Philip Larkin.

This poem explores the speaker's attitude to the Church and to the place in society of religious belief. You don't necessarily have to be a churchgoer or hold deep religious convictions in order to appreciate and respond to this poem but if it is a topic to which you have given some thought, on which you perhaps share the speaker's apparent uncertainty, then it will be an ideal choice for this question.

A possible opening might be as follows:

> *One poem which has certainly makes me reflect seriously on an important issue is Philip Larkin's mid-1950s poem "Church Going". In this poem Larkin explores attitudes to religion and to the place of religious observance in modern Britain. His speaker demonstrates throughout the poem an ambivalent, almost contradictory point of view: on the one hand he makes fun of the church and dismisses its importance, yet he seems remarkably interested in and knowledgeable about churches and the importance some people attach to them. I think this reflects rather accurately the way many of us, including myself, think about religion today. As*

church attendance figures show, regular worship has declined markedly over the last two hundred years or so and in our "modern", sceptical, scientific age, religion might seem out of date, or even a little quaint. Yet even among all these "non-believers", the Church still seems to hold some kind of sway and command a lot of respect, as the numbers wanting baptisms, church marriages, and religious funerals seem to suggest. To me, Larkin's poem captures perfectly this uncertainty, the idea that on the face of it religion is old-fashioned, superstitious nonsense, but you're glad it's there if you need it and that, deep down, it does serve an important role in our lives.

Possible points to develop:

★ The first stage of the poem: disrespectful, mocking (with language points to support) – but why is he visiting a church in the first place and is there any significance in his touching the font?

★ The second stage ("Yet stop I did"): thoughtful reflection on churches and the Church; mixture of mockery ("the crew that tap and jot and know what rood lofts were"/"randy for antique"), but a sense of questioning underneath

★ The final stage "A serious house on serious earth it is …": acceptance of importance of the Church, that it is "special", that it provides comfort and solace at important times, that there is some higher power that recognises our "destinies"; the style of the final verse: elegant, flowing iambic pentameter (Shakespearean/Biblical sounding) contrasting with the jerky, fractured sentences (and non-sentences) in the opening section

★ The verse form: elaborately structured, complex, but unobtrusive (the rhymes are barely noticed for example); does this perhaps mirror a point of view about the Church: it is there, solid, structured, reassuring, yet we hardly notice it?

Points to Note and Remember:

1. Keep a sensible balance between the **personal** (your reflections on the "serious issues") and close study of **the language** of the poem.

2. When writing about **Church Going** it is easy to gloss over (or even miss out) the "middle verses"; a good answer will always have at least two or three important points to make about these. You are expected to know, and be able to quote from the whole poem.

Question 14

Choose a poem which seems to you to end in an unexpected or mysterious way.

Explain what is unexpected or mysterious about the way the poem ends and go on to discuss how effective you think it is as a conclusion to the poem as a whole.

As with all poetry questions, the key here will be to select a poem which genuinely "fits" the question. There are poems for which you *could* make something of a case, e.g.

★ it is "unexpected" that the ending of **Dulce et decorum est** shifts from describing the soldiers to an attack on the patriots back home

★ it is "unexpected" that **Assisi** ends by describing the dwarf's voice a "sweet as a bird" when before the poem has focused on his deformities

★ the last line of **Church Going** is rather "mysterious"

However, in all these cases your argument would never be strong and you would just be "going through the motions" of writing a Critical Essay instead of genuinely exploring a poem in terms of the question you have chosen.

> Wiser choices might be some of Ted Hughes' animal poems, which often end rather mysteriously (**Esther's Tomcat**, **Pike**, **Crow Tyrannosaurus**, **The Jaguar**, for example). The conclusion of Larkin's **The Whitsun Weddings** would be a very good choice.

Suggested Approaches:

Witch Girl by Douglas Dunn.

Douglas Dunn is a contemporary Scottish poet, (who, coincidentally, was a colleague of Larkin when they both worked at the University Library in Hull, and who admired Larkin's poetry).

Witch Girl is about the persecution of an alleged witch and her daughter. It is based on the true story of Janet Horne, of Kintradwell in Sutherland, the last "witch" to be killed in Scotland. Her daughter was born with a deformed hand and her neighbours accused her of witchcraft, alleging she transformed her daughter into a horse and rode her to witches' meetings. She was convicted at Dornoch in 1722 and burned inside a barrel of boiling tar.

In a poem of nine four-line stanzas all except the last two and a half lines describe the burning of the mother and the wanderings of the daughter afterwards. Then, quite unexpectedly, the last three lines say:

> By Gryfe, by Deveron,
> By Cree and Tay, I see her wash her lameness,
> And hear her breathing in the wood and stone.

The poet has jumped dramatically from the past to the present and in so doing has clarified a key point of the poem as a whole: that prejudice and fear of those who are different is not something of the past but is still evident in the country.

Possible opening paragraphs

For all but the last two and a half of its 36 lines, Douglas Dunn's poem **Witch Girl** *tells the story of a woman convicted of and executed for witchcraft and the wanderings afterwards of her handicapped daughter. The events are quite obviously set in Scotland's past. Quite unexpectedly in the last two and a half lines the poet jumps to the present day and makes clear what is, I think, the central concern of the poem: the treatment of those who are different and outcast – not just in the past but in the present day.*

The unexpectedness of the conclusion is underlined by the sudden change from past tense ("She hawked her flowers… she slept…") to present ("I see… and hear…") which dramatically drags the reader away from some distant tale into the present day and a consideration of the way society treats those who are different. Also the poem changes abruptly from a third person narrative ("No one to help her; no one saw her die") to one in which the poet himself becomes involved:"I see her wash her lameness…" It is almost as if recounting the events surrounding the Witch Girl has prompted the poet to realise the extent to which persecution and demonisation of minorities are not just features of history but are still with us.

These paragraphs focus well on the ending of the poem and what makes it "unexpected", so you are now in a position to consider the rest of the poem. You would need to take care, however, not simply to provide a "guided tour", but to direct your comments as much as possible to the idea of the way the witch girl and her mother are persecuted for no rational reason and the way the poet points out the hypocrisy of those who carry out the persecution.

For example, a small but important point from near the beginning of the poem:

The repetition in the first verse of "they said" emphasises the idea of constant rumour among the community, and the irony that the only "proof" they need of the mother's being a witch is that her daughter has a physical deformity.

Points to Note and Remember:

1. The focus must be on the ending, but you have to link it effectively with key points in the rest of the poem

2. When writing about **Witch Girl**, it is easy to concentrate too much on the mother and her suffering; remember that it is through the girl that Dunn develops a key idea of the poem

Question 15

Choose a poem in which features of structure play an important part.

Describe these important structural features and show how they enhance your appreciation of the poem as a whole.

Quite often in the poetry section there is a question which deals with some of the more technical aspects of poetry. Such questions should be avoided by anyone who does not have a good grasp of these technicalities in general and a detailed understanding of how they work in the poem he wants to write about.

In this particular question you are asked to look at "features of structure". This is an open enough description to allow a number of aspects to be relevant: the verse form, the structure of the poem as a whole, the use of repetition, the use of rhyme, rhythmical/metrical patterns, unusual word order.

It is not, however, an invitation simply to define some "techniques" and give a list of examples; the question requires, as every poetry question does, that you see these in the context of an overall understanding of the poem.

Suggested Approaches:

O What Is That Sound (sometimes called **The Quarry** or **The Deserter**) by W.H. Auden.

It features, for example, a great deal of repetition:

★ every verse begins with the word "O"

★ the word at the end of every second line is repeated

★ the word "dear" occurs at the end of every third line – and a rhyme (or half-rhyme) for it at the end of every first line

★ the word "only" at the start of the third line in the first three verses

In addition, the whole poem is structured in the style of an old-fashioned ballad:

★ the question and answer/dialogue structure, with the first two lines a question asked by one person and the last two lines the response

★ the deliberate lack of clarity about who is asking and who is answering

★ the sparse/non-existent details of setting etc.

★ the abrupt time shifts from verse to verse

Also, the last verse departs radically from the pattern established in the previous eight verses – and this sudden change becomes an important structural feature in itself:

★ a third voice (the poet's) narrates the last verse

★ the question/answer structure is abandoned

★ the verse, a scene of sheer terror and menace, is the culmination of the advancing threat described in the preceding verses

So there would be no difficulty in carrying out the first part of the question; "Describe these important structural features…", but how will you tackle the second part?

Firstly, you will need to have your own clear idea of what the poem is "about". As with all good literature, there is no one "right answer" to this. It could be about any of the following:

★ the fears of an army deserter

★ betrayal within a relationship

★ the approach/advance of war and militarism in general

The last of these is probably the easiest to write about. The poem was written in the mid-1930s when all of Europe was becoming aware of the increasing power and threat from the build up of armies in Germany and Italy, and of the increasing powers of the dictators. In a way, the poem represents the relentless advance not just of the actual soldiers in the poem, but of militarism and fascism in general.

What do the structural features emphasise?

★ the repetition in general suggests the predictability and relentlessness of the advance

★ the repeated words (in the second line) sound like a drum beat, imitating the march of the soldiers

★ the question/answer structure builds up a tension which conveys the impending horror of the arrival of the military forces

★ the sudden change in the last verse dramatically conveys the brutality which the remaining character in the poem has to face

Points to Note and Remember:

1. **You must do more than simply describe and list a number of "features"; your conception of the central idea of the poem must be at the heart of the essay.**

Question 16

Choose **two** poems with a similar setting.

Compare the way the setting is evoked in the poems, making clear which you find more effective in conveying the central concern(s) of the poems.

Most years there is a question which invites you to refer to two poems. While this obviously requires more knowledge, it does mean that you have more material to work with. A helpful tactic is to have at least one suitable "pair" of poems well prepared: if there is a suitable question you can use them in a comparison question; if there isn't, then you have at least those two poems you can possibly use for the other questions, which will all ask for one poem only.

> Possibilities for this question:
>
> Two of Edwin Morgan's poems based in Glasgow (e.g. **Glasgow Sonnet**, **Trio**, **The Starlings in George Square**, **Glasgow Green**)
>
> Two poems by different poets with a similar setting (e.g. in a zoo: **Au Jardin des Plantes** by John Wain and **The Jaguar** by Ted Hughes; or in a windy countryside: Hughes' **Wind** and Larkin's **Wedding Wind**)
>
> Two poems from the First World War battlefields (e.g. Owen, Sassoon, Rosenberg)

Suggested Approaches:

Brooklyn Cop and **Hotel Room 12th Floor** by Norman MacCaig.

In the opening paragraphs of an answer to this question the concern(s) of the two poems should have been discussed. The following paragraphs might appear in the body of your essay:

In both poems MacCaig depicts the city as violent. In **Hotel Room** *he refers to*

> *…the broken bones, the harsh screaming*
> *from coldwater flats, the blood*
> *glazed on the sidewalks.*

where the harsh alliteration in "broken bones" conveys the aggressiveness the poet senses in the city and the use of the slightly onomatopoeic "screaming" adds to the fear. There are no people in this part of the poem, only objects ("bones… flats… blood… sidewalks") – the violence seems to have dehumanised the city. In **Brooklyn Cop** *similarly there are "clubbings" and "gunshots", and the cop walks the "thin tissue over violence." The imagery here reflects how fragile, how wafer-thin is the hold of civilised society. This is an idea developed, I think, more effectively in* **Hotel Room**, *which makes a more general point about the nature of uncivilised behaviour: that it is everywhere – "The darkness is never somewhere else".*

Both poems are rich in effective word choice and imagery. In **Brooklyn Cop**, *the cop is described as "Built like a gorilla" – suggesting he is not only large, but threatening, animalistic, primitive, perhaps a little slow but representing enormous force. He is "thick-fleshed" and* *"steak-coloured" both of which descriptions continue the primitive, animal impression and have an internal alliteration that sounds harsh and abrasive. In* **Hotel Room** *the imagery is even more startling: the Empire State Building, symbol of technological achievement and civic pride is reduced to "that jumbo-sized dentist drill" – capturing not just the shape of the skyscraper, but mocking its importance by comparing it to something extremely small, and suggesting that, like a dentist's drill, it is an object associated with pain and discomfort – something to be feared. Both descriptions effectively set the tone for the remainder of the poems, but more so with* **Hotel Room** *where the questioning of how "civilised" we really are develops well from this early image.*

The essay would then go on, in its discussion of the final sections of each poem, to come to a conclusion as to which you thought the more effective.

Points to Note and Remember:

1. When writing about these poems a common failing with "Hotel Room" is to spend too much time on the descriptions in the first verse (the helicopter, the Empire State Building) and not enough on the "big picture" of the poem, i.e. the ideas contained in the last three lines, and with "Brooklyn Cop" few students explore adequately the last five lines – and especially the last two.

Section D – Film and TV Drama

Question 17

Choose a **film or ★TV drama** which presents a disturbing or upsetting or alarming picture of a society.

Show how the film or programme makers create the impression and discuss to what extent there is any optimism in the text as a whole.

Suggested Approaches:

The Boys from the Blackstuff: Episode 3 – **Shop Thy Neighbour**.

Any of the words "disturbing" or "upsetting" or "alarming" could be applied without any difficulty, e.g.:

★ the stresses on Chrissie and Angie's marriage; the poverty they are facing; the run-down appearance of the area they live in; Angie's plea for Chrissie to "fight back"; Chrissie's rage at the conclusion of the play; the bizarre and confused behaviour of the Department of Employment officials; the home life of Miss Sutcliffe

However, we must look at the entirety of the instruction in the second sentence, which asks not just for an account of the way the society is presented, but to assess "to what extent there is any optimism in the text as a whole". The formula "to what extent" is always useful – if you are prepared to *think*, and don't just have a pre-prepared line of thought to trot out. For **Shop Thy Neighbour**, you could refer to:

★ the apparently irrepressible humour of several of the characters

★ a pervading sense of humanity in many of the characters

★ the way that the DoE officials are beginning to target the "big fish" (Molloy) and not the "little guys" (Chrissie and Loggo)

★ Chrissie's pride in his skills (scene 40)

★ Angie's response ("laughter and tears") at the end

The opening of an answer might start as follows:

> *A TV drama which presents a disturbing and at times alarming picture of a society is Alan Bleasdale's* **Shop Thy Neighbour**, *the third in a series of five plays known collectively as* **Boys from the Blackstuff**. *Directed by Philip Saville, they were first broadcast on BBC2 in October/November 1982. The society in question is working class Liverpool of the time, suffering heavily with the high unemployment and consequent poverty brought about by the economic policy of the then government under Margaret Thatcher. Despite the very bleak picture it presents, it is still possible to see an element of optimism.*

There would follow a discussion of the negative points (from the list above). For example:

> *The title* **Shop Thy Neighbour** *refers to the calls received by the Fraud Section at the Dept of Employment giving anonymous information about people cheating the system, for example, by working while claiming "dole". The frequency with which such calls come in suggests a society in which people are more than willing to "shop" others who, as we see from the example of Chrissie and Angie, cannot get a legitimate job and are actually going hungry. The distortion of the better known phrase "Love Thy Neighbour", with its Christian message of tolerance and compassion is an early and clear indication of a society which is in turmoil.*

Next might come the behaviour of the Department of Employment officials e.g. Miss Sutcliffe's arbitrary decision not to prosecute Chrissie and Loggo, Moss's bizarre dialogue with Chrissie (scene 24) comparing them to combatants in World War I – obvious suggestion of wasteful, stupid…

The effect is to suggest a society in which the supposed forces of law and order are in a state of as much confusion as everyone else.

> *During a climactic scene (scene 40) in the bedroom Angie eventually erupts at Chrissie inertia. To remind him of their shortage of money, she has shown him the hole in one of her shoes. All he can reply is "Yeah, well – walk on one leg you'll be alright". This prompts Angie's outburst:*
>
> > *"It's not funny, it's not friggin' funny. I've had enough of that – if you don't laugh, you'll cry – I've heard it for years – this stupid soddin' city's full of it – well why don't you cry – why don't you scream – why don't you fight back, you bastard. Fight back."*
>
> *The picture presented here of a city full of men stripped of their dignity, unable or unwilling to stand up for themselves and reduced to seeing everything as a joke is deeply disturbing. The power and rhetoric of Angie's words are almost like a battle-cry.*

An example of a positive point would be Angie's response at the end:

> *The action at the end freezes on Chrissie and Angie in the aftermath of his slaughter of some of the pets in the back garden: pigeons, chickens, geese. We see a blood-splattered rabbit and Chrissie's last words are: "Somebody'd better wash the blood off that rabbit", which causes*

Angie to laugh and cry at the same time, so our final image is a mixed one, but there is in the laughter some hope for their relationship.

Points to Note and Remember:

1. Remember to address the second part of the question. This question is very similar to many Critical Essay questions at Higher: a relatively straightforward "explain" part followed by a more demanding "discuss" part; a high-scoring essay will always tackle the second part in detail.

Question 18

Choose a **film or TV drama** which explores childhood or adolescence.

Show how the film or programme makers explore the subject and discuss to what extent they create a convincing depiction of the stage of life.

Suitable texts for TV drama:

P'Tang Yang Kipperbang (Jack Rosenthal); **Blue Remembered Hills** (Dennis Potter); **The Lost Prince** (Stephen Poliakoff); **One Summer** (Willy Russell); **Bar Mitzvah Boy** (Jack Rosenthal)

Suggested Approaches:

Leaving by Daniel Boyle (available on DVD as part of Scottish Writers' Collection – BBC 2008).

A possible opening:

> *Daniel Boyle's TV play* **Leaving** *explores adolescence by telling the story of three 15 year old boys in their last days at school in Greenock in 1960. Boyle, who wrote and directed, presents a very convincing depiction of the issues and problems facing adolescent boys, not just in 1960, but today also. His main focus is Nick, whose childhood has been affected by the desertion of his father and the suicide of his mother. Nick is fiercely loyal to his best friends, Gus and Jada, and the strains on their friendship are an important feature of the text. Despite an ending which involves death and separation, Boyle introduces a hint of optimism, and throughout the play he lightens the mood with some very amusing scenes of school life.*

As an introduction, this is fairly long, but it effectively sets up the structure and development of the whole essay, whose key sections would be:

★ Nick's "past"

★ the friendship group

★ the ending, in which you would refer to:

  ★ the death of Gus

  ★ Jada's decision to go to Canada with his uncle

  ★ Nick's joining the "weather ships" as a preface to becoming a Merchant Seaman

  ★ the advances of "the girl" in the final sequence

★ One of the comic scenes, e.g.:

   ★ the lesson on "The Achievements of Civilisation" in which a class of scruffy, bored 15 year old boys in a run-down classroom are lectured about Herodotus, Babylon and Nebuchadnezzar by a teacher who ends up belting those who can't remember the name of Nebuchadnezzar's wife; the sheer uselessness of the information for these boys' lives becomes more and more obvious; and the irony of the teacher's less than "civilised" behaviour becomes more and more amusing

   ★ and show how this lightens the mood, in a way that humour in the face of adversity is a common feature of adolescence

Question 19

Choose a **film or ★TV drama** which deals with a serious subject in a comic or light-hearted way.

Show how the comic or light-hearted elements are created but yet allow an exploration of the serious subject.

Suitable TV texts for this question:

Leaving Daniel Boyle

Down Among the Big Boys Peter McDougall*

The Elephants' Graveyard Peter McDougall*

One Summer Willy Russell

Boys from the Blackstuff Alan Bleasdale

Ready When You Are, Mr McGill Jack Rosenthal

Appropriate Situation Comedy:

Extras Ricky Gervais and Stephen Merchant (especially the final "Special" episode)

Blackadder Goes Forth Richard Curtis and Ben Elton (especially "Goodbyeee")

If You See God, Tell Him Andrew Marshall and David Renwick

   ★ Some other works by Peter McDougall, e.g. **Just A Boys' Game** and **Just Another Saturday**, certainly deal with serious subjects and have some funny one-liners, but it would be hard to argue they explore the serious subject "in a comic way".

Suggested Approaches:

Takin' Over the Asylum by Donna Franceschild.

An Outline:

1. This six-part drama was written by Donna Franceschild and directed for BBC Scotland in 1994 by David Blair. It stars Ken Stott as Eddie McKenna, an unsuccessful double-glazing salesman whose main interest is in being a DJ. He resurrects the hospital radio service at a Glasgow psychiatric hospital and builds strong relationships with a number of the patients, especially the manic depressive Campbell (the TV debut of David Tennant).

2. The serious subject explored is mental illness and how to treat it, e.g.

   ★ how to channel the manic depressiveness of Campbell

   ★ the plight of the self-harming Francine

   ★ reintegrating the obsessive-compulsive Rosalie into society

   ★ the tragedy of the schizophrenic Fergus, whose skills as an electronic engineer are essential to the radio station

   ★ the varying attitudes of staff members, e.g. the caring Isabel and the aggressive Stuart

   ★ the impact on patients' families, e.g. Campbell's father and Rosalie's husband

   ★ Eddie's alcoholism

3. The comedy is generated largely by the constant confusion of who is "mad" and who isn't, e.g. the behaviour of Eddie's boss, Mr Griffin in the "real" world. The confusion is flagged up very early when Eddie mistakes Campbell for a staff member, because he doesn't seem in any way "mad". There is also the tour de force of the fund-raising fete and the "Spot the Loony" competition. Most of the exchanges between Eddie and Campbell are riddled with fast one-liners.

Question 20

Choose a **film or ★TV drama** in which a key scene or sequence is intensified by the use of sound and/or visual effects.

Describe how the sound and/or visual effects intensify the scene or sequence and assess the importance of the scene to the text as a whole.

Suggested Approaches:

This is the most "technical" of the questions in the Film and TV Drama section of this Paper, and is likely to be easier for film than for TV Drama since the former tends to make more use of "special effects", which are often quite expensive and therefore more likely on a film's budget. Nevertheless, many quality TV Dramas make subtle use of sound and/or visual effects and if you have a firm knowledge of how these are used and can write sensibly about the central concerns of the text as a whole, then you should be able to construct a good answer.

Some suggestions:

Shooting the Past by Stephen Poliakoff.

The long sequence in Part 3 when Marilyn shows Anderson the series of photographs about his family's past: the use of haunting violin, piano and synthesiser background music mixed with sounds suggested by the photographs (seagulls, the type of music played by Hettie's orchestra, café sounds, a woman's laughter, running water, snatches of French…) intensifies the storytelling; as more and more photographs are presented in quick succession to Anderson, sometimes an unbroken sequence of picture after picture, it has an almost hypnotic effect not just on Anderson but on the viewer as the camera lingers on small details and faces.

The scene is vital to the text as a whole as it shows the power, beauty and significance of the collection Anderson's company is destroying; it opens up to Anderson the importance of the past; it brings to a climax the relationship between Marilyn and Anderson; it causes Anderson to change his mind about breaking up the collection.

Just a Boys' Game by Peter McDougall:

The fight sequence in the container yard at the climax of the play is intensified by the sights and sounds of the heavy machinery and containers moving around as the men fight.

Important to suggest the brutality not just of the fight but of the society in which Jake lives, where violence appears to be a substitute for companionship.

Takin' Over the Asylum by Donna Franceschild:

Campbell's breakdown towards the end of Part 2 "Fly like an Eagle" is intensified by a cacophony of sounds such as distorted music, shouting voices, breaking glass, stuck records.

Gives audiences some sense of the disturbed nature of Campbell's mind; is a major factor in Eddie's decision to carry on at the hospital; in plot terms, leads to Campbell's continued stay in the hospital and commitment to the radio station.

The Lakes by Jimmy McGovern:

The drowning sequence at the end of the first part is made intense by a vivid mixture of sound and visual effects: the terrified screaming of the girls, the loud swirling of the water and the roar of the low-flying jet; the distorted underwater visuals of the young girls floundering to get to the surface, of the boat disappearing and then hitting the floor of the lake, of Danny swimming underwater in a frantic but hopeless rescue attempt, the shot from below the surface of a floating Alice band.

This sequence is the key to the plot and ties in all the hidden, uncontrollable passions which form the basis of the play.

G.B.H. by Alan Bleasdale

Any of the flashback sequences in which Murray recalls his childhood and his involvement with Eileen Critchley could be discussed in terms of the way the flashback is created visually (soft, dreamlike, contrasting her comfortable upper middle-class background with his working class background), and linked to its importance in the unravelling of Michael Murray's disturbed psyche.

Points to Note and Remember:

1. Description of "the sound and/or visual effects" and the "importance to the text as a whole" would have to be in a fair balance in this answer, so it is essential that you not only know the sequence in detail, but you have to remember the second half of the question is equally important.

Critical Essay Paper 3
Section A – Drama

Question 1

Choose a play in which the cruelty or corruption or carelessness of a character causes difficulties within the play.

Show how the cruelty or corruption or carelessness affects other people in the play and discuss to what extent the character reforms his/her behaviour by the end of the play.

Corruption:

Hamlet (Claudius); **A Man for All Seasons** (Richard Rich/Cromwell); **All My Sons** (Joe Keller); **Othello** (Iago); **King Lear** (Edmund)

Cruelty:

A Streetcar Named Desire (Stanley); **Death of a Salesman** (Howard); **Macbeth** (Macbeth); **King Lear** (Cornwall/Regan/Goneril); **The Birthday Party** (Goldberg and McCann)

Carelessness:

Twelfth Night (Sir Toby Belch); **A Midsummer Night's Dream** (Puck); **The Tempest** (Prospero)

Suggested Approaches:

If you choose to answer this question using **King Lear**, you have a choice as to which character and which fault you choose to focus on. All four of the villainous characters could be called corrupt, and equally they could be seen as cruel.

Possibly Edmund would offer the most scope for an answer, and probably the fault best explored would be his corrupt nature rather than his cruelty. He betrays his brother, dupes his father, betrays him to Cornwall, woos Goneril in despite of Albany, transfers his allegiance to Regan after Cornwall dies and eventually has Lear and Cordelia in his power.

The second part of the question should take into account his confession of his treachery, and his last minute but vain attempt to redeem himself by telling of his instructions to kill Lear and Cordelia.

Points to Note and Remember:

1. Lear is a big play in all senses of the word. You should be prepared to answer a question such as this which does not focus on Lear himself. It means you have to have a very good general knowledge of the play and the ability to select relevant parts of the play, relevant characters/ relationships and relevant quotations. You have to know much more than you will be able to use in an answer. There is no substitute for studying the text again and again from a variety of angles.

Question 2

Choose a play which has as a central feature a conflict between generations, or couples or social classes.

Show how the situation and/or personalities contribute to the conflict. To what extent do you find the resolution of the conflict satisfying in terms of the play as a whole?

Generations:

All My Sons; **The Glass Menagerie**; **King Lear**; **A View from the Bridge**; **Romeo and Juliet**

Couples:

Macbeth; **A Streetcar Named Desire**; **A Doll's House**; **A Midsummer Night's Dream**; **Much Ado about Nothing**; **The Crucible**

Social classes:

Pygmalion; **A Streetcar Named Desire**; **Twelfth Night**

Suggested Approaches:

Consider **A Streetcar Named Desire**.

The most obvious conflict here is between Blanche and Stanley. But they do not fit the category of "couples". They do, however, fit the category of "social class" conflict. The following points would provide a basis for the first part of the question.

The situation:

★ Blanche's background of "old money" in the South – the family estate, her social aspirations

★ The fact that she has fallen on hard times, and has had to move to a working class cosmopolitan area, in cramped living conditions with her sister and Stanley

★ Stanley's background – working class, independent, macho culture, immigrant stock…

★ Stanley's suspicions about the "loss" of Belle Reve

Personalities:

★ Blanche: insecure, vain, desperate for "love" or any sort of relationship, using sex as a weapon in the battle between the sexes.

★ Stanley: dominant, plain-speaking, violent, suspicious, controlling…

The second part of the question asks for your opinion of the "satisfying" nature of the resolution to the conflict. "Satisfying" does not mean "enjoyable"; in its literary sense it means that the resolution is dramatically satisfying, that it fulfils the expectation that the play has built up; that somehow what was inevitable has been demonstrated. Stanley and Blanche's relationship seems likely to have a violent resolution.

Stanley's rape of Blanche and her subsequent descent into insanity is the shocking culmination of the conflict – as Stanley says "We've had this date with each other from the beginning". Blanche's use of sex as a weapon has finally backfired on her and Stanley's "punishment" is extreme and violent. But he needs to regain control over his wife and his home. The rape exacerbates Blanche's increasing detachment from reality, leading to her acceptance of the Doctor's hand, in the belief that he is being "kind" to her. The audience, although shocked by the ending, sees in it a kind of inevitable resolution between the old and the new, as represented by Blanche and Stanley. The class conflict between the anachronistic and effete "Old South" with its outdated views on manners and inherited position has succumbed to the "new" cosmopolitan, democratic, thrusting and successful (although more brutal) America represented by Stanley.

Question 3

Choose a play in which a single scene illustrates a reversal of fortune for one of the characters.

Describe in detail how the scene shows the reversal and discuss to what extent this reversal in fortune makes the character's fate inevitable.

Suitable texts would include:

Macbeth – second weird sisters' scene, the banquet scene or Macduff's revelation of his birth

Hamlet – the death of Polonius – the play within the play

The Merchant of Venice – trial scene (for Shylock or Antonio)

Twelfth Night – the letter scene

King Lear – Goneril's (or Regan's) rejection of Lear

Much Ado About Nothing – Beatrice's (or Benedick's) "arbour" scene

As You Like It – Rosalind's banishment from court

Othello – Iago's poisoning of Othello's thoughts (Act 3 Scene 3)

Romeo and Juliet – Romeo's killing of Tybalt

Suggested Approaches:

Consider **Macbeth**: The Banquet Scene.

Macbeth's behaviour at the banquet is so strange that despite Lady Macbeth's efforts to distract attention, the Scottish lords are left with grave suspicions that he might be guilty of the murder of Duncan. The inevitable consequences unfold as we see various scenes suggesting that a conspiracy might be in the offing: Act 3 Scene 6 between Lennox and another Lord; Macduff's flight to England; Macbeth's revenge on Lady Macduff and her children. This makes Macduff's case stronger, and increases the chances of English help being given to Malcolm. Further repression on the part of Macbeth leads to the inevitable rebellion against him and his defeat at the hands of Macduff. If you know the Banquet Scene well, your description of its events will justify the statement that this scene marks a reversal in Macbeth's fortunes. You can then concentrate on the extent to which you think this scene seals Macbeth's fate.

Points to Note and Remember:

1. In many plays there is a choice of scene. The scenes from the list of plays (above) are only a few of the possible choices. Choosing the best for the question is important.

Question 4

Choose a play which deals with a social or political or religious issue.

By referring to two or more of the following features – structure, setting, language, soliloquy, use of narrator – show how each contributes to your understanding of the thematic concerns of the play.

Social:

Death of a Salesman; A View from the Bridge; All My Sons; A Doll's House; Pygmalion; The Slab Boys; Yellow Moon; The Merchant of Venice; Under Milk Wood

Political:

Macbeth; Hamlet; King Lear; Mary Queen of Scots got her Head Chopped Off; The Cheviot, the Stag and the Black, Black Oil; Bold Girls

Religious:

The Crucible; A Man for All Seasons; The Devil's Disciple; The Royal Hunt of the Sun

Note: some of these plays would be equally at home under one of the other headings.

Suggested Approaches:

You are asked to refer to **two or more** features.

★ Structure could include references to key scenes, climax, denouement, pace.

★ Setting in time and culture is vital to questions about these issues.

★ Language – poetic, biblical, rhetorical or comic – can make an important contribution.

★ Soliloquy – its use as a clear statement of the ideas of the play.

Use of narrator (an aspect of staging) – often a commentator on the events of the play, helping the audience to process the ideas.

The Cheviot, the Stag and the Black, Black Oil by John McGrath.

In this inventive play there are many features which impact on the central issue – the constant exploitation of Scotland's resources and people. The three part structure allows for an exploration of each of these in turn: The Cheviot represents the Clearances of the 18th and 19th Centuries when the people were cleared from the land to make way for sheep; The Stag represents the beginning of the tourist invasion and the invention of "romantic" Scotland with its Monarch of the Glen symbol, and the Black, Black Oil deals with the American invasion of, mainly, Aberdeen.

Each of the following points (among others) could be expanded and integrated with the exploration of the main concerns of the play. Often two or three of these features contribute to the success of one sketch or sequence.

★ The framing structure of a ceilidh allows a fast moving sequence of music, sketches, songs

★ Direct address between the actors and audience, breaking the barriers of conventional theatre

★ Language: the use of Gaelic song to recall past glories; the use of "vox pop" to show the strength of local feeling; the use of comic language such as "The Frying Scotsman All Night Chipperama" and "Fingal's Café" show the debasement brought about by tourism when in the hands of guys on the make.

Section B – Prose Fiction

Question 5

Choose a **novel** in which the mood or atmosphere created in the opening section is important to a central theme of the novel as a whole.

Describe how the writer creates the mood or atmosphere and show how it is important in the exploration of the theme.

Possible texts:

The Handmaid's Tale	repression and sexuality
The Cone-Gatherers	good and evil in the forest
Greenvoe	strength of the community/nameless authority
The Inheritors	unfallen man
Nineteen Eighty-Four	totalitarian power/repression
Brick Lane	emotional growth
A Farewell to Arms	futility of war
Brighton Rock	good v evil/the theory of sin
The Trick is to Keep Breathing	search for identity/sanity
Jane Eyre	isolation/independence
Bleak House	corruption of justice/false hopes

Suggested Approaches:

The Grapes of Wrath by John Steinbeck.

The question asks for the "mood or atmosphere" created by the setting – not just a description of the setting, Steinbeck creates a scene in which everything piles up against the farmers – the heat, the dust, the wind – all undermining the hope they had in their crop, but the effect is to create not a mood of despair, but one of resistance among the farmers. "After a while the faces of the watching men lost their bemused perplexity and became hard and angry and resistant." This quotation provides evidence for the assertion that the mood is one of "resistance" in the face of their difficulties.

This part of the answer should give quite detailed evidence. You could use quotation (as shown above); you can also use other references to the text in the form of description of incident or conversation. The better you know your text, the more easily you will be able to call in your evidence. There are places where you will want to quote, because the actual words make your point most clearly. The quotation above from the first chapter of **The Grapes of Wrath** is extremely helpful, because it really encapsulates the central concern of the text – what happens to that resistance when it is put under intolerable pressure.

The essay would now go on to follow the idea of resistance under pressure by tracing the effects of the dust bowl and the migration on the Joad family, which is really quite a straightforward task.

Points to Note and Remember:

Two specific points to remember about quotation when answering questions on the novel:

1. A few well chosen quotations illustrating key points in the text, or delineating key character points can help your essay by making the argument more fluent and convincing, but reference to specific incidents, characters, ideas is equally valuable.

2. In most cases, quotations like the one above need no further comment. To add "This shows that the men changed from being puzzled to being determined" is repetitive, intrusive and time-wasting "micro analysis".

Question 6

Choose a **novel** or **short story** in which one of the central concerns is injustice or cruelty, perpetrated by the state, the community, the family or the individual.

Show how the injustice or cruelty affects one of the main characters. Discuss how the character's attempts to cope with the injustice or cruelty add to your appreciation of injustice or cruelty in the text.

Nineteen Eighty-Four – injustice and/or cruelty perpetrated by the state towards Winston and/or Julia

The Handmaid's Tale – injustice perpetrated by the state towards Offred

One Day in the Life of Ivan Denisovich – injustice and /or cruelty perpetrated by the state towards Ivan

The Grapes of Wrath – injustice of the political/economic system towards the Joads

Oliver Twist – injustice/cruelty of (poor law) system towards Oliver

The Great Gatsby – injustice/ cruelty of the social "aristocratic" community

Oranges are not the only Fruit – cruelty of the (religious) community towards Jeanette

Small Island – injustice (caused by prejudice) of the community towards Hortense

Sunset Song – cruelty/injustice of the community towards Long Rob (or even Ewan) or of the cruelty of John Guthrie towards his wife/Will/Chris?

Lord of the Flies – cruelty of Roger and/or Jack towards Sam'n'Eric, Ralph, Piggy…

The Woman Who Walked Into Doors – cruelty of Charlo towards Paula

Tess of the D'Urbervilles – cruelty of Alec D'Urberville towards Tess

Consider the Lilies – cruelty of the landowners/indifference of the Church

Suggested Approaches:

This question looks quite long, and seems to demand a complex answer. It does have several parts, but this kind of question can actually be easier to answer because it gives you a structure for your essay.

★ What is the effect of the injustice or cruelty on one or more character(s)?

★ How well does the character cope with it?

★ What does this add to our understanding of the injustice or cruelty?

Nineteen Eighty-Four – George Orwell.

The effects of the injustice of the totalitarian society on Winston are (physically) his poor living conditions and (spiritually) the repression of his free thought. Some details of the physical conditions – the clothes, the food, the buildings. Some details of the terror of surveillence – the Thought Police, Big Brother, the pioneers… and the effects of manipulation – the Two Minute Hate, the alteration of History, Newspeak…

Initially we feel that Winston might just be coping. He seems to be willing to defy the State/Big Brother – the diary, the affair with Julia, the joining of The Brotherhood – but later, when it all explodes in his face, he is completely ground down until his personality has all but disappeared – his betrayal of Julia, his capitulation to Big Brother

Our understanding is extended by the recognition of the fact that for Winston there never was any hope, because the totalitarian nature of the ruling power is just that. A possible last paragraph might run as follows:

> *By the end of the novel we realise the all pervading nature of the tyranny governing Oceania (and perhaps the other two continents, about which we know absolutely nothing – even their existence is not proven). Winston's ability, in the beginning of the novel, to hang on to fragments of a life "before" – a better life – has been destroyed, as will such memories in any who have them. "Who controls the past controls the future. Who controls the present controls the past." Winston's capitulation to Big Brother, and his eventual death – at least of his spirit if not of his body – has been destined from the beginning, as he thought in Chapter 1, "Whether he wrote DOWN WITH BIG BROTHER, or whether he refrained from writing it, made no difference… You might dodge successfully for a while, even for years, but sooner or later they were bound to get you." Our journey with Winston through his rebellion and hope lets us see just how pervasive and powerful and dangerous a totalitarian society is.*

If you chose the short story option see pages 106–7.

Question 7

Choose a **novel** or **short story** in which a gradual revelation of crucial information is an important factor in your appreciation of the central concerns of the novel or short story.

Show how crucial information is gradually revealed and how this process enhances your appreciation of the central concern(s) of the text.

A few of the more suitable novels are:

Greenvoe; The Inheritors; The Trick is to Keep Breathing; Jane Eyre; Great Expectations; Oliver Twist; Atonement; Never Let Me Go; The Quiet American; Lord of the Flies; Nineteen Eighty-Four; The Cone-Gatherers; A Prayer for Owen Meany

Most Victorian novels would be appropriate, simply because the "revelation" is a major ingredient of the genre, and the fact that many were serialised means that hints and hooks were necessary.

Suggested Approaches:

Jane Eyre – Charlotte Brontë.

A possible beginning:

> In **Jane Eyre** by *Charlotte Brontë*, the concept of good moral choice is one of the main concerns of the novel. Jane is faced with two major moments of decision: the first is her decision to leave Rochester when she finds out he is already married; and the second is her decision not to marry St John Rivers and go with him as a missionary to India.
>
> The occasion of the first of these choices is the culmination of a gradual revelation of information about Rochester's first wife, Bertha Mason. The fact that the revelation is partial and gradual allows the reader to journey with Jane through her early relationship with Rochester only vaguely affected by the knowledge that there is something being hidden from her in Thornfield Hall.

The gradual revelation is effected by the following incidents:

★ the eerie laugh on her first arrival at Thornfield Hall, with the explanation that it is a servant Grace Poole, who is a bit eccentric

★ the fire in Mr Rochester's bedroom – again blamed on Grace Poole

★ Grace's high salary discussed among the other servants

★ the appearance of Mr Mason and its unsettling effect on Rochester

★ the request to Jane to bandage up Mr Mason's wounds after he has been attacked in the attic

★ Rochester's attempt to tell Jane his own story under the guise of being about "a young man he knew"

★ the wedding veil torn in two

★ Mr Briggs and Mr Mason intervening at the wedding

★ and, finally, the visit to the attic to see Bertha, his wife

> *Each of these incidents has a progressively disturbing effect on Jane, although parallel to that is her growing happiness in her relationship with Rochester. It is the coming together of these two threads at the wedding which makes the impact of her decision so effective in the reader's understanding of her dilemma.*

The second set of circumstances which is revealed only gradually is Jane's relationship with John Eyre, and her eventual financial independence created by his death. This impacts on her relationship with St John, as he turns out to be her cousin, but it also allows her to pass another test – marriage without love, no matter what high moral value St John sets on her Christian duty, seems a betrayal. At the moment when she might just be about to capitulate to St John's wishes, she "hears" Rochester calling her, reminding her what love really is. On finding him a widower, and being now secure in her own independence, financial and spiritual, she can give herself freely to him as an equal.

Points to Note and Remember:

1. By definition, all novels reveal crucial information in the course of the plot, and therefore any novel you have studied could be appropriate; but the thrust of this question is really designed for novels where the writer tantalises the reader with shadowy/unexplained/partial information, the full import of which is kept concealed by the writer until it contributes to an important climax, denouement, reversal…

If you have chosen the short story option, see pages 106–7.

Question 8

Choose a **novel** with an incident involving two or more main characters which creates a turning point in the novel.

Describe the incident and show how its outcome is important to your appreciation of the main concern(s) of the novel.

The following suggest possible incidents from a variety of novels:

The deer drive in **The Cone-Gatherers**

Lok's last meeting with the New People in **The Inheritors**

Frederic Henry's meeting with two battle police in **A Farewell to Arms**

Gatsby's meeting with Daisy/meeting in the New York hotel in **The Great Gatsby**

Chris and Ewan's weekend on his leave in **Sunset Song**

Tess telling Angel about her past in **Tess of the D'Urbervilles**

Heathcliff overhearing Cathy's conversation with Nelly in **Wuthering Heights**

Lizzie's meeting with Lady Catherine in **Pride and Prejudice**

Miss Abbott's meeting with Gino and his baby in **Where Angels Fear to Tread**

Suggested Approaches:

Lord of the Flies – William Golding.

Selection of materials:

★ The incident about the fire occurs about a third of the way through the novel. You have to decide how much (if any) of the material you know about the novel up to this point is relevant to your answer. If you start at the beginning of the novel and recount events until you reach this incident, you are either going to be writing stuff which is not relevant, or you are going to leave yourself little time to deal with the main thrust of the question – probably both. As we saw in Questions 2 and 8 in Paper 1, you should start with the incident.

★ the appearance of the ship, and the realization that the fire is out

★ Jack's appearance in all his euphoria at the success of the hunt

★ the reaction of the crowd to the news of the boat

★ the shifting of allegiance between Ralph and Jack

★ Jack's "apology" putting him (unfairly) in the right according to misplaced schoolboy codes

★ Ralph's refusal to move while the fire is built

★ the important outcome of the incident "By the time the pile was built they were on different side of a high barrier."

The beginning of Jack's power to tempt all the boys into his gang are shown here. The cruel treatment of Piggy foreshadows the terrifying violence to come. The descriptions of the hunt show the lack of inhibition, the breakdown of the veneer of civilisation, the cruelty of "the mob" – all illustrating ultimately "the darkness of man's heart".

Your answer would go on to show how the rest of the novel portrays the playing out of this antagonism, concluding with the return of "normality" brought about by the naval officer which deepens the horror of all that has passed.

Prose – Non-fiction

Question 9

Choose a **biography** or **autobiography** which presents the life of a vibrant and/or influential personality.

Show how the writer's presentation of the person effectively conveys the vibrant and/or influential nature of her or his personality.

Suggested Approaches:

This is a fairly straightforward question, but remember that you are not just recounting the life of the subject, you are looking at how the writer presents him/herself or his or her subject showing how the "vibrancy" or the "influence" is demonstrated. Possibly discussion of such features as use of anecdote, strength of evidence, choice of detail, would be appropriate here, but other approaches and features are equally possible.

Points to Note and Remember:

1. The thrust of this question is really towards a full-length biography or autobiography. A single incident is unlikely fully to represent the "life" of such a subject.

Question 10

Choose an **essay** or a **piece of journalism** which employs a particular tone to reinforce the central ideas of the essay.

Show how successfully the writer uses tone to help you to see the ideas from her/his point of view.

Suggested Approaches:

Possible tones could include sceptical, celebratory, persuasive, satirical…

Tone is created through features such as word choice, sentence structure, the use of question and exclamation, climax and various other techniques with which you are familiar from the Close Reading Paper.

In dealing with the creation of the tone, you would have to link your examples with the ideas presented, and also show to what extent you are brought to share the writer's point of view.

Points to Note and Remember:

1. In an essay such as this, there is a need to analyse the language quite closely, because the question is on "techniques" – those which contribute to tone.

Question 11

Choose a **work of non-fiction** which explores the wonder of travel, or the extremes of human endeavour.

Show how the writer creates the sense of wonder, or an appreciation of the extreme lengths to which the participants are driven.

Possible texts dealing with the "wonder" include Paul Theroux's **Great Railway Bazaar** which include the wonder of the great "romantic" railway journeys and the delight in the diversity of people he meets. Palin and Bryson also seem to welcome people and places with enthusiasm.

"Wonder" and "extremes of human endeavour" are not, of course, mutually exclusive. Some travel books, such as Rory Stewart's **The Places in Between** combine extreme danger with a sense of wonder, and other books such as **The Ascent of Annapurna** by Maurice Herzog combine the extreme nature of the dangers they faced with wonder at the high Himalaya.

Suggested Approaches:

The question itself is fairly straightforward. Description of place, people and incident, and the writer's response to them will form the main thrust of your answer.

Section C – Poetry

Question 12

Choose a poem which portrays the natural world as spiritual or uplifting.

Identify what aspect of the natural world the poet is describing and discuss to what extent he or she is successful in bringing into focus its spiritual or uplifting effects.

Inversnaid and **Pied Beauty** (Hopkins)

On a Croft by Kirkaig (MacCaig)

The Horses (Hughes)

Snake (D.H. Lawrence)

Horses (Edwin Muir)

Hamnavoe (George Mackay Brown)

At the Firth of Lorne (Iain Crichton Smith)

Poem in October (Dylan Thomas)

Ode to Autumn and **Ode to a Nightingale** (Keats)

Tintern Abbey (Wordsworth)

Suggested Approaches:

The Windhover by Gerard Manley Hopkins.

The Windhover, or falcon, is the subject of this poem. Hopkins talks of seeing the hawk wheeling and diving against the rising sun one morning.

The description of the movement, the effects of the wind on the bird and the effects of the bird's flight on the poet are all the subject of the octave of the sonnet.

The sestet, while continuing the praise of the hawk moves onto a more emotional level, touching on pride, fire, danger in the first three lines, moves to contrast with the earthbound in the last three lines, but still sees the power of the hawk to spark fire.

The identification of the hawk with Christ (signalled in the dedication) becomes more overt in the sestet – a kindling fire brought to earth.

Each of these headings would be expanded by reference to the actual words and structure of the poem, and you would have to show how they create uplifting feelings in the poet. For example you might say:

> *...then off, off forth on swing,*
> *As a skate's heel sweeps smooth on a bow-bend:*

An impression of speed given by the repetition of the "off, off" and "swing" gives the direction as that of a parabola. This sets up the comparison with a skate's heel – not the skater – which he wants us to focus on: the sharpness of the skate and its speed, and its skill matching that of the falcon's flawless flight. The skill of the movement is emphasised in the phrase "sweeps smooth" where the long vowels and the alliteration of the hissing "s" sound adds an auditory image to the pictorial one, suggesting a flawless trajectory. The last part of the skating simile "on a bow-bend" gives not only the curving quality of a bow, but also suggests the speed at which an arrow could be launched, and possibly the hidden power and danger within the hawk

Points to Note and Remember:

1. Take care that the analysis of any aspect of the poem is directed at the main thrust of the question – the uplifting or spiritual effect of the natural world.

Question 13

Choose a poem in which you can recognise a point where the poem moves from description into reflection.

Identify that point in the poem and show how effectively the poet uses the description (of place, person, or experience) to provide a springboard for her or his reflection on the central ideas of the poem.

Many of the poems you have studied will fall into this category. Almost all classical and many modern sonnets have this structural point built into their form. Other poems of this kind are typical of many writers such as Larkin (**The Whitsun Weddings**), Heaney (**Death of a Naturalist**), Hughes (**Thrushes**), MacCaig (**So Many Summers**), Burns (**To a Louse**).

Suggested Approaches:

Fern Hill by Dylan Thomas.

The beautiful, evocative description of childhood which Thomas gives us in this poem is optimistic in tone and exhilarating in language. The opening line "Now as I was young and easy under the apple boughs" is the topic for the next four stanzas of the poem. The simplicity of the language, the underlying recollection of folk-song, gives the reader expectations of pleasure to come. Only towards the end of the poem is the mood altered to show the shadow of time cast over the child's life.

The contrast between the warmth and joy in the description of the child's experience in the first two thirds of the poem is contrasted with the sense of loss in the last stanza where the child's realisation that time is limited reminds the reader of his own mortality.

Points for development:

★ Time is personified through out the poem – repetition of the permissive – "Time let me…" through to the more prescriptive – "time allows", "time held me"

★ the happiness of childhood pursuits and his feeling of invincibility

★ the wonder of a new creation felt in the dawning of a new day:

> So it must have been after the birth of the simple light
> In the first, spinning place, the spellbound horses walking warm
> Out of the whinnying green stable
> On to the fields of praise

★ The beginning of a transition in "In the sun born over and over" suggesting the passing of time leading to the inevitable understanding that time is limited: "so few and such morning songs"

All these points should be developed by referring to the poetic techniques Thomas uses, especially his trademark use of words slightly "shifted" from their normal place or order – e.g., "happy as the grass was green"; "all the moon long" "high hay". Important also are his use of the colours e.g. "green" and "golden", his use of Biblical allusion and his use of evocative sound "And the Sabbath rang slowly…"

The final stanza, in contrast with the warmth and enthusiasm of the previous stanzas, has a much colder feel with references to "shadow", "the moon that is always rising" leading to the saddest line in the poem, "And wake to the farm forever fled from the childless land" which has echoes of his earlier joyful awakenings – "the sun born over and over" The idea of time not being endless and unlimited (the child's vision) is encapsulated in the powerful line, "Time held me green and dying" (the adult's understanding of our mortality). The poem does, however, recapture some of its optimism in the last line, "Though I sang in my chains like the sea." The appreciation that life will end seems to enhance the value of time remaining.

Points to Note and Remember:

1. The important thing to remember in tackling this kind of question is that it is not an open invitation to run straight through the poem, identifying in passing the point in question. A better approach Is to start from appropriate point in the poem and then refer, in this case, to the contrast, which you then develop in your argument.

Question 14

Choose **two** poems on the same theme.

Compare the approaches taken to the theme and discuss which you feel to be more effective in increasing your understanding and appreciation of the central concern(s) of the poems.

Suggested Approaches:

Counting the Beats by Robert Graves and **Night Marriage** by Carol Ann Duffy.

These two poems are both love poems; both are set during the night, when the lovers are thinking of each other. In **Counting the Beats**, the lovers are in bed, sleepless, wondering what their end will be…will their love survive death? In **Night Marriage**, the lovers are apart in distance but together in dream and imagination.

In the opening of **Night Marriage**, the speaker is waiting for her lover to appear in her dreams, when she switches off the light, "You slip from yourself/to wait for me"

But over the lovers' heads threats loom: the "huge storm" in **Counting the Beats** and the reality of her lover's absence ("I wake bereaved") in **Night Marriage**.

Further points for discussion:

★ The use of repetition in **Counting the Beats**

★ The use of imagery in **Night Marriage**

★ The similarity in the final verses – the lovers are "face to face"

★ The dissimilarity in the final lines – the threat versus the confidence

The evaluative part of your answer is entirely your own. Do you prefer the optimism (although possibly only temporary) of **Night Marriage**, or do you prefer the shared realism of the conclusion to **Counting the Beats**?

Question 15

Choose a poem in which the writer creates an interesting character or persona.

Show by what means the writer creates the character or persona and discuss how effectively the concerns of the poem are developed through the presentation of the character or persona.

Suggested Approaches:

Holy Willie's Prayer by Robert Burns.

Central idea concerns hypocrisy (of an ostensibly God-fearing character) illustrated by:

★ Willie's self-aggrandisement and pride (shown in the Invocation)

★ His blindness to and denial of his own faults (shown in the Confession)

★ His spite and curses on Gavin Hamilton and others (shown in the Supplication)

Each of these sections should be developed to show how his personality is revealed:

1. His praise of God for having "chosen" him to be one of the elect;

His delight in the terrors of Hell, which will affect other people – not him:

"In burnin lakes…chained to their stakes."

His exaggerated sense of his own position and goodness- "example/to a Thy flock" "zeal I bear/when drinkers drink…"

2. which he immediately negates in his "confession" where he reveals that he drinks himself (that Friday I was fou…) and is "fashed wi' fleshly lust".

His self delusion allows him to blame anyone else but himself – he blames original sin, and comforts himself with the idea that he sees his obsession with sex as a way of keeping him humbled even though he is privileged, or that he is being "tested" so has to put up with the consequences, or even that his sinning is God's will.

3. His real nastiness and small-mindedness is more clearly revealed in his asking God to call down curses on his enemies. He works himself into a fury ending with a climactic – "destroy them/ an" dinna spare". This contrasts ridiculously with the last stanza where he returns to his self–congratulatory mode in an unctuous request that he should be "Excelled by nane" in which case he might let God take some of the credit – "And a' the glory shall be Thine" followed by a thoroughly self-satisfied double Amen

In the course of your essay, you will deal with Burns' poetic techniques, by showing how effective they are in increasing our sense of the hypocritical nature of Willie, and probably, by extension, his Church. For example, word choice and sound in "fashed wi' fleshly lust" deserve comment. And there are many more aspects such as structure, imagery, Biblical language, stanza form, rhyme scheme ("Strong as a rock… To a' Thy flock" – the strong rhyme here builds Willie up to a peak of virtue, only to send him tumbling further in the next few stanzas).

Points to Note and Remember:

1. Compare this question with the Question 16, Paper 1 on page 114 which looks very similar, but is actually very different:

> Choose a poem in which the poet creates a convincing character.

> Show how the poet, by skilful use of technique, brings the character alive.

The task is **entirely** different: one concentrates on **characterisation**, the other on the **ideas/concerns** of the poem.

This demonstrates yet again, that the important part of the question is the second part, the task.

Section D – Film and TV Drama

Question 16

Choose a **film or TV drama** which is set in the future.

Show to what extent setting it in the future facilitates the discussion of an important theme.

Suggested Approaches:

Blade Runner (Ridley Scott).

The setting in a future where androids/replicants have been created to provide (among other things) an extra labour force makes possible the discussion of one of the central themes – what is it to be human? Who are the human beings and who are the replicants. If there is a need for a test…

Question 17

Choose a **film or TV drama** in which an act of betrayal (e.g. of friends, of family, of country) is central to the theme of the text.

Describe what impact the betrayal has on the betrayed and show how it is important in developing the theme of the text.

Suggested Approaches:

On the Waterfront (Elia Kazan).

Terry realises that he has been betrayed by his brother Charlie in the prize fighting world (revealed during the sequence in the taxi): that he has, for short term gains, been prevented from realising his potential in the ring. This opens his eyes to the bigger moral picture, and prompts him to consider speaking to the Crime Commission about the death of Joey. His subsequent actions lead to his crusade against the corruption created by Johnny Friendly and the mob, and to the breaking of the stranglehold they had over the longshoremen. The struggle between corruption and truth which is one of the central concerns of the text is illustrated by the movement of Terry from the corrupt (Johnny Friendly etc.) to the truth in the persons of Edie and Father Barry.

Question 18

Choose a **film or TV drama** in which one important sequence focuses on a moment of decision for the hero/heroine.

By examining the sequence in detail, show how the moment of decision is portrayed, and go on to show the impact of that decision on the rest of the text.

Suggested Approaches:

The Godfather (Coppola).

The hospital sequence in which Michael Corleone finally commits himself to an alliance with "The Family" is obviously an extremely important decision. The construction of the scene, the sound effects, the shots showing abandoned food, empty chairs, the tracking camera in corridors... and many other details would be required for the first part of the question. The second part – the impact of that decision on the rest of the film – follows through to the relentless and single-minded running of the Family (far more ruthless than the Godfather himself).

Question 19

Choose a **film or TV drama** in which one of the main characters is a flawed hero.

Show how the film or programme makers present the character as flawed and discuss how your reactions to her or his role in the text as a whole are manipulated by the film or programme maker.

Suggested Approaches:

Schindler's List (Spielberg).

Oskar Schindler's original presentation – womanising, mercenary, good time guy – is gradually transformed throughout the film as he comes to sympathise more and more with the Jewish people whom he tries to save. The effect of massacres and the hounding of the Jews strengthens his resolve to save them. His original factory designed to make him rich, is eventually drained of all its resources because of the bribes he has had to pay the Germans. An interesting aspect of his presentation is the life he leads with the Germans, where he assumes the same attitudes as they, and makes friends of Amon Goeth. There is, however, still some ambiguity about his personal life which undermines his "heroic" portrait.

Appendix 1
What to Choose?

Drama

You are unlikely to have more than one play well prepared, so the choice you make from the four or five questions will be very important to your success. Assume for the moment that the play you have studied is **The Crucible** by Arthur Miller. Even although you may not have studied this play, you should go on reading this section because the principles governing choice are important and the principles apply to any play you actually have studied. (If you're not familiar with The Crucible, it will help if you look at a synopsis of the play on an internet site such as Wikipedia or Spark Notes.)

The first principle is that you must look at all the questions in the section.

> 1. ... a character other than the hero/heroine plays a crucial role in affecting the thoughts and actions of the hero or heroine.

The hero is obviously Proctor, so which characters could be the "other"? – Abigail is probably the most obvious, although Elizabeth, Hale or even Rebecca Nurse are possible candidates.

But this is only the starting point for the question. The "real" question, the task, is described in the **second** part.

The second principle, therefore, is that you must also look carefully at the task you are being asked to do in each of the questions:

> By referring closely to the part played by your chosen character show how important he or she is in affecting the thoughts and actions of the hero/heroine in the course of the play.

Do you know enough about your chosen character in relation to Proctor? At which points in the play do they interact? What effect does the interaction have on Proctor's thoughts and actions?

Even though you may be satisfied that you do know something about all of these aspects, you should go on to read Question 2. It might suit you better.

> 2. ...a scene... in which a main character is persuaded or forced to act against his/her wishes or conscience.

Main characters would commonly be thought to be Proctor, Abigail, Elizabeth. Acting against... wishes or conscience? Abigail can probably be deleted from the list. What about a scene?

Proctor: the scene in the courthouse where he is forced to declare that he has slept with Abigail; or the scene in Salem jail where he goes against his conscience and admits to witchcraft.

Elizabeth: the scene in the courthouse where her love for John forces her to tell a lie, as she thinks, for his good.

But, again, look at the "real" question – the part you have to answer:

> Describe the scene in detail and discuss to what extent the character's decision in this scene continues to reverberate throughout the play as a whole.

Given that you understand the question, do you know any of the scenes mentioned above (or any other appropriate scene) in enough detail?

What decision(s) are taken, and how do these decisions govern events, actions and relationships later in the play?

Now move on to Question 3.

> **3.** …has as one of its main concerns loss of respect, or of honour, or of status.

All of these could be said to apply to Proctor, but you have to choose the best one– and that is probably going to be "loss of honour".

But, as before, look at the real question, the second part:

> Identify which loss you have chosen and show how the playwright's exploration of this loss is important in your appreciation of the play as a whole.

There are several excellent opportunities to demonstrate this "loss of honour" – in the court scene where he reveals his shame with Abigail, and in the prison scene where he allows his "confession" to be written down.

Finally, Question 4.

> **4.** …a seemingly strong relationship or marriage which deteriorates throughout the course of the play.

Elizabeth and Proctor? A strong relationship, but not a deteriorating one. So this question is not suitable for this text.

The final stage for this section is to make a firm choice.

In theory you should know the play well enough to tackle three of these questions, but the one which stands out most clearly as a good option for this play is Question 3. Question 2 would also be a good choice, if you have a detailed knowledge of the scene you choose, but Question 1, although you could probably write an answer, is not straightforward.

If you had plunged into Question 1 without looking further, you would have missed the two better options out of the four.

But the third principle of choice is that you must go on to read the questions in the other Sections for which you have studied. It may be that there are two other questions in the paper as a whole which you can answer better than the one you have provisionally chosen for Drama.

You should approach the other sections in the same way.

For example, for Section C – Poetry, you should have a choice of poems available. Using the following four poems – Church Going, Valentine, Anthem for Doomed Youth and Futility (all of which are printed in Appendix 3) try to fit these to the poetry section of this paper which you will find on page 80.

Appendix 2 – Texts

Please note that this is a guide to the texts mentioned in this book and that, while all are eminently suitable, it is not intended as an exclusive list of "recommended texts". In all Sections many perfectly suitable texts are not mentioned, but their omission should not be seen as any kind of slur. It is simply not possible to list every appropriate text for Critical Essay study.

Section A – Drama

(a) Texts which are discussed in the book (numbers indicate the page(s) on which the text is discussed):

Byrne: *The Slab Boys*	121	Shakespeare: *King Lear*	146
Ibsen: *A Doll's House*	99	Shakespeare: *Macbeth*	148
McGrath: *The Cheviot, the Stag, and the Black, Black Oil*	149	Shakespeare: *Othello*	93
Miller: *All My Sons*	97	Shakespeare: *The Merchant of Venice*	125
Miller: *Death of a Salesman*	123	Williams: *A Streetcar Named Desire*	147
Miller: *The Crucible*	165	Williams: *The Glass Menagerie*	95
Shakespeare: *Hamlet*	120		

(b) Other suitable texts which are referred to in the book:

Albee: *Who's Afraid of Virginia Woolf*	Shakespeare: *A Midsummer Night's Dream*
Arden: *Serjeant Musgrave's Dance*	Shakespeare: *As You Like It*
Bolt: *A Man for All Seasons*	Shakespeare: *Much Ado About Nothing*
Greig: *Yellow Moon*	Shakespeare: *Romeo and Juliet*
Lochhead: *Mary Queen of Scots got her Head Chopped Off*	Shakespeare: *The Tempest*
Miller: *A View from the Bridge*	Shakespeare: *Twelfth Night*
Munro: *Bold Girls*	Shaw: *Pygmalion*
Pinter: *The Birthday Party*	Shaw: *The Devil's Disciple*
Russell: *Educating Rita*	Thomas: *Under Milk Wood*
Shaffer: *The Royal Hunt of the Sun*	

Section B – Prose

(i) *Fiction – Novels*

(a) Texts which are discussed in the book (numbers indicate the page(s) on which the text is discussed):

Brontë, C: *Jane Eyre*	153	Gaskell: *North and South*	130
Forster: *Where Angels Fear to Tread*	105	Grassic Gibbon: *Sunset Song*	102
Galloway: *The Trick is to Keep Breathing*	101	Golding: *Lord of the Flies*	155

Golding: *The Inheritors*	104	Orwell: *Nineteen Eighty-Four*	152
Huxley: *Brave New World*	128	Salinger: *The Catcher in the Rye*	127
Jenkins: *The Cone-Gatherers*	131	Steinbeck: *The Grapes of Wrath*	150

(b) Other suitable texts which are referred to in the book:

Ali: *Brick Lane*	Hardy: *Far From the Madding Crowd*
Angelou: *I know Why the Caged Bird Sings*	Hardy: *Tess of the d'Urbervilles*
Atwood: *The Handmaid's Tale*	Hartley: *The Go-Between*
Austen: *Emma*	Hemingway: *A Farewell to Arms*
Austen: *Pride and Prejudice*	Hemingway: *For Whom the Bell Tolls*
Banks: *Espedair Street*	Irving: *A Prayer for Owen Meany*
Boyd: *The Blue Afternoon*	Ishiguro: *Never Let Me Go*
Bronte, E: *Wuthering Heights*	Ishiguro: *The Remains of the Day*
Burgess: *A Clockwork Orange*	Jenkins: *Leila*
Crichton Smith: *Consider the Lilies*	Jenkins: *The Changeling*
Dickens: *Bleak House*	Kesey: *One Flew Over the Cuckoo's Nest*
Dickens: *Dombey and Son*	Lee: *To Kill a Mockingbird*
Dickens: *Great Expectations*	Levy: *Small Island*
Dickens: *Hard Times*	Mackay Brown: *Greenvoe*
Dickens: *Nicholas Nickleby*	MacLaverty: *Cal*
Dickens: *Oliver Twist*	MacLaverty: *Grace Notes*
Doyle: *The Woman Who Walked into Doors*	MacLaverty: *Lamb*
Drabble: *The Millstone*	McCarthy: *The Road*
Fitzgerald: *The Great Gatsby*	McEwan: *Atonement*
Forster: *A Room with a View*	Paton: *Cry, the Beloved Country*
Forster: *Howards End*	Solzhenitsyn: *One Day in the Life of Ivan Denisovich*
Fowles: *The Collector*	Spark: *The Prime of Miss Jean Brodie*
Frazier: *Cold Mountain*	Stevenson: *Dr Jekyll and Mr Hyde*
Greene: *A Burnt-out Case*	Waugh: *A Handful of Dust*
Greene: *Brighton Rock*	Waugh: *Brideshead Revisited*
Greene: *The Power and the Glory*	Waugh: *The Loved One*
Greene: *The Quiet American*	Winterson: *Oranges are not the Only Fruit*
Gunn: *The Silver Darlings*	

(ii) *Fiction – Short Stories*

(a) Texts which are referred to in the book:

Asimov: *Nightfall*	107	Hemingway: *In Another Country*	131
Ballard: *Billennium*	107	Hemingway: *The Battler*	131
Bradbury: *A Sound of Thunder*	107	Joyce: *Eveline*	106
Bradbury: *The Murderer*	107	Joyce: *The Boarding House*	106
Bradbury: *The Pedestrian*	107	Kennedy: *What Becomes*	106
Chopin: *The Story of an Hour*	131	Lawrence: *Odour of Chrysanthemums*	106
Clarke: *The Nine Billion Names of God*	107	Lessing: *Flight*	106
Clarke: *The Star*	107	Lessing: *Through the Tunnel*	131
De Maupassant: *The Vendetta*	131	London: *The Law of Life*	131
Donovan: *A Ringin Frost*	106	Mackay Brown: *Andrina*	106
Gillman: *The Yellow Wallpaper*	106	Mansfield: *The Lady's Maid*	106
Grassic Gibbon: *Smeddum*	106		

(b) Other suitable texts:

Desai: *A Devoted Son*
Poe: *The Fall of the House of Usher*
Walker: *Everyday Use*

(iii) *Non-fiction*

The following writers and types of writing are referred to in the book:

Travel:	Bill Bryson Bruce Chatwin Michael Palin Rory Stewart Paul Theroux Colin Thubron	**Exploration/ Expedition:**	Andrew Greig Maurice Herzog Alfred Lansing Robert Falcon Scott Joe Simpson
Journalism:	Yasmin Alibhai-Brown Ian Bell Ian Hislop Howard Jacobson Malcolm Muggeridge Melanie Phillips Will Self Polly Toynbee Keith Waterhouse	**Biography/ Autobiography:**	Peter Ackroyd Simon Callow Hunter Davies Michael Holroyd C.S. Lewis Lawrence Olivier Arthur Miller Dava Sobel Claire Tomalin
Political/ sociological Issues:	Tony Benn Richard Holmes Barack Obama Tom Wolfe	**Foreign Correspondents:**	James Cameron John Simpson

Section C – Poetry

(a) Texts which are reproduced in Appendix 3 and numbers (where applicable) indicating the page on which the text is discussed:

Arnold: *Dover Beach*	110		Jamie: *The Thaw*	112
Auden: *O What Is That Sound*	137		Larkin: *Church Going*	134
Burns: *Holy Willie's Prayer*	160		MacCaig: *Brooklyn Cop*	139
Duffy: *Night Marriage*	160		MacCaig: *Hotel Room 12th Floor*	139
Duffy: *Valentine*			Morgan: *Trio*	111
Dunn: *Witch Girl*	136		Owen: *Anthem for Doomed Youth*	
Eliot: *The Love Song of J. Alfred Prufrock*	114		Owen: *Futility*	
Graves: *Counting the Beats*	160		Paterson: *The Thread*	112
Hopkins: *The Windhover*	157		Thomas, D: *Fern Hill*	158

(b) Other suitable texts which are referred to in the book:

Browning: *My Last Duchess*	Larkin: *Wedding Wind*
Burns: *To a Louse*	Lawrence: *Snake*
Crichton Smith: *At the Firth of Lorne*	MacCaig: *Assisi*
Heaney: *Death of a Naturalist*	MacCaig: *On a Croft by Kirkaig*
Hopkins: *Pied Beauty*	MacCaig: *So Many Summers*
Hopkins: *Inversnaid*	MacCaig: *Visiting Hour*
Hughes: *Crow Tyrannosaurus*	Mackay Brown: *Hamnavoe*
Hughes: *Esther's Tomcat*	Morgan: *Glasgow Green*
Hughes: *Pike*	Morgan: *Glasgow Sonnet*
Hughes: *The Horses*	Morgan: *The Starlings in George Square*
Hughes: *The Jaguar*	Muir: *Horses (not The Horses)*
Hughes: *Thrushes*	Owen: *Dulce et Decorum est*
Hughes: *Wind*	Thomas, D: *Poem in October*
Keats: *Ode to a Nightingale*	Wain: *Au Jardin des Plantes*
Keats: *Ode to Autumn*	Wordsworth: *Tintern Abbey*
Larkin: *The Whitsun Weddings*	

Section D – Film and TV Drama

(i) Film

(a) Texts which are discussed in the book (numbers indicate the page(s) on which the text is discussed):

Coppla: *The Godfather*	163	Kubrick: *Dr Strangelove*	117
Eastwood: *The Unforgiven*	115	Polanski: *Knife in the Water*	119
Hitchcock: *Rear Window*	118	Scott: *Blade Runner*	162
Kazan: *On the Waterfront*	162	Spielberg: *Schindler's List*	163

(b) Other suitable texts which are referred to in the book:

Anderson: *If...*	Losey: *The Servant*
Boyle: *Trainspotting*	Lumet: *Twelve Angry Men*
Coppola: *Apocalypse Now*	Scott: *Thelma and Louise*
Hitchcock: *Psycho*	Trumbull: *Silent Running*
Kubrick: *2001: A Space Odyssey*	

(ii) TV Drama

(a) Texts which are discussed in the book (numbers indicate the page(s) on which the text is discussed):

Bleasdale: *Boys from the Blackstuff*	140	McDougall: *Just a Boys' Game*	145
Bleasdale: *GBH*	145	McGovern: *The Lakes*	145
Boyle: *Leaving*	142	Poliakoff: *Shooting the Past*	144
Franceschild: *Takin' over the Asylum*	143		

(b) Other suitable texts which are referred to in the book:

Curtis/Elton: *Blackadder Goes Forth*	Potter: *Blue Remembered Hills*
Gervais/Merchant: *Extras*	Rosenthal: *Bar Mitzvah Boy*
Marshall/Renwick: *If You See God, Tell Him*	Rosenthal: *P'Tang Yang Kipperbang*
McDougall: *Down Among the Big Boys*	Rosenthal: *Ready When You Are, Mr McGill*
McDougall: *The Elephants' Graveyard*	Russell: *One Summer*
Poliakoff: *The Lost Prince*	

Appendix 3
Poems

Dover Beach by Matthew Arnold

The sea is calm to-night.
The tide is full, the moon lies fair
Upon the straits; on the French coast the light
Gleams and is gone; the cliffs of England stand;
Glimmering and vast, out in the tranquil bay.
Come to the window, sweet is the night air!
Only, from the long line of spray
Where the sea meets the moon-blanched land,
Listen! you hear the grating roar
Of pebbles which the waves draw back, and fling,
At their return, up the high strand,
Begin, and cease, and then again begin,
With tremulous cadence slow, and bring
The eternal note of sadness in.

Sophocles long ago
Heard it on the Ægæan, and it brought
Into his mind the turbid ebb and flow
Of human misery; we
Find also in the sound a thought,
Hearing it by this distant northern sea.

The Sea of Faith
Was once, too, at the full, and round earth's shore
Lay like the folds of a bright girdle furled.
But now I only hear
Its melancholy, long, withdrawing roar,
Retreating, to the breath
Of the night-wind, down the vast edges drear
And naked shingles of the world.

Ah, love, let us be true
To one another! for the world, which seems
To lie before us like a land of dreams,
So various, so beautiful, so new,
Hath really neither joy, nor love, nor light,
Nor certitude, nor peace, nor help for pain;
And we are here as on a darkling plain
Swept with confused alarms of struggle and flight,
Where ignorant armies clash by night.

O What Is That Sound by W.H. Auden

O what is that sound which so thrills the ear
Down in the valley drumming, drumming?
Only the scarlet soldiers, dear,
The soldiers coming.

O what is that light I see flashing so clear
Over the distance brightly, brightly?
Only the sun on their weapons, dear,
As they step lightly.

O what are they doing with all that gear,
What are they doing this morning, morning?
Only their usual manoeuvres, dear,
Or perhaps a warning.

O why have they left the road down there,
Why are they suddenly wheeling, wheeling?
Perhaps a change in their orders, dear,
Why are you kneeling?

O haven't they stopped for the doctor's care,
Haven't they reined their horses, horses?
Why, they are none of them wounded, dear,
None of these forces.

O is it the parson they want, with white hair,
Is it the parson, is it, is it?
No, they are passing his gateway, dear,
Without a visit.

O it must be the farmer that lives so near.
It must be the farmer so cunning, so cunning?
They have passed the farmyard already, dear,
And now they are running.

O where are you going? Stay with me here!
Were the vows you swore deceiving, deceiving?
No, I promised to love you, dear,
But I must be leaving.

O it's broken the lock and splintered the door,
O it's the gate where they're turning, turning;
Their boots are heavy on the floor
And their eyes are burning.

Night Marriage by Carol Ann Duffy

When I turn off the light
and the dark mile between us
crumples and falls,
you slip from your self
to wait for me in my sleep,
the face of the moon sinking into a cloud;

or I wake bereaved
from the long hours
I spend in your dreams,
an owl in the forest crying its soft vowels,
dark fish swimming under the river's skin.

Night marriage. The small hours join us,
face to face as we sleep and dream;
the whole of the huge night is our room.

Valentine by Carol Ann Duffy

Not a red rose or a satin heart.

I give you an onion.
It is a moon wrapped in brown paper.
It promises light
like the careful undressing of love.

Here.
It will blind you with tears
Like a lover.
It will make your reflection
a wobbling photo of grief.

I am trying to be truthful.

Not a cute card or a kissogram.

I give you an onion.
Its fierce kiss will stay on your lips,
possessive and faithful
as we are,
for as long as we are.

Take it.
Its platinum loops shrink to a wedding ring,
if you like.
Lethal.
Its scent will cling to your fingers,
cling to your knife.

Witch Girl by Douglas Dunn

For evermore, they said, that girl was lame
In hands and feet, and that, they said, was proof
The lightless Devil spelled her into horse,
Moulding her hands and feet in solid hoof.

Poor girl, her mother saddled her, then rode
Through Sutherland until the outraged Law
Attended to the giddy-ups of gossip,
Force-feeding both of them on Tolbooth straw.

Only her mother was condemned. A pious mob --
Citizens and presbyters – whinnied, neighed,
Clip-clopped, as, standing in their fear of God,
There too were men who watched but also pitied.

Cold day in Dornoch... Shivering, the witch
Relieved her freezing round that fire which burned
To burn her up. Crowds psalmed with horror.
She blistered in the tar and, screaming, burned.

They spoke in Dornoch how the horses mourned
And how that lame girl, wandering, was heard
Tearing at the grass; and how she sat and sang,
As if the Devil made her bird;

And how she washed her lameness in the rivers
From Oykell to the Clyde and Tweed and Forth,
Notorious as something to be pitied,
A girl to look at but a beast in worth.

No one could see her but would think he saw
Hoof in her fumbling hands her staggering gait.
They spurned her flowers, as if they'd grown
    from her;
They barbed their righteous charity with hate.

She hawked her flowers in Glasgow, by the Trongate;
In Edinburgh, selling flowers, she slept
Beside the braziers of the City Guard.
The earth and animals within her wept.

No one to help her; no one saw her die,
If she is dead. By Gryfe, by Deveron,
By Cree and Tay, I see her wash her lameness,
And hear her breathing in the wood and stone.

The Love Song of J. Alfred Prufrock by T.S. Eliot – extract

S'io credesse che mia risposta fosse
A persona che mai tornasse al mondo,
Questa fiamma staria senza piu scosse.
Ma perciocche giammai di questo fondo
Non torno vivo alcun, s'i'odo il vero,
Senza tema d'infamia ti rispondo.

Let us go then, you and I,
When the evening is spread out against the sky
Like a patient etherised upon a table;
Let us go, through certain half-deserted streets,
The muttering retreats
Of restless nights in one-night cheap hotels
And sawdust restaurants with oyster-shells:
Streets that follow like a tedious argument
Of insidious intent
To lead you to an overwhelming question…
Oh, do not ask, "What is it?"
Let us go and make our visit.

In the room the women come and go
Talking of Michelangelo.

The yellow fog that rubs its back upon the window-
    panes,
The yellow smoke that rubs its muzzle on the
    window-panes
Licked its tongue into the corners of the evening,
Lingered upon the pools that stand in drains,
Let fall upon its back the soot that falls from chimneys,
Slipped by the terrace, made a sudden leap,
And seeing that it was a soft October night,
Curled once about the house, and fell asleep.

And indeed there will be time
For the yellow smoke that slides along the street,
Rubbing its back upon the window-panes;
There will be time, there will be time
To prepare a face to meet the faces that you meet;
There will be time to murder and create,
And time for all the works and days of hands
That lift and drop a question on your plate;
Time for you and time for me,
And time yet for a hundred indecisions,
And for a hundred visions and revisions,
Before the taking of a toast and tea.

In the room the women come and go
Talking of Michelangelo.

And indeed there will be time
To wonder, "Do I dare?" and, "Do I dare?"
Time to turn back and descend the stair,
With a bald spot in the middle of my hair
[They will say: "How his hair is growing thin!"]
My morning coat, my collar mounting firmly to
    the chin,
My necktie rich and modest, but asserted by a simple pin
[They will say: "But how his arms and legs are thin!"]
Do I dare
Disturb the universe?
In a minute there is time
For decisions and revisions which a minute will
    reverse.

Counting the Beats by Robert Graves

You, love, and I,
(He whispers) you and I,
And if no more than only you and I
What care you or I ?

Counting the beats,
Counting the slow heart beats,
The bleeding to death of time in slow heart beats,
Wakeful they lie.

Cloudless day,
Night, and a cloudless day,
Yet the huge storm will burst upon their heads one day
From a bitter sky.

Where shall we be,
(She whispers) where shall we be,
When death strikes home, O where then shall we be
Who were you and I ?

Not there but here,
(He whispers) only here,
As we are, here, together, now and here,
Always you and I.

Counting the beats,
Counting the slow heart beats,
The bleeding to death of time in slow heart beats,
Wakeful they lie.

The Windhover by Gerard Manley Hopkins

To Christ Our Lord

I CAUGHT this morning morning's minion, king-
dom of daylight's dauphin, dapple-dawn-drawn
    Falcon, in his riding
Of the rolling level underneath him steady air, and
    striding
High there, how he rung upon the rein of a wimpling
    wing
In his ecstasy! then off, off forth on swing,
As a skate's heel sweeps smooth on a bow-bend: the
    hurl and gliding
Rebuffed the big wind. My heart in hiding
Stirred for a bird, – the achieve of, the mastery of the
    thing!

Brute beauty and valour and act, oh, air, pride, plume,
    here
Buckle! AND the fire that breaks from thee then, a
    billion
Times told lovelier, more dangerous, O my chevalier!

No wonder of it: shéer plód makes plough down
    sillion
Shine, and blue-bleak embers, ah my dear,
Fall, gall themselves, and gash gold-vermilion.

Thaw by Kathleen Jamie

When we brought you home in a taxi
through the steel-grey thaw
after the coldest week in memory
-even the river sealed itself-
it was I, hardly breathing,
who came through the passage to our yard
welcoming our simplest things:
a chopping block, the frost-
split lintels; and though it meant a journey
through darkening snow,
arms laden with you in a blanket,
I had to walk to the top of the garden,
to touch, in a complicit
homage of equals, the spiral
trunks of our plum trees, the moss,
the robin's roost in the holly.
Leaning back on the railway wall,
I tried to remember;
but even my footprints were being erased
and the rising stars of Orion

denied what I knew: that as we were
hurled on a trolley through swing doors to theatre
they'd been there, aligned on the ceiling,
        ablaze with concern
for that difficult giving,
before we were two, from my one.

Church Going by Philip Larkin

Once I am sure there's nothing going on
I step inside, letting the door thud shut.
Another church: matting, seats, and stone,
And little books; sprawlings of flowers, cut
For Sunday, brownish now; some brass and stuff
Up at the holy end; the small neat organ;
And a tense, musty, unignorable silence,
Brewed God knows how long. Hatless, I take off
My cycle-clips in awkward reverence,

Move forward, run my hand around the font.
From where I stand, the roof looks almost new-
Cleaned or restored? Someone would know: I don't.
Mounting the lectern, I peruse a few
Hectoring large-scale verses, and pronounce
"Here endeth" much more loudly than I'd meant.
The echoes snigger briefly. Back at the door
I sign the book, donate an Irish sixpence,
Reflect the place was not worth stopping for.

Yet stop I did: in fact I often do,
And always end much at a loss like this,
Wondering what to look for; wondering, too,
When churches fall completely out of use
What we shall turn them into, if we shall keep
A few cathedrals chronically on show,
Their parchment, plate, and pyx in locked cases,
And let the rest rent-free to rain and sheep.
Shall we avoid them as unlucky places?

Or, after dark, will dubious women come
To make their children touch a particular stone;
Pick simples for a cancer; or on some
Advised night see walking a dead one?
Power of some sort or other will go on
In games, in riddles, seemingly at random;
But superstition, like belief, must die,
And what remains when disbelief has gone?
Grass, weedy pavement, brambles, buttress, sky,

A shape less recognizable each week,
A purpose more obscure. I wonder who
Will be the last, the very last, to seek
This place for what it was; one of the crew
That tap and jot and know what rood-lofts were?
Some ruin-bibber, randy for antique,
Or Christmas-addict, counting on a whiff
Of gown-and-bands and organ-pipes and myrrh?
Or will he be my representative,

Bored, uninformed, knowing the ghostly silt
Dispersed, yet tending to this cross of ground
Through suburb scrub because it held unspilt
So long and equably what since is found
Only in separation – marriage, and birth,
And death, and thoughts of these – for whom was built
This special shell? For, though I've no idea
What this accoutred frowsty barn is worth,
It pleases me to stand in silence here;

A serious house on serious earth it is,
In whose blent air all our compulsions meet,
Are recognised, and robed as destinies.
And that much never can be obsolete,
Since someone will forever be surprising
A hunger in himself to be more serious,
And gravitating with it to this ground,
Which, he once heard, was proper to grow wise in,
If only that so many dead lie round.

Brooklyn Cop by Norman MacCaig

Built like a gorilla but less timid,
thick-fleshed, steak-coloured, with two
hieroglyphs in his face that mean
trouble, he walks the sidewalk and the
thin tissue over violence. This morning
when he said, 'See you, babe' to his wife,
he hoped it, he truly hoped it.
He is a gorilla to whom 'Hiya, honey' is no cliché.

Should the tissue tear, should he plunge through
into violence, what clubbings, what
gunshots between Phoebe's
Whamburger and Louie's Place.

Who would be him, gorilla with a nightstick,
whose home is a place
he might, this time, never get back to?

And who would be who have to be
his victims?

Hotel Room, 12th Floor by Norman MacCaig

This morning I watched from here
a helicopter skirting like a damaged insect
the Empire State Building, that
jumbo size dentist's drill, and landing
on the roof of the PanAm skyscraper.
But now midnight has come in
from foreign places. Its uncivilised darkness
is shot at by a million lit windows, all
ups and acrosses.

But midnight is not
so easily defeated. I lie in bed, between
a radio and a television set, and hear
the wildest of warwhoops continually ululating through
glittering canyons and gulches –
police cars and ambulances racing
to the broken bones, the harsh screaming
from coldwater flats, the blood
glazed on sidewalks.

The frontier is never
somewhere else. And no stockades
can keep the darkness out.

Trio by Edwin Morgan

Coming up Buchanan Street, quickly, on a sharp
        winter evening
a young man and two girls, under the Christmas
        lights –
The young man carries a new guitar in his arms,
the girl on the inside carries a very young baby,
and the girl on the outside carries a chihuahua.
And the three of them are laughing, their breath rises
in a cloud of happiness, and as they pass
the boy says, "Wait till he sees this but!"
The chihuahua has a tiny Royal Stewart tartan coat
        like a teapot-holder,
the baby in its white shawl is all bright eyes and mouth
        like favours in a fresh sweet cake,
the guitar swells out under its milky plastic cover, tied
        at the neck with silver tinsel tape and a brisk
sprig of mistletoe.
Orphean sprig! Melting baby! Warm chihuahua!
The vale of tears is powerless before you.
Whether Christ is born, or is not born, you
put paid to fate, it abdicates
                        under the Christmas lights.
Monsters of the year
go blank, are scattered back,
can't bear this march of three.

-And the three have passed, vanished in the crowd
(yet not vanished, for in their arms they wind
the life of men and beasts, and music,
laughter ringing them round like a guard)
at the end of this winter's day.

Anthem for Doomed Youth by Wilfred Owen

What passing-bells for these who die as cattle?
Only the monstrous anger of the guns.
Only the stuttering rifles' rapid rattle
Can patter out their hasty orisons.
No mockeries now for them; no prayers nor bells,
Nor any voice of mourning save the choirs, -
The shrill, demented choirs of wailing shells;
And bugles calling for them from sad shires.

What candles may be held to speed them all?
Not in the hands of boys, but in their eyes
Shall shine the holy glimmers of goodbyes.
The pallor of girls' brows shall be their pall;
Their flowers the tenderness of patient minds,
And each slow dusk a drawing down of blinds.

Futility by Wilfred Owen

Move him into the sun –
Gently its touch awoke him once,
At home, whispering of fields unsown.
Always it woke him, even in France,
Until this morning and this snow.
If anything might rouse him now
The kind old sun will know.

Think how it wakes the seeds, –
Woke, once, the clays of a cold star.
Are limbs, so dear-achieved, are sides,
Full-nerved – still warm – too hard to stir?
Was it for this the clay grew tall?
– O what made fatuous sunbeams toil
To break earth's sleep at all?

The Thread by Don Paterson

Jamie made his landing in the world
so hard he ploughed straight back into the earth.
They caught him by the head of his one breath
and pulled him up. They don't know how it held.
And so today thank what higher will
brought us to here, to you and me and Russ,
the great twin-engined swaying wingspan of us
roaring down the back of Kirrie Hill

and your two-year-old lungs somehow out-revving
every engine in the universe.
All that trouble just to turn up the dead
was all I thought that long week. Now the thread
is holding all of us: look at our tiny house,
son, the white dot of your mother waving.

Fern Hill by Dylan Thomas

Now as I was young and easy under the apple boughs
About the lilting house and happy as the grass was
    green,
The night above the dingle starry,
Time let me hail and climb
Golden in the heydays of his eyes,
And honoured among wagons I was prince of the
    apple towns
And once below a time I lordly had the trees and leaves
Trail with daisies and barley
Down the rivers of the windfall light.

And as I was green and carefree, famous among the
    barns
About the happy yard and singing as the farm was home,
In the sun that is young once only,
Time let me play and be
Golden in the mercy of his means,
And green and golden I was huntsman and herdsman,
    the calves
Sang to my horn, the foxes on the hills barked clear
    and cold,
And the sabbath rang slowly
In the pebbles of the holy streams.

All the sun long it was running, it was lovely, the hay
Fields high as the house, the tunes from the chimneys,
    it was air
And playing, lovely and watery
And fire green as grass.
And nightly under the simple stars
As I rode to sleep the owls were bearing the farm away,
All the moon long I heard, blessed among stables, the
    nightjars
Flying with the ricks, and the horses
Flashing into the dark.

And then to awake, and the farm, like a wanderer white
With the dew, come back, the cock on his shoulder:
    it was all
Shining, it was Adam and maiden,
The sky gathered again
And the sun grew round that very day.

So it must have been after the birth of the simple light
In the first, spinning place, the spellbound horses
    walking warm
Out of the whinnying green stable
On to the fields of praise.

And honoured among foxes and pheasants by the gay
    house
Under the new made clouds and happy as the heart
    was long,
In the sun born over and over,
I ran my heedless ways,
My wishes raced through the house high hay
And nothing I cared, at my sky blue trades, that time
    allows
In all his tuneful turning so few and such morning
    songs
Before the children green and golden
Follow him out of grace.

Nothing I cared, in the lamb white days, that time
    would take me
Up to the swallow thronged loft by the shadow of
    my hand,
In the moon that is always rising,
Nor that riding to sleep
I should hear him fly with the high fields
And wake to the farm forever fled from the childless
    land.
Oh as I was young and easy in the mercy of his means,
Time held me green and dying
Though I sang in my chains like the sea.

Appendix 4
Commentary on Close Reading 'Bad Answers'

Paper 1: Social Networking

1 *(a)* Simply quotes from the passage – no attempt to use "own words".

  (c) Simply says what **any** parenthesis does – no reference made to what **this** parenthesis is doing in **this** sentence.

2 *(a)* What this answer says is true and is in "own words"; however, it is not answering the question about what makes one more "perilous" (dangerous).

  (b) Only two words **and** only identifies them – no comment made on what these words **suggest** and **how** they convey the writer's attitude.

3 A completely "empty" answer which shows no understanding of **why** the writer is describing a slaughterhouse – and a strong suggestion that the word "analogy" has not been understood. Some appropriate words are quoted but there is no consideration of what they **suggest**.

4 Seems to be doing the right thing: identifies features and comments on them sensibly enough. However, neither comment is linked in any reasonable way to the idea of 'threat'.

5 *(b)* Identifies two features of sentence structure (semicolon and dashes), but the comments are not acceptable. A semicolon cannot show disapproval! Perhaps the relationship between what comes before it and what comes after it could be relevant, but not the piece of punctuation itself. Similarly, it is not enough just to say there is "extra information" – you must say what the extra information **is** and explain **how** it conveys, in this case, disapproval.

  Picking out "big words" is unlikely to be helpful, and the comment here certainly isn't. Note also that you shouldn't make a single comment on three words in this way: one word – one comment.

8 *(b)* Not in "own words" – has simply quoted "starved for real community" and added on a bit about Twitter.

9 *(b)* A really silly answer. For a start, the sentences are not all that long, and just having a lot to say does nothing to clarify what the writer is saying.

Paper 2: Responding to Change

1 *(a)* No attempt to use "own words", so no marks.

1 *(b)* Quotes words and repeats the question; no attempt to "show how…"

1 *(c)* Both points are "true" and expressed in own words, but neither is an answer to the question.

2 *(a)* A good explanation of why the doctor is making the proposal, but does not explain why people reacted the way they did.

3 *(b)* Makes a good start by explaining what a blizzard is, but doesn't make any connection with "the writer's point" – indeed doesn't even say what the writer's point is.

4 *(a)* Makes three apparently good points by identifying three words/expressions and making comment about their connotations. However, the question is about "'our' attitude" and this answer is about the **writer's** views not what she thinks **"ours"** are.

4 *(b)* The comment about dashes is very vague, and simply having a "lot to say" doesn't "clarify her argument". The point about the use of "And" is quite interesting, but being "conversational" doesn't "clarify her argument". Moreover, neither point shows any understanding of what her "argument" actually is.

7 *(a)* The first point identifies a suitable area for comment, but then simply repeats the question with no attempt to explain the connection. The second point is very debatable: it is hard to accept that the writer is being tongue-in-cheek here.

7 *(b)* Has missed the point of the question; simply repeats some of the statistics, with nothing at all on the "spin" the writer is putting on them.

Paper 3: Shopping

1 *(a)* Mostly "lifts" from the passage; no understanding shown; no clear reference to "consumerism".

1 *(b)* Not a terrible answer, but not likely to score any marks, because the quotation is too long and it is not clear which word is being dealt with, and the comment, while by no means stupid, is simply too vague. (Note also the unnecessary repetition of the question at the beginning of the answer.)

2 *(a)* True up to a point, but not addressing the question, especially the words "our place in society".

2 *(b)* There are no marks just for spotting a colon, some commas, or a minor sentence. There must be an explanation of their **effect** and a clear link to what the writer is saying.

4 *(b)* Simply restates what the writer says – no attempt to say anything about the "**effect**".

6 Much too reliant on the words of the passage. It is possible that there is understanding, but it is not shown satisfactorily, and there is no attempt to explain.

7 The first point has no connection with the question – and it's debatable how "rhetorical" this question is. The second point is true, and in the use of the word "concedes" shows good understanding, but it also has no connection with the question. The last point at least mentions the word "myth" but says nothing about the way the writer illustrates it.

8 Own words? [Such an answer shows good understanding in that it correctly and succinctly isolates the key points, but answering it in this way disregards the requirement to answer in "own words".]

10 *(b)* A sensible observation but there is no effort to explore the connotations of the key words, and this answer is contrasting the two types instead of looking at the impression given of **one** type.

11 *(a)* Much too vague. In the first sentence it's not enough just to mention "airport" as the link back – there must be understanding of what point the writer is making about airport shops. The second sentence is even weaker: no specific word(s) chosen and no sense of what the other paragraph is about.

11 *(b)* Correct meaning of "rational" but not a sensible or acceptable link with the power of the computer's design.

14 The word "alluring" is used of the white computer not the black one.

16 This answer shows a very good understanding of the main argument of the passage, but it doesn't answer the question, which is about the "writer's attitude to his own consumerist habits".